REASONING IN ETHICS AND LAW

0180475

SM 99007048
04/00
£40.00 171.2
→ (mus)
✓

This book is due for return on or before the last date shown below.

Don Gresswell Ltd., London, N.21   Cat. No. 1208   DG 02242/71

Reasoning in Ethics and Law

The role of theory, principles and facts

Edited by
ALBERT W. MUSSCHENGA
WIM J. VAN DER STEEN

Ashgate

Aldershot • Brookfield USA • Singapore • Sydney

Published by
Ashgate Publishing Ltd
Gower House
Croft Road
Aldershot
Hants GU11 3HR
England

Ashgate Publishing Company
Old Post Road
Brookfield
Vermont 05036
USA

Ashgate website: http://www.ashgate.com

British Library Cataloguing in Publication Data
Reasoning in ethics and law : the role of theory,
    principles and facts. - (Avebury series in philosophy)
    1. Reasoning 2. Judgement (Ethics) 3. Judgement (Logic) 4. Law
    - Moral and ethical aspects 5. Principle (Philosophy)
    I. Musschenga, Albert W. II. Steen, Wim J. van der, 1940-
    171.2

Library of Congress Catalog Card Number: 99-73627

ISBN 0 7546 1045 4

Printed and bound by Athenaeum Press, Ltd.,
Gateshead, Tyne & Wear.

Contents

v

List of Contributors

H.J.M. Boukema is Member of the Bar of Amsterdam. Recent publications: Law for the Vanquished, *Rechtsfilosofie en Rechtstheorie* (1993), no. 2; Excuses in Court, *Rechtsfilosofie en Rechtstheorie* (1995), no. 3; Rechtszekerheid in het burgerlijk procesrecht, *Rechtsfilosofie en Rechtstheorie* (1998), no. 3.

Govert A. den Hartogh, formerly a professor of legal philosophy in the Faculty of Law and a professor of medical ethics in the Faculty of Medicine, is now professor of ethics and its history in the Faculty of Humanities of the University of Amsterdam. His publications include: The Slippery Slope Argument. In: Peter Singer, Helga Kuhse eds., *Companion to Bioethics*, Blackwell, Oxford 1998, 280-290; Priorities in Health Care: Why the Search for Criteria Failed. In: G.A. den Hartogh ed., *The Good Life as a Public Good*, Kluwer, Dordrecht forthcoming; *Law as Convention*. Law and Philosophy Library, Kluwer, Dordrecht, forthcoming.

Harm Kloosterhuis studied Dutch language and literature (specialisation argumentation theory), and law at the University of Amsterdam. He is presently working at the Faculties of Law of the Erasmus University of Rotterdam and of the University of Aruba. He is preparing a dissertation on analogical reasoning in the law. Recent publications: Analysing Analogy Arguments in Judicial Decisions. In: Frans H. van Eemeren & Rob Grootendorst, *Studies in Pragma-Dialectics*, SicSat, Amsterdam 1994, 238-245; The Study of Analogy-Argumentation in Law: Four Pragma-Dialectical Starting Points. In: Frans H. van Eemeren, Rob Grootendorst, J. Anthony Blair & Charles A. Willard (eds.), *Proceedings of the Third ISSA Conference on Argumentation*, Vol. IV, Special Fields, SicSat, Amsterdam 1995, 138-145; Lijdt de Hoge Raad in Nederland nog steeds aan een analogie-fobie? In: E.T. Feteris e.a. (red.), *Op goede gronden*, Ars Aequi Libri, Nijmegen 1997, 115-122.

Cees W. Maris is professor of legal philosophy at the Faculty of Law of the University of Amsterdam. He is Editor in Chief of *Dutch Magazine of Legal Philosophy and Legal Theory*. He published the following books: *Critique of the Empiricist Explanation of Morality* (1981) and *Horror Vacui* (1990). Recent articles: Franglais; On liberalism, nationalism and multiculturalism. In: T. van Willigenburg, F.R. Heeger & W. van der Burg (eds.), *Nation, State and the Coexistence of Different Communities,* Kok Pharos Publishing House, Kampen 1995, 57-98; Dutch Weed and Logic, *International Journal of Drug Policy* 7(1996), Part I: 80-87; Part II: 142-152; The Tao of Jurisprudence, *Law and Critique* VII (1996), 115-126.

Albert W. Musschenga is professor of ethics at the Faculty of Philosophy of the Vrije Universiteit of Amsterdam. He is Editor in Chief of *Ethical Theory and Moral Practice*, an European Forum, published by Kluwer Academic Publisher, Dordrecht, The Netherlands. Recent publications: The Relation between Concepts of Quality of Life, Health and Happiness, *Journal of Philosophy and Medicine* 22(1997), 11-28; Intrinsic Value as a Reason for the Preservation of Minority Cultures, *Ethical Theory and Moral Practice* 1(1998), pp. 201-225; Intrinsic Value and Intrinsic Valuing. In: Marcel Dol a.o. (eds*.), Recognizing the Intrinsic Value of Animals: Beyond Animal Welfare,* Van Gorcum, Assen 1999 (Animals in Philosophy and the Sciences, Vol. II).

Wim J. van der Steen is professor of philosophy of biology, Faculties of Biology and Philosophy, Vrije Universiteit, Amsterdam. Among his recent publications are: *A Practical Philosophy for the Life Sciences*, SUNY Press, Albany 1993; *Facts, Values, and Methodology: A New Approach to Ethics,* Rodopi, Amsterdam and Atlanta 1995; Forging links between philosophy, ethics, and the life sciences: A tale of disciplines and trenches, *History and Philosophy of the Life Sciences*, in press.

Henri Wijsbek studied philosophy in Lund, Sweden, and in Amsterdam. His main topics were philosophy of language and ethics. He is currently dividing his time between a European medical-ethical project at Faculty of Medicine of the Erasmus University of Rotterdam and his thesis on moral and legal reasoning about euthanasia in the Netherlands. So far, work on the latter has resulted in an article about the famous Chabot-case.

Theo van Willigenburg is professor of ethics in the faculty of Philosophy of the Erasmus University in Rotterdam, and Socrates professor of medical ethics at the Academic Medical School of the University of Amsterdam. His main research is in the fields of meta-ethics and ethical methodology, medical ethics and business ethics. Recent publications: Morally Relevant Facts: Particularism and Intuitionist Rationality. In: W. van der Burg & T. van Willigenburg (eds.), *Reflective Equilibrium*, Kluwer, Dordrecht 1998, 41-54; New Casuistry: What's New? *Philosophical Explorations*, 1/2 (1998), 41-54; Is the consumer always right? Subject-relative valuations and inherent value. In: R. Norman (ed.), *Ethics and the Market*, Ashgate, Aldershot 1999.

Introduction

ALBERT W. MUSSCHENGA
WIM J. VAN DER STEEN

Human beings rely on the cognitive capacity of reasoning in all sorts of endeavours. Reasoning comes in different kinds. In ethics and the law, modes of reasoning are distinct for two reasons. First, mere canons of pure logic do not suffice to characterise reasoning in ethics and the law since modes of reasoning should be tailored here to practical settings. Second, normative modes of reasoning for guiding human behaviour are at centre stage. Because reasoning takes a practical, normative turn in ethics and in law, these areas share much methodology, and they address similar problems. This volume charts two shared problems, the relation between principles, rules and particular judgements, and the role of facts and factual assertions in normative settings. The contributions in part I deal with the first problem. The second problem is taken up in the contributions in part II.

Theory, Principles, Judgements

Commonalties should ensure that legal philosophy can benefit from exchanges with moral philosophy, and the other way round. However, the recognition of potential benefits appears to be unbalanced. Discussions about the relevance of ethical theory for legal philosophy are well-represented in the literature. But systematic accounts transferring insights from legal philosophy to moral philosophy are rare.

Ethics should affect the law for the simple reason that existing legal rules do not suffice to solve all legal problems. The philosopher of law Neil MacCormick argues that existing law may be compatible with different rulings in a given case and thereby with different normative judgements regarding human behaviours. This invites extra-legal modes of argument. The

1

question whether a particular ruling does 'make sense in the world' calls for an appraisal of its consequences. The judge thus needs to rely on a consequentialist type of argument in line with an ethical theory known as 'rule utilitarianism' (MacCormick 1978, 104 f.).

Legal philosophy has a long tradition of theorising about argumentation. Theorising is commonly inspired by reasoning practised by lawyers and judges. The conviction that moral philosophers can benefit from this tradition has been an important motive for producing this volume.

Many studies in meta-ethics and normative ethics do account for moral reasoning. But relations between these theoretical accounts and practices of moral reasoning are much more elusive than those between theories of legal reasoning and the practice of legal arguments. Indeed, the relation between 'theory' and 'practice' has become highly controversial in moral philosophy. In the still ongoing debate, some authors grant that legal philosophy, unlike moral philosophy, exhibits a balanced view on the relation between 'theory' and 'practice'. But they do not articulate how the example of legal argumentation could help us improve the theory of moral argumentation.

Indeed, many ethicists nowadays tend to dispense with the traditional varieties of ethical theory instead of aiming to improve it. Adherents of traditional theorising, in the Kantian as well as in the utilitarian tradition, characteristically aim at an overarching theory as a source of universal principles binding all rational beings. They regard such principles as superior to the customs, conventions, and rules of local moral traditions. In their view, critical moral reasoning amounts to the subsumption of cases under universal principles. The subsumption model characteristically takes the form of deductivism. Proper reasoning thus conceived proceeds by valid deductive arguments, that is, arguments that logically transfer truth from the premises to the conclusion. In the last two decades, resistance against this type of ethical theorising and the allied subsumptive model of moral reasoning has evolved into a movement known as 'anti-theory'.

Commonalties and differences among participants in this movement are well-documented in *Anti-Theory in Ethics and Moral Conservatism*, edited by Stanley G. Clarke and Evan Simpson (1989). In their introduction, the editors state that anti-theorists reject normative (ethical) theory as unnecessary, undesirable, or impossible, usually for all the three reasons (1989, 3). *Unnecessary*, because moral reasoning can do without foundational moral principles. *Undesirable*, because moral reasoning, if limited to the application of abstract universal principles, cannot account for the unique particulars of a situation. Further, mere application of principles would reduce the moral actor to a passive executor of manual-like prescriptions. *Impossible*, because no philosopher has come up with an ethical theory that convinces all concerned.

Traditionalists among the anti-theorists argue for the primacy of moral practices over ethical theory. They reject the opposition which 'rationalist' moral philosophers have construed between reason and tradition. Alisdair MacIntyre, a well-known traditionalist, sees traditions as the bearers of reason. In his view, moral reasoning is a tradition-dependent, contextual practice taking many forms (MacIntyre 1988). Traditionalists oppose not only the search for universal, foundational principles, but also the subsumption model of moral reasoning. In their account of moral reasoning, the emphasis shifts from principles to qualities required for moral agency, to Aristotelian practical wisdom.

The traditionalists often refer to legal reasoning as a paradigm for moral reasoning. Legal rules are contextual. They only bind those who live within the jurisdiction of the legislators in their state. Judges need to know about the rules. But over and above this, their salient function is to exercise practical wisdom in the interpretation of the rules. This invites an anti-foundationalist stance and a rejection of the subsumptive model of moral reasoning.

Michael Walzer has mounted an extensive defence of this view. He argues that lawyers and judges addressing the question 'What is the legal or constitutional thing to do?' can but resort to a particular body of laws or a particular constitutional text. Neither the body of laws nor the text has ' ... the simplicity and precision of a yardstick against which we might measure the different actions urged by the contending parties. Deprived of a yardstick, we rely on exegesis, commentary, and historical precedent, a tradition of argument and interpretation. Any given interpretation will be contentious, of course, but there is little disagreement about what we are interpreting or about the need for the interpretative effort' (1985, 23).

In taking legal reasoning as a model for moral reasoning, Walzer assumes that legal reasoning is interpretative and non-subsumptive, and that it has no place for theory. We will argue that this needs to be qualified. First, we consider whether morality contains an equivalent to 'a particular body of laws or a particular constitutional text'.

Legal reasoning always draws on a system of positive law that contains two kinds of rules, primary rules of obligation and secondary rules of recognition for identifying valid primary rules. Judges need to interpret these rules such that they fit particular applications. The verdict of the judge is binding, at least within a certain jurisdiction. In morality, authorities like judges do not exist. Nobody's judgement is authoritative here because of the position they hold. Further, a 'positive morality' analogous to positive law does not exist. True, we might conceptualise primary moral rules as a system of generally accepted normative social expectations that regulates social behaviour within a group or community. But no generally accepted rules of recognition exist to determine which primary rules should be valid. Therefore, moral reasoning is rarely restricted to the identification and interpretation of valid rules applying to a particular case. Controversies over the validity of rules are indeed common in ethics. Of course, in practice, every community will endorse some moral rules. But unlike judges who are obliged to apply the law, moral persons remain free in principle to reject any rule as immoral. Authority allotted to a moral tradition anyhow fails to generate the equivalent of the force that laws and texts have in legal reasoning. Any attempt to construe an analogy between legal and moral reasoning should account for the absence of uncontested authoritative moral rules and texts.

Walzer's view of moral reasoning as interpretation amounts to a rejection of ethical theorising and subsumptive argumentation. This is contestable. Let's consider theorising first. Why should we dismiss ethical theorising? Walzer argues that the discoveries and inventions of ethical theorists are superfluous interpretations in disguise (1987, 21). We would argue that, even when one concedes that ethical theories are in fact interpretations, the conclusion need not be that they are superfluous. Ethical theories may provide distinctive philosophical contributions to the process of interpreting morality. This point is convincingly elaborated by Michele Moody-Adams in *Fieldwork in Familiar Places* (1997). She argues, as we would, that Walzer and other 'anti-theorists' rightly oppose the view that ethical theorising overrides all non-philosophical interpretative efforts. But this does not imply that moral philosophy cannot generate fruitful interpretations of morality. 'First, the discipline of philosophy inculcates special appreciation of (and usually special commitment to) standards of reasonableness in argument. Second, the moral philosopher's knowledge of alternative ways of interpreting moral experience may sometimes enable her to produce the kind of thought experiments which can stimulate moral imagination – but which, unlike real experiments, need not sacrifice real human beings' (164). When we drop the claim that conceptions of ethical theorists are rationally superior, discrepancies among philosophical conceptions need not be a cause for great concern. Theorising in ethics would be superfluous only on the assumption that it never contributed to consensus. That assumption is patently false.

This modest view of ethical theory is in line with views of legal theorists on the role of legal theory. True, as we indicated, relations between theory and practice are more balanced in legal philosophy than in ethics. But regarding the force of theory, limitations of the law resemble those of ethics. According to MacCormick, legal reasoning as public argumentation draws on normative canons with varying degrees of clarity and explicitness. The study of legal reasoning is an attempt to explicate and explain criteria for distinguishing between acceptable and unacceptable arguments in the law (1978, 12). A theory of legal reasoning needs to be both reconstructive and prescriptive: '(...) I set forth an account of certain features of legal argumentation which are actually instantiated within the law reports, and explain the reasons why I think they ought to be fundamental features of legal argumentation given its function ... My conclusions therefore present a double face: they are both in their own right normative and yet I believe them to describe norms actually operative in the systems under study. In the latter I am offering eminently falsifiable hypotheses' (1978, 13). This comes close to the traditionalist's view of moral reasoning, but it is at odds with their wholesale rejection of theory.

Walzer, in considering moral reasoning as interpretation, also dismisses subsumptive arguments. He regards legal reasoning as a paradigm for moral reasoning. Interpretation should be the 'path' in either kind of reasoning (1985). It cannot amount to the subsumption of cases under 'abstract' universal rules and principles, since it aims at judgements that account for unique features of concrete cases. The thesis that rules are essential for moral reasoning, according to Walzer, is refuted by the observation that conflicting principles may apply to a particular case.

According to traditionalists, the subsumption model with its emphasis on principles, abstracts not only from the particulars of a situation, but also from the qualities which a person needs for wise decisions. Traditionalists insist that, in moral judging, only persons endowed with the wisdom of 'experience and fine-tuned perception' can properly attend to unique features of particular situations (Nussbaum 1990). Thus understood, a moral judgement is the perception of the right and proper thing to do rather than a conclusion reached by the application of a principle.

Against this view, we would hold that judgements as fine tuned perceptions are entirely compatible with judgements on the basis of principles. A judgement, attained by perception or any other means, can always be logically reconstructed as a conclusion of an argument with a principle among the premises. We would contend that such reconstructions are indispensable in full-fledged assessments of judgements.

Considering wisdom, traditionalists tend to view principles as mere 'rules of thumb' for the inexperienced. Wise and experienced persons allegedly do not need principles to determine what is right in concrete situations. We would object here that even the most sensitive among us still need principles to guide their actions and to justify their decisions, 'to navigate among descriptions of situations' (O'Neill 1987, 64). These need not be the principles like those searched for by rationalist universalists. Instead, we may agree with John Kekes that principles are 'born out of the practice they subsequently guide, and are born through the midwifery of judgement' (Kekes 1989, 129). This is not to deny that principles require interpretations that fit concrete situations. As O'Neill states: 'Principles and rules must be indeterminate, so cannot specify all the boundary conditions or all the details of their own application in varying contexts. We cannot deduce their applications' (O'Neill 1987).

All in all, we sympathise with many points made by traditionalists. But we deplore their dismissal of the subsumption model and allied theorising. Their focus is almost exclusively on *processes*, not least psychological ones, that result in judgements. We should also attend to a proper reconstruction of *results*. Practical judgements, in ethics or the law, must be satisfactory in a psychological sense. In addition to this, they must allow of justification by logically proper means.

The contributions in part I of this volume concern the relation between theory, principles and judgements. Govert A. den Hartogh discusses the attacks of particularists and casuists on standard methodology, especially in 'practical' or 'applied' ethics with principles at the core. Den Hartogh defends this methodology, transforming criticisms into a tool for understanding it better. In his analysis of casuistry, he shows that cases allow moral analysis only if they function as models or paradigms representing general considerations. Casuistry cannot be meaningful unless it recognises that moral truth resides not in the particular case as such, but in clusters of cases. Particular cases have heuristic value only in relation to general considerations. Cases *fix the meaning* of these considerations, and as such they have indispensable informational value. That is why the deductivism of the subsumption model is wrong. In his view, principles are always qualified by open-ended chains of exception clauses. He calls this view 'default-generalism'. Principles are part of a network of general considerations that calls for holistic applications. Applications can never be mechanical; they require judgement. The exercise of judgement can either defeat or override a principle.

Theo van Willigenburg criticises Den Hartogh's views. Considering theories of moral argumentation, he distinguishes between 'top-down' approaches such as principlism, specificism and deductivism, and 'bottom-up' approaches such as casuistry. All approaches claim guidance toward justifiable conclusions. Top-down approaches focus on rules or principles, bottom-up approaches focus on precedents. Adherents of rule-based methods argue that we need rules to make our decisions consistent and coherent, and our actions predictable. Van Willigenburg contends that moral rules would have guiding power only if they were specified in detail. But their relevance would decrease with specification. To be relevant, a rule must be general. These considerations combine to render the entire idea of guidance by rules problematic. Hence, Van Willigenburg denies that cases are relevant only to the extent that they represent general considerations. Generalists such as Den Hartogh wrongly assume that descriptions which make a precedent relevant for a new case, need to be informed by a general rule. Van Willigenburg sympathises with particularists, who hold that morally relevant 'salient features' cannot always be captured by general rules.

Analogical reasoning has an important place in the methodology of particularists. Particular cases are not connected by general principles. New cases are resolved by analogies between old and new cases. In the words of Jonsen & Toulmin: 'Thus the first feature of casuistic method is the ordering of cases under a principle by paradigm and analogy' (1988, 252). Henri Wijsbek and Harm Kloosterhuis both chart the method of analogical reasoning.

Henri Wijsbek analyses the structure and the strength of analogies in much detail. Analogies enable us to transfer, via similarity relations, available information about a 'base' to a partially unknown situation, the 'target'. The nature of similarity is a contentious issue in literature about analogical reasoning. According to Wijsbek, we need a criterion for *relevant* similarity. Wijsbek's point of departure is the most promising theory of relevant similarity, the theory of *structural* similarity developed by Derder Gentner et al. The base has a certain structure. The structure can be transferred to the target. Therefore the same conclusion holds for the target. Wijsbek rejects Hemple's view in which analogies might be psychologically effective and rhetorically effective, but logically speaking irrelevant. Contrary to Hempel, he argues that analogical arguments can be valid, if one modifies the concept of validity. This concept works with default rules. If I have no evidence to the contrary, I am entitled to infer that the same properties in the target lead to the same conclusion as in the base. Due to the default-character of the rules, the conclusion can be false, even when all the premises are true, without thereby invalidating the inference. His conclusion is that analogies provide a method for incorporating new or contested phenomena consistently into an existing conceptual framework. So apart from their heuristic function, they have a justificatory role to play as well. Their devious nature suggest that they will find employment principally when the target-inference cannot be applied directly due to ignorance or bias on the part of the addressee. Knowledge is useful because it enables us to find our way in the natural and social world. If we can gain genuinely new knowledge by satisfying ourselves with something less than absolute certainty, then that is a price we should gladly pay. It's the kind of knowledge we always had about the world anyway. For a large part, it is gained through analogies.

In his influential *Moral Notions* Julius Kovesi endorses the common view that analogies in moral reasoning serve to elucidate and elaborate the meaning of concepts, rules and principles (1967, esp. 32 ff.). Their meaning is not exhausted by applications in paradigm cases. Paradigm cases merely represent undisputed applications of concepts, rules, and principles. Analogical reasoning serves to explore their applicability in new cases. The function of analogies is both heuristic and justificatory. From a logical point of view, analogical arguments are inconclusive. However, analogical arguments can be turned into valid ones by adding a premise. In Kloosterhuis' contribution, the legal philosopher Ilmar Tammelo figures as a representative of this position.

Tammelo's approach is wrong, according to Kloosterhuis, because he abstracts from the communicative and interactional context of analogical arguments. Judges, in the context of the cases before the court, always take counter-arguments of actual or hypothetical antagonists into account. Thus, the acceptability of an analogical argument does not exclusively depend on logical validity.

Kloosterhuis uses the pragma-dialectical argumentation theory of Frans van Eemeren and Rob Grootendorst to develop a more comprehensive and systematic reconstruction of analogical arguments. According to them, analogical reasoning represents a relationship between arguments and a standpoint defended in a discourse procedure. The nature of the relationship depends on the aim to convince those who militate against the standpoint. Argumentation schemes such as analogical reasoning allow of critical evaluation. Our evaluations should cover both the acceptability of schemes as such and the correctness of applications. Kloosterhuis elaborates standards for both aspects of evaluation regarding analogical arguments in legal reasoning.

Facts, Judgements, Theories

In discussions about legal reasoning, the role of facts is underestimated. If, in a legal argument, a factual statement linking the conclusion with a rule is false, then the conclusion is not supported by the rule. Likewise for moral reasoning.

Judges and lawyers cannot afford to abstract from the facts of the case. They not only argue points of law, but also the facts of the case. These are often difficult to establish. The memories and perceptions of even honest and reliable witnesses can distort reality. Criminal cases, for example, require proof beyond reasonable doubt that the accused has committed a crime under a legal rule. That explains why rules of evidence are an important subject in legal theory.

Moral philosophers who are not involved with real-life practical ethics, tend to illustrate their reasoning with hypothetical examples. Wijsbek discusses, in part I, Judith Jarvis Thomson's famous example of an analogical argument by which she tries to justify the decision of a woman who becomes pregnant after being raped, to abort the foetus. These examples are often construed such that no doubt exist about the facts of the case.

Considering more realistic settings, moral philosophers often concentrate on normative principles, while leaving disputes about facts to scientists. Thus, they engage in lengthy discussions about the principle of the preservation of the integrity of animals. Should it supplement the principle of preventing and not inflicting harm and pain? This is indeed a difficult issue. But the empirical issues involved are at least as difficult. We should know which species of animals really experience pain and what actions cause pain in these animals. Confronted with such matters, moral philosophers have to turn to empirical science. What does biology tell us about the capacity of an animal species to experience pain? Would the experience of animal species differ from pain in humans? No consensus about these issues exists in biology. But educated guesses based on similarities and differences between humans and other species are feasible in principle. Ethicists should anyhow be acquainted with relevant scientific evidence, to know the potential domain of application of normative principles. Considering the treatment of animals, say in husbandry, ethicists may hold that we should err on the safe side in attributing pain to animals. If so, then biologists can at least offer them suggestions about the location of the safe side.

In passing, we note that the role of empirical issues in normative reasoning should strengthen our comments above on traditionalism. We argued that the overemphasis on experience and wisdom which characterises much traditionalism is misguided. Imagine traditionalists not knowing about biology, who visit a zoo. Suppose they wish to know if chimpanzees kept there are treated well. If they perceived that the animals often show broad grins with teeth bared, for example in interactions with visitors, they would presumably regard this as a sign of well-being. That would be a serious mistake. Chimpanzees resemble human beings in many respects, but important dissimilarities exist not least in facial expressions. 'Grinning', in chimpanzees, is a sign of *fear*. Biologists do know that much about the animals. Experience and wisdom in moral matters would be singularly unhelpful in this case if not informed by reliable arguments from biology.

Contributions from empirical science in normative settings are not limited to controversial opinions. Uncertainties do exist in science, but science can also deliver hard evidence and well-confirmed theories. Indeed, we would not regard controversy within science as the main source of trouble for ethics and the law. The main problem is rather that it is increasingly difficult to locate evidence and well-confirmed theories that properly bear on our normative concerns. Science nowadays provides us with huge amounts of information from rapidly increasing numbers of disciplines. Thus, most scientists are unable to oversee their own discipline, and they seldom have adequate knowledge about other disciplines covering similar territories. Therefore, it would be unwise for ethicists simply to rely on opinions about empirical matters voiced by experts from science. It is desirable that ethicists somehow arrive at an overview of science, however superficial, that allows them to locate appropriate sources of evidence to be studied in more detail. The two examples below illustrate this.

Two anthropologists, James Fairhead and Melissa Leach (1996) have recently performed an in-depth study of landscapes in Guinea in western Africa. They offer convincing evidence showing that common opinions about the origin of the landscapes are flawed. Common views have it that the current mosaic pattern of forest patches amidst savannah represents desertification, or at least deforestation, in progress. Further, it is generally assumed that the inhabitants of small villages wreak havoc by inappropriate methods of agriculture. Fairhead and Leach show that these views are based on dogma rather than evidence. Administrators in the colonial past simply *assumed* that Guinea had been fully covered by forest in recent times, and that the mosaic landscape is a sign of deforestation. The dogma has been perpetuated over decades without a proper search for evidence. It has led to disastrous policies promoted by so-called developed countries, with the putative aim of improving the environment in Guinea. Local populations have been indicted of mismanagement, and their agricultural practices have been replaced, forcibly so, by modern methods aiming to improve on the situation. In reality, the mosaic pattern has existed over the centuries, and villagers have actually increased forest areas by prudent management. Needless to say, common policies have invoked all sorts of legal and moral principles. In the case of Guinea, the application of these principles has been entirely inappropriate since they were combined with empirical claims that are demonstrably false.

Common views of some medical treatments also appear to exhibit this pattern. Ethicist have a role to play in the evaluation of treatments by cost-benefit analyses. Considering the facts about costs and benefits they will mostly rely on experts from medicine. That may not be wise in all cases. We should realise that intimate links exist nowadays between medicine and the pharmaceutical industry. A huge amount of literature *outside* medicine convincingly shows that such links at times benefit the industry while they harm patients. This indicates that bias in scientific research about medical treatments, and bias in policies based on research, are much more common than the average medical professional would have it. Governmental organisations which are legally responsible for marketing decisions, often reveal bias in favour of the industry even to the extent that they act against their own guidelines. A good source illustrating this in a shocking way is a book by John Abraham (Abraham 1995). We should not be surprised that bias exists. We all know that the consumption of officially prescribed drugs has exhibited a massive increase over the last few decades. The quantities of drugs consumed should indeed suggest, oddly so, that populations in western countries are mostly composed of ill persons. Shouldn't ethics and the law be concerned with biased science, pure and applied, as a potential source of this situation?

The examples cast doubt on the common assumption that science is generally the most reliable source of knowledge. This assumption is linked with the view that science is value-free, albeit in a limited sense. Wim van der Steen argues that value-freedom cannot exist in any sense. In addition to constitutive, methodological values, contextual values play a legitimate and unavoidable role within scientific research. He shows by examples that researchers can but resort to contextual values to justify priorities among divergent methodological criteria which scientific theories have to meet. It is impossible for theories to satisfy all criteria at the same time. Therefore, moral philosophers should not simply rely on scientists for empirical information to make their principles operative. Theories and data are intrinsically selective. Moral philosophers who deal with practical questions and who participate in public debates about such questions, should uncover selectivity in reports written by experts from science and determine what selections are adequate for their purposes.

Considering the role of facts within legal reasoning, H.J.M. Boukema argues that presentations of facts, not least by lawyers, are unavoidably selective. In trials, lawyers aim to establish a selection of relevant facts so as to maximise the chances that rules of law secure a legal conclusion fitting their purposes. As Boukema puts it, lawyers have an ingrained respect for facts and only a subordinate interest in truth. Advocates try to present facts and use applicable rules in a manner most favourable to their clients. Likewise for prosecutors *vis-a-vis* the public interest. Judges are very much interested in the truth and in *all* the facts, but civil and criminal procedure limit their access to facts, and hence, the truth. They are confined to the case as presented by litigants or prosecutor and defendant.

Accusations of incest belong to the most difficult cases brought before the court. Incest is commonly committed with girls below the age of 14 by fathers or other male persons within the intimate circle of the family. Some authors contend that, because of its traumatic nature, experiences of incest tend to be repressed or dissociated. Victims often suffer from all kinds of psychic and psychosomatic symptoms. In psychotherapy, the victim allegedly becomes aware again of the repressed or dissociated memories of incest. The psychotherapist recognises the symptoms as possible signs of incest, suggests this explanation to the client, and tries to uncover lost memories. The problem with incest cases is that evidence for the accusations is hard to obtain. Cees Maris uses the example of incest to discuss the merits of narrative legal theories. According to these theories, all human knowledge consists of narratives which cannot be assessed through correspondence with an independent empirical reality. They replace the criterion of correspondence by narrative coherence among diverse stories. For the narrative legal theorist, incest cases do not constitute a specific problem, because it is anyhow impossible to check factual assertions of diverse parties in a legal case against empirical reality. The reliability of the victims' memories in incest cases is a hotly disputed issue. Experimental psychologists contend that lost memories are fabricated by the therapists. Some clinical psychologists respond that the laboratory experiments by which experimental psychologists test human memory, cannot do justice to their clinical practice. Should one give the benefit of the doubt to the clinical psychologists who usually support the stories of the victims? Some feminists do plead for a reversal of the burden of proof in incest cases, on grounds of positive discrimination. The position of women is vulnerable. Their stories about abuse usually meet unbelief and defence reactions. Incest is a wide-spread phenomenon. A reversal of the burden of proof would strengthen the position of incest victims. Maris rejects this argument. A reversal of the burden of proof would result in an unacceptably high percentage of unjust convictions. Maris finally concludes that the criterion of narrative coherence is not sufficient. Although every assertion about reality may be a construction, the building blocks of the construction cannot be mere fictions. We need extra-narrative evidential support, even in incest cases.

Factual assertions not only figure as premises in normative arguments. They also play a role in background convictions supporting the plausibility of normative theories. In his contribution Albert W. Musschenga discusses whether the plausibility or implausibility of empirical background assumptions affects the justification of an ethical theory and its basic moral principles. He concludes that the impact on a theory's justification of the discovery that certain of its empirical background beliefs are false or very implausible, depends on the nature of the evidentiary relation between these beliefs and the theory. Hardly any ethical theory has disappeared because its empirical background assumptions proved to be implausible. What has happened again and again is that problematic empirical background assumptions are dropped or replaced by other, more plausible ones.

In the last section of his contribution he discusses another way to make the findings of empirical science relevant for ethical theorising and practical ethics: empirical science can tell us whether what 'ought' to be done also 'can' be done. His conclusion is that the standard of feasibility is only relevant for a general evaluation of theories and principles which aim to guide other-regarding, interpersonal actions, and not for supererogatory ones. He argues that perhaps much more relevant than the *general* feasibility of theories and principles is whether these are feasible in *particular contexts*. Empirical research is needed to determine whether empirical background assumptions and presuppositions can be met in a specific context. He illustrates this by examining whether assumptions presupposed by the doctrine of informed consent, apply to decisions of very ill patients regarding participation in clinical research. The assumptions concern the capacity of humans to grasp and understand information and make autonomous decisions.

References

Abraham, J. (1995), *Science, Politics and the Pharmaceutical Industry*, UCL Press, London.

Clarke, S.G. & E. Simpson (1989), *Anti-Theory and Moral Conservatism*, SUNY Press, Albany.

Fairhead, J. & M. Leach (1996), *Misreading the African Landscape*, Cambridge University Press, Cambridge.

Jonsen, A. & S. Toulmin (1988), *The Abuse of Casuistry*, University of California Press, Berkeley.

Kekes, J. (1989), *Moral Tradition and Individuality*, Princeton University Press, Princeton.

Kovesi, J. (1967), *Moral Notions*, Routledge & Kegan Paul, London.

MacCormick, M.N. (1978), *Legal Reasoning and Truth*, Oxford University Press, Oxford.

MacIntyre, A. (1988), *Whose Justice? Whose Rationality?*, Duckworth, London.

Moody-Adams, M.E. (1997), *Fieldwork in Familiar Places*, Harvard University Press, Cambridge, Mass.

Nussbaum, M.C. (1990), *Love's Knowledge*, Oxford University Press, New York/ Oxford.

O'Neill, O. (1987), 'Abstraction, Idealization, and Ideology in Ethics', in J.D.G. Evans (ed.), *Moral Philosophy and Contemporary Problems*, Cambridge University Press, Cambridge, pp. 55-70.

Walzer, M. (1987), *Interpretation and Social Criticism*, Cambridge University Press, Cambridge, Mass./London.

Part I:
Theory, Principle, Judgement

1 General and Particular Considerations in Applied Ethics

GOVERT A. DEN HARTOGH[1]

In spite of sustained criticism, principles still form the core of the usual methodology of applied ethics. People usually assume that the area they study is governed by a set of principles, that problems can be analysed as conflicts between principles, and that solution, even if argued only by intuitive 'weighing', will consist in some form of arbitration between their competing claims. In this paper I argue that this is how it should be. That doesn't mean, however, that the criticisms are simply mistaken. They help us understand the standard methodology more clearly.

The paradigm of this approach in bioethics, which has shaped the outlook of an entire generation of ethicists, and even to some extent of the workers in the field, is *Principles of Biomedical Ethics* by Beauchamp & Childress (1994), with its four principles of non-maleficence, beneficence, respect for autonomy and justice, widely known as the Georgetown mantra. Problems in bioethics often are alleged to arise from conflicts between the principles of respect for people's autonomy and of benificence. A sophisticated example of the approach is Joel Feinberg's monumental quattrology on the moral foundations of the criminal law, which lists and evaluates the possible grounds for encroaching upon an individual's freedom, with the conclusion that freedom should be restricted only to prevent harm and offence to others. The argument for this conclusion consists in the detailed discussion of hard cases, which at the same time results in a specification of the meaning of the principles, both the accepted and the rejected ones. Most studies of distributive justice likewise focus on principles. Indeed, the most significant (and to my mind most worrying) characteristic of work in this area is that the claims of justice are usually derived from one basic principle only, say equal or leximin 'real freedom'. Recent work fortunately reinstates pluralism; Michael Walzer (1983), for instance, recognises principles of need, desert, and the recognition of 'membership', and his discussion of the distributive problems of concrete 'spheres of justice' (health care, leisure time, jobs, education) takes the usual 'principlist' format: deciding which principles govern any particular sphere, and solving apparent, or arbitrating real conflicts between them.[2]

Principlism is usually criticised on the following grounds. (1) The appeal to principles doesn't help to solve actual practical problems, for these arise precisely when principles conflict with each other. (2) Principles don't offer any significant guidance in concrete cases anyway because of their inherent vagueness and indeterminacy. (3) For any rule or principle, we know that situations will or at least may emerge requiring us to break it, but that is something we can only decide by looking at the case at hand. There is an obvious tension between these objections: principles must be practically informative to some extent, in order either to conflict with each other, or to stand in the way of what 'the situation requires'. But we cannot dismiss any particular objection simply because it belongs to an incoherent set. So I consider them all, in separate sections respectively. In between I take a hard look at the alleged superiority of the casuistic method in providing determinate guidance.

How to Decide Conflicts

The most common criticism of the appeal to principles is the following. Applied ethics, if it is to be of any use, should help us 'solve' problematic cases. At the very least it should enable us to reduce the range of acceptable solutions. Principles are no use whatsoever in achieving this aim. For problematic cases typically involve conflicting principles. Thus we have to turn to other considerations to make any progress. In concrete cases these considerations usually derive from the careful observation of relevant characteristics of the case; no 'codebook' of general rules and principles can generate them.

The argument means to suggest that applied ethics should forget about rules and principles, and rather attend to the similarities and differences between the relevant aspects of concrete case descriptions. That is the method of casuistry, which allegedly improves on principlism.

But this conclusion doesn't follow from the argument at all.

In one of the more forceful presentations of the argument, Earl Winkler (1993) usefully (and consistently) gives us an example. He compares two cases in which physicians have to decide whether or not to proceed with medical treatment of a patient against his own will. The first patient suffers from multiple sclerosis, and refuses to have his meningitis treated. His past history indicates a rather successful adjustment to his condition, and his MS has not worsened. It turns out that his refusal of treatment results from a family crisis which has caused some relatives to withdraw their usual concern and support. The physicians decide to give the patient antibiotics to save his life and inform him accordingly. They also tell him how to deal with what they think is his real problem. (When they have done so, Winkler writes, '(t)he patient is silent'. What would they have done, if he had protested vehemently, had asked for an attorney etc.?) Family counselling starts, it restores the internal peace of the family, 'and everyone is happy'.

The second patient is paraplegic as a result of a motorcycle accident, which has made him embittered against the whole world. Having refused all efforts at rehabilitation before, he now refuses to eat. But his general tendency to blame everyone else for his condition even prevents him from taking full responsibility for this decision. Force-feeding is considered, but decided against.

In both cases the principle of respect for autonomy is relevant, but the details of the cases invite us to honour the principle in the second case, but not in the first. This cannot be explained, Winkler believes, by the assumption that some initial condition of application of the principle isn't fulfilled in the first case, while it is fulfilled in the second. The principle requires the patient to be competent for making his decision, in some sense of competence (to be specified!). But whatever criterion of competence we suggest, the first patient is more likely to satisfy it than the second. It could be argued, Winkler goes on to suggest, that the refusal of the first patient isn't really an authentic choice. It doesn't fit well with the basic values and commitments of this patient, given the actual circumstances (as opposed to the circumstances as he perceives them). But the same point can be made, he believes (I am not so sure about this), about the second patient.

This case-study shows that we cannot simply decide such issues by taking the principle of respect for autonomy as our premise and deriving a solution from it by Modus Ponens. We should look at the cases carefully, and this may cause us to have doubts which in the first case – for Winkler at least, and presumably for most of his American readers – cannot be silenced.[3] But the case-study does not show that we can forget about the principle, and look at the cases *instead*.

Why do we want to abstain from force-feeding in the second case? Clearly because that would be a brutal infringement of the patient's autonomy. Moreover, both cases presumably confront us with *genuine* moral conflicts, not only apparent ones. We have to choose between two alternatives, and the reason to prefer one alternative is respect for the patient's autonomy, the reason to prefer the other is that this will serve the best interests of the patient. (Again, this seems debatable to me in the second case, but that is besides the point.) And these are genuine reasons: even if they are overruled, they are not simply set aside. In that case they leave 'moral traces' (Nozick 1968) which should be reflected in the agent's actions and feelings. For instance, the principle of autonomy at least requires the physicians to fully explain their choice to the first patient.

So the principles to a large extent provide us with the reasons for our eventual choices, or, as I will put it, the principles *rationalise* our choices.[4] On this point the criticism of principlism has an air of absurdity. 'Principles are of no use, for they don't help to solve real problems.' Could that be a good defence for a doctor who simply disregards his patient's autonomy or does not even try to act in his best interests?

Interestingly, and for the critics exceptionally, Winkler to some extent recognises the point. But, he argues, this 'deductive' construction of justification 'is irredeemably *ex post facto* and retrospective. In a far more important, essential, and primary sense, justification is a *process*.' And in this process the real work is done by case-driven considerations.

It is true that when we are asked to offer a justification of a decision, the question can have different meanings. For example, the meaning of such a question might be: why is it true that we have to abstain from force-feeding? The answer to this question is: force-feeding would violate the principle of respect for autonomy. This amounts to justification in the sense of rationalisation. A second possible meaning of the same question is: how do we arrive at the insight that we have to abstain from force-feeding? This epistemological question is still ambiguous, it can be taken in two different senses. In the first sense it is a question about the justification of our belief, it asks for a *warrant*. In the second sense it asks for a *heuristic*, and it is answered by a reconstruction of an actual thought process. So far, the critical argument has only established that 'looking at the case' has a heuristic value.

What is the relation between the quest for a rationalisation (a reason for choosing one option rather than another) and the quest for a warrant (a reason for the belief that our choice is right)? Both may appeal to the same consideration(s). But it is also possible that we are sure that something is wrong while being unsure about the reason why it is wrong. Thus our belief that something is wrong need not depend on accepting any particular explanation of the fact that it is wrong. Indeed, a rationalisation may be warranted by the very judgement which it rationalises: a reason may derive part of its plausibility from the fact that it *covers* a judgement about which we are intuitively sure.[5]

However, this doesn't seem to be the case in either of Winkler's two cases. In so far as the autonomy principle and the best interests principle figure in the rationalisation judgements for these cases, they seem to be part of the answer to the epistemological question as well. We have doubts about simply doing the best for the first patient, and we strongly feel that it would be wrong to force-feed the second one. These epistemic attitudes can only be defended by appeal to the principle of respect for autonomy. If we 'forget' about the principles, we loose both: our sense of a conflict in both cases, and also the way of finding the proper solution to the second one. (As well as a guide to action in innumerable cases which we now reckon to be unproblematic ones.) So, even on the epistemological issue, the principles form a large part of the story, even if not the whole of it.

What more do we need? I have already mentioned considerations of competence and authenticity. Other relevant considerations include the following.

(1) What the patient 'really' wants, is not wholly clear in the first case, as is testified by his silence after the physicians' announcement of their intention. Expressed death wishes can 'mean' – be intended to communicate – many things, and often more than one thing at the same time. What a competent speaker of the language knows the utterances to mean is not all, and some-

times not at all what they mean. In the first case we may wonder whether the patient really wants to be dead at all. In the second case this is less doubtful, even though 'wishing to be dead' is here a form of accusation or revenge as well. (I don't so much doubt the authenticity of the patient's refusal as its integrity.)

(2) What exactly does the alleged personal value of the life of the second patient (the value of his life for himself) amount to?

(3) The option of not-respecting his autonomy in this case involves the highly invasive and brutally coercive action of force-feeding.

(4) Lastly, while in the first case we may reasonably hope that the patient will eventually agree with our decision, as a result of a personal development which doesn't compromise the rationality of his agreement, no such hope seems to be warranted in the second case.

These considerations are almost as general as the appeal to principles, they are relevant to classes of cases. (Note that Winkler describes his own concrete cases in terms which cover other possible, and quite probably actual, cases as well.) They are also *related* to the notions of autonomy and best interests. This is obviously true for considerations (1) and (2), for they are relevant to deciding what these principles exactly require. Correctly interpreting the will of the patient is required by the principle of respect for autonomy itself. So the need for this interpretation can hardly be an argument for the redundancy of the principle. To identify what is required by each principle, we may need to answer many subsidiary questions; that is part of what we mean when we say that applying a principle requires judgement. Considerations (3) and (4) are relevant in a different way. Violations of the norm of respecting a person's autonomy come in degrees. It makes a difference whether we disregard only the person's present will, or his durable will for the foreseeable future. And to use physical force means 'violating' autonomy in a stronger sense than to insist on giving antibiotics. Such considerations help us when the relevant principles cannot be jointly satisfied, for in such cases we should inquire which package of actions and attitudes do satisfy them to the largest possible extent. This is not merely a matter of the comparative evaluation of available options. Our task is rather to *design* such a package of actions.[6] Executing that task requires creativity and imagination.[7]

To begin with, we should differentiate between several aspects or dimensions of the value protected by a principle. For example, what is it about autonomy that makes it worth respecting? The fact that each individual knows best what is in his own best interests? Or that he knows best what is most consonant with his basic values and commitments? Or is it the intrinsic value of his sovereignty over his own life, of his being 'at the steering wheel'? Each of these considerations invites us to determine its relative force and to chart the limits of its area of application. Second, we should make sure we understand the intrinsic nature or 'social meaning' of the things or actions to which the principle is applied. This is obviously true about principles of distribution,[8] but it applies also to the notion of 'brutality' which differentiates Winkler's two cases of possible violations of autonomy. Third, we should realise that principles should not be applied one by one, in an atomistic way, but rather holistically, as a network of interrelated considerations. For instance, if autonomy is only one of people's interests among others, however basic, it should be weighed against those others, but if it is constitutive of a person's moral standing, it should be given additional weight, perhaps even lexical priority.

It is because of the fact that principles are to be considered holistically, that we should sometimes allow ourselves to get involved in ethical 'theory', for theory aims at reconstructing coherent sets of rationalising general considerations. But we should not expect too much from theory. Progress with a practical problem need not depend on our ability to tackle the theoretical issues underlying it. If ethical theory aims at reconstructing the interrelations between values and principles, the plurality of competing theories suggests that its success is rather limited. (Though the understandable focus on the area of disagreement may be somewhat misleading.) Epistemologically speaking, most of the warrant theories claim derives from their ability to account for lower-level judgements. For these reasons it is generally an unattractive program to try to find solutions to practical problems by deducing them from comprehensive ethical theories. Such theories don't have sufficient authority to deliver the goods. That doesn't rule out, however, that particular questions require us to consider problems from 'high theory', as for instance the truth of the doctrine of double effect, the legitimacy of agent-relative considerations etc.[9] As Williams said in his influential criticism of high theory, there is no reason to expect the truth about the subject matter of ethics to be simple. 'Perhaps we need as many concepts to describe it as we find we need, and no fewer' (Williams 1985, 17).[10] We can be interested in ethical theory for practical reasons without believing it to be the starting point of all, or even most arguments in applied ethics.[11]

I have argued that, to solve conflicts of principles, we have to supplement the principles by subsidiary considerations of two kinds: considerations of application (exemplified by (1) and (2) above) and considerations of specification (e.g. (3) and (4)). 'Specifying principles' has recently been put forward as a way of saving principlism in an amended form (Richardson 1990, 1994; DeGrazia 1992).[12] In my view this is something applied ethicists have always done, even if some (Feinberg, Walzer) are far more expert in doing it than others. We will even find later that the method is equivalent to the method recommended by those who want to replace principlism by casuistry.

Specifying considerations again invites the sceptical comment we found Winkler making to principles: perhaps we may use them in explaining our achievements *ex post facto*, but they are no use at all in making those achievements. (The comment recalls similar sceptical views of legal realists and others on the justification of courts' verdicts.) Rather, it is only by attending to the details of the case at hand that we find the 'solution' which we afterwards defend in terms of the ambivalence of death wishes, grades of brutality of the violation of autonomy etc. My answer to the sceptic again consists in distinguishing between two questions. The first question is *why it is* that we should decide to respect the patient's autonomy in the second case, but not in the first. Which aspects of the cases actually *make* them relevantly different? Answering this question of rationalisation we point to the general considerations I listed and similar ones. The second question is *how we know* that we should make those different decisions in both cases. At this point the critic could insist that we know by looking, and that this knowledge is prior to any commitment to the general considerations which, admittedly, rationalise our judgement. But this position is implausible. Perhaps, in simply attending to the details of the second case, we immediately had a strong intuition that in this case force-feeding would be unacceptable. Still that would be an epistemologically unsatisfactory state to be in. We would feel the urge to find good reasons for our judgement, convincing for ourselves and *in foro externo,* for others. And when someone suggests those reasons, we will respond by feeling more confident of our judgement.

Usually, I suggest, these are not distinct stages. Our very first 'intuition' will already be a judgement about the case in terms of reasons.[13] The first sentence in which Winkler presents his conclusion is a case in point: 'attempting to force-feed this patient would be perfectly brutal and without foreseeable end'. Most case-driven considerations already appeal either to principles or to general considerations that specify them.

The Guiding Power of Principles

The second standard criticism of principlism has it that, due to the vagueness of general terms and the complexity of the world, principles are too indeterminate to provide any guidance. This line of criticism, as I said, is hardly consistent with the first one. But the answer to both objections is roughly the same, so I will be brief about the second one.

Principles, as we saw, have to be supplemented by subsidiary specifying considerations, to flesh out such abstracts concepts as 'autonomy', 'competence', 'harm', 'need' etc., and to design packages of actions which optimally satisfy sets of competing principles. So it is true that in applying principles judgement is needed. But it hardly follows that we can snugly do with the judgement alone and forget about the principles.

Judgement is needed not least because many concepts used in principles have threshold values. How good should a performance be to count as competent? How important should a setback to interests be to count as harm? To answer such questions, we must draw a line on a continuum. The continuum is relevant again when we cannot satisfy all relevant principles jointly, for if we cannot stay at the thresholds, we want to stay as close to them as possible. It is true that these questions cannot be decided by appeal to the principles themselves, because they make no sense outside the context of the enterprise of applying them.

Perhaps the basic misunderstanding involved in this second line of criticism is identifying a principle with a formula. Knowing a principle is similar to understanding a general prescription, issued by authority, even if actually there is no authority 'behind' the principle at all. If you know what the words 'respect' and 'autonomy' mean, you know what it means to respect autonomy, and therefore you are able to recognise each case in which respect is required. On this view, by the way, it is hard to see what the special expertise of an ethicist might possibly consist of. His task is apparently limited to 'conceptual analysis', which should be distinguished from substantial moral judgement. I have no idea what such an analysis would look like. It is simply impossible to apply the principle of respect for autonomy without an appreciation of the value of autonomy, and the moral relevance of this value, which goes far beyond the understanding of the lexical meaning of words. We should rather put it the other way around: you only fully understand the way a principle is expressed if you are able to apply it correctly.

My arguments sofar may foster the suggestion that I believe all the real work in applied ethics to be done by general considerations: providing rationalisations and warrants. Careful attention to cases merely has a heuristic value. However, I have not denied that 'brute' (i.e. non-rationalised) intuitions about cases may provide part of the warrant for our final judgements. More importantly, I would grant that looking at particular case may be a necessary stage on the way of finding the specifications we need. There is more to competence in applying norms than knowledge of the meanings of words. What exactly is involved in this 'more'?

The Alleged Superiority of Casuistry

The usual alternative to principlism is casuistry. Confronted with a hard case, unable to decide between, say, two seemingly equally attractive and equally objectionable alternatives, we are advised not to look for general considerations which will only rationalise our conflict, but rather for cases which are comparable to the present one in most respects, but in which the first or the second of our alternatives are obviously to be preferred. Even better, we might construct a whole range of such cases on a continuum between the two 'clear' ones. Then we have to judge how close our present case is to either end of the continuum.

It is hard to imagine someone going through this procedure in its pure form.[14] How do we identify relevant 'clear cases'? How are we to measure closeness? The answer seems to be that, implicitly at least, we appeal to general considerations. Our predicament is a conflict (real or apparent) between two principles, the clear cases are paradigmatic instantiations of each of these principles not conflicting with the other, and our judgement of 'closeness' derives from a cumulation of similarities and differences which all can be shown to be relevant by specifying considerations.

Casuistry has been most strongly defended, as an alternative to the 'tyranny of principles', by Jonsen and Toulmin (1988) in *The Abuse of Casuistry*, in which they argued that the casuistic method as practised by (mostly) catholic theologians in the sixteenth and seventeenth century, is an exemplar to be followed by present-day applied ethicists (see also Brody 1988; Van Willigenburg 1991). But the 'old' casuistry as they describe it turns out to appeal to principles in precisely the way I suggested to be unavoidable.

By and large, the method consisted in the following steps. The point of departure is some particular item from an established code of behaviour, e.g. the Ten Commandments or the Seven Deadly Sins. This item defines a certain ethical domain. The first step in treating the problems of the domain is to present some paradigmatic and unproblematic examples of conduct in accordance with duty and of conduct violating it. Next, a range of possible cases is constructed having more and more dissimilarities in comparison with the paradigm cases. For each of these cases the dissimilarities are specified, and their weight is then adjusted in terms of two types of considerations: opinions of moral authorities (fathers of the church, the highest esteemed casuists from the tradition), and so-called 'maxims'. Cases are then decided (with a specified degree of 'probability') on the cumulative force of these considerations.

This, of course, is not what I called 'pure casuistry' at all, it is casuistry with the general considerations in the background made explicit. Except for the appeal to authority, the approach is virtually indistinguishable from the procedure of specifying principles in confrontation with hard cases which I recommended in the first section. And so, again, it is not a forgotten method to be rediscovered, it is the method actually followed by all good work in applied ethics. It is worth observing that it is also the method generally practised in legal dogmatics.[15] In any reasonably comprehensive treatise on, say, contract law or fiscal law, the domain is organised by appealing to some basic rules and/or principles, which may or may not be explicitly stated in any statute. Paradigmatic applications of these principles, in statutory prescriptions and case law, are presented. We then move on to hard cases, most of them analysed as conflicts of basic rules and principles. Finally, solutions of these cases are offered in terms of specifying considerations which maximally restore coherence over the entire domain.

So, contrary to the usual interpretations of the great debate on the proper method of applied ethics, we don't have two alternative methods here at all. (Of course, I don't deny that many authors are sinning: some on account of their monism and atomism, subsuming cases under their favourite principle without considering the acceptability of the outcomes; others on account of their unorganised pluralism, recognising 'tragic moral dilemmas' wherever a plurality of relevant considerations are found pointing in different directions.) What we have, rather, are different interpretations of the same procedure. Probably these interpretations make some difference in practice, but they hardly result in totally incompatible ways of arguing.

The interpretations differ along the following dimension. At one end we find the position, which I introduced already, according to which the appeal to cases has nothing but a heuristic (and, we may add, didactic) value. Problems are, in the end, decided by appeal to the subsection of relevant general considerations from the total network of valid ones. It only happens that the inescapable limitations of our understanding make it impossible for us to always have this entire network, or even the subsection, before our minds. But at some level the relevant considerations exert their force, and so it happens that when we are confronted with hard cases, we get an intuitive idea, in which these considerations are unconsciously applied. On the guidance of this idea, we will eventually be able to make the relevant considerations explicit as well.

On the opposed reconstruction, the category of general considerations would be dispensable but for the deficiencies in our understanding. The 'locus of certitude', as Jonsen and Toulmin call it, is always in the judgement on the particular case. But this judgement can only be relied upon if we 'see' the case in its correct shape, and here rules and principles may help us to attend to relevant details. They are to be seen as rules of thumb, summaries of our earlier concrete judgements. However, we can never be sure of their validity without assessing it in the concrete case itself (cf. Nussbaum 1986, ch. 10; Dancy 1993, ch. 4).

As I have presented these positions, they provide different answers to the epistemological question. 'Generalists' and 'particularists' also disagree on the rationalisation issue. I discuss this issue in the next section.

Both positions are deficient.[16] As to the first, it is a complete mystery, how attending to a particular case helps us find a relevant norm which otherwise eludes us. How can we have intuitions in which 'the norm exerts its force unconsciously'? There must be a closer connection between 'knowing a norm' and 'knowing what to do in a concrete case' than this account assumes.

The second position is even more unsatisfactory. If in some particular case the answer, on looking at the case in its right shape, is clear, how does this help us find the answer in another case, in which, so far, the answer is unclear? The point is not only that the defenders of the superiority of casuistry cannot answer this question, since the appeal to principles covering both cases is closed to them. The point is that any strong epistemological claim for the casuistic method is incompatible with (epistemological) particularism.[17] On a consistent particularist understanding the precedent case can have no authority at all; taking it into consideration does not warrant any growth of our confidence in the solution it suggests. We can only say that the similarities are more important than the differences or *vice versa after* having made up our mind on the problem case itself. For if the first judgement presented us with any support for the second, the locus of certitude would not fully be in the particular case at all.[18] Hence the precedent does not even create a presumption.

So what is the use of considering a precedent case? The most radical view is that it only has a heuristic use: it helps us fix attention on aspects of the case which may or may not be relevant; the proper use of the appeal to precedent is only that of an aide-memoire or checklist, (Dancy 1993, 66ff). That is clearly less than defenders of casuistry such as Jonsen and Toulmin claim for their favourite method. Moreover, it is precisely what the second view claimed to be the proper use of principles as well. So this conception surrenders the claim to superiority for the casuist method and concedes its equivalence to principlism.

But even this rather unambitious view is more than the epistemological particularist is entitled to. For why is it that of all the possible selections of possibly relevant properties of the problem case, some particular selection has a stronger claim on our attention than any other arbitrary one? There is no satisfactory answer to this question which doesn't claim some degree of *probability* that this selection determines the correct judgement of the problem case. We don't make checklists of mere possibilities. Particularism, however, cannot allow any claim to probability. If this is true, no form of the appeal to precedent is compatible with particularism.

The analogy with induction, often made, serves to underline the point. For an inductive generalisation is nothing but a statistical coincidence, which we shouldn't apply to the next case, unless we assume it to be traceable to an underlying universal causal pattern. If (*per impossibile*) we were to believe that no such causal patterns exist, we would have to stop making inductive generalisations. That the sun will rise tomorrow, would not even be a hypothesis.

Finally, it is worth noting that the practice of casuistry, as described by Jonsen and Toulmin, is in direct contradiction with any particularist interpretation. For the theologians working in this tradition always discussed *classes* of possible cases. Toulmin himself is very much inspired by his experience in a government committee on bioethical issues in which he found the members time and again to disagree strongly about 'principles', but to agree nevertheless about 'cases', (Toulmin 1981, 31; Jonsen & Toulmin 1988, 16-19).[19] Committees, however, don't discuss particular cases which all members are personally acquainted with, but rather classes of cases. Even if this is sometimes done by reference to reports of particular cases, the reports will describe these cases in general terms applicable to other cases as well.

Is any stable position to be found in-between these extremes? To answer this question, let us ask: how do we teach a person to follow a norm? It seems that there are two possibilities (Hart 1961, 121 ff): we can either communicate a statement of the norm in general terms, which we may expect a competent speaker of the language to understand, or we can present this person with a series of relevant cases, pointing out the required behaviour in each. How do we know that our pupil has understood the lesson? This is clear in the last case: he has understood it, if he is able without further guidance, to recognise a new relevant case, and to identify the required behaviour in it. But this is also the correct answer in the first case; if our pupil only knows the formula we have taught him, and is (mysteriously) able to explain its meaning by giving adequate reformulations, but doesn't know what to do in a concrete case, we would consider our lessons to have been in vain. This means that fully knowing the meaning of the statement of the norm consists in being able to continue the series. On the other hand, in using the second method, our aim hasn't been to teach our pupil something about the 'particular cases' we present, but rather about *extrapolations* from these to an indefinite number of new cases. If we are using statements in general terms as a vehicle, our aim is exactly the same, for to understand the meaning of such statements already involves being able to refer to paradigmatic cases, and to extrapolate from these to new ones.[20] Cognitive psychology tells us that our mastery of general concepts is like this; my suggestion is that our appeal to general considerations in practical judgement isn't at all different.

Note, however, that talk of 'particular' cases should not necessarily be taken literally; abbreviated sketches of such cases which stand for classes of cases, may be sufficient. The point is only that a grasp of the general always consists in the ability to extrapolate or project from some of its instantiations to others. That is not, as suggested in the claims for the superiority of casuistry over principlism (cf. McDowell 1979), a form of knowledge alternative to knowing a rule; it *is* knowing a rule.

We have now found the kernel of truth in the particularist criticism of principlism. Pointing to particular cases (or to descriptions of relatively concrete classes of cases) has more than a heuristic value only: it fixes the meaning of general (or higher-level) considerations, and as such it has an indispensable informational value. Even if in any particular case this value is dispensable, that is only because the relevant consideration is part of a network of beliefs which is fixed in this way at innumerable places. On the other hand, cases are only relevant as models or paradigms, as representatives of general considerations. All the operations of casuistry derive their sense from the fact that moral truth is not in the particular case as such, but only in clusters of cases.

The Order of Rationalisation

One argument for the epistemological priority of the general is the following. In each particular case in which an action is right or wrong, praiseworthy or blameworthy, some properties of the action and of the context of action combine to make it right, wrong etc. This presupposes a valid norm in virtue of which these properties are right-making etc. In itself, this is an insight about rationalisation, not about warrant. But if it is true, it also simply and elegantly explains how it is that we (often, usually) know what is right, wrong etc. in a new situation which we haven't thought of before. For this new situation will have some properties which are picked out by a rule which we already know, and by appealing to the rule we also come to have warranted moral beliefs about the new situation.

Something like this must be true, provided that 'knowing the rule' is explained as I did in the last section: we know the rule if we recognise that the 'new' situation resembles situations which we are familiar with, either by experience or by thought or by imagination. But it is only 'something like this' which is true. The argument itself is invalid.

For even if a 'new' situation has the same properties as an old one, and in the old one action A was obligatory or virtuous, it doesn't follow conclusively that action A is obligatory or virtuous in the new one: this situation may also have some properties which *defeat* that conclusion.

This insight seems to have far more threatening consequences for generalism than the idea I rejected, that principles are no use when conflicts between them arise. For if an action is obligatory on account of one principle, but should nevertheless, all things considered, not be done in a case in which this principle *conflicts* with another, that doesn't mean that A isn't obligatory after all. Nor is this a kind of inert moral fact: it may well exert its force in some substitute actions (or at least feelings) being required of the agent. Therefore the occurrence of moral conflict doesn't undermine the adequacy of proceeding by subsumption of particular cases under universal rules: if a principle states that under conditions C, an action has a certain moral characteristic, this may be true for all conditions C, even if the deliberative conclusion the moral agent eventually has to draw isn't fully determined by this. But *defeasibility* really undermines the adequacy of the subsumption model of argument. For if we add to the premises the statement that not only conditions C obtain, but conditions C-1 as well, our original conclusion doesn't follow any more, not even as an input to further moral deliberation.[21]

This threatens generalism in the following way. Think again of Winkler's paraplegic patient. I said in section 1 that the question *why* we should refrain from force-feeding this patient is answered by saying that force-feeding would (brutally) violate his autonomy. I held this to be a point in favour of principlism; so I implicitly assumed that this reason was a reason *in virtue of* the principle that a person's autonomy should be respected. But this, it seems, cannot be true, for in some cases the fact that an action violates a person's (let's say, a tyrant's) autonomy may not provide any reason against it; it may even provide a reason to do it. Since the principle is out-ruled by a counter-example, it seems we can only return to the original insight: violation of the patient's autonomy is a reason against force-feeding in this particular case, not necessarily in another. These are truths about particular cases, and they are (fallibly) known by inspecting the cases. If we attempted to arrive at these truths by appealing to a principle, we would go wrong in an unpredictable number of cases. So it is safe to trust such a principle as a heuristic at most.

Generalising, we can state this particularist argument in the following way:

(1) Moral characteristics are supervenient, i.e. if a state of affairs, an action or an agent has some moral property, this is always on account of other proper-ties it has.

(2) Supervenience, however, works in a *holistic* way. If we are only looking at some of the properties of the action etc., we can never conclude that it has a certain moral property as well. We have to inspect the other properties, and any one of these may be relevant to the final judgement.

(3) Therefore, moral judgement can only be particularist. For general consid-erations require us to abstract from at least some properties of the actual case, but these may always be relevant. Moral properties depend on other proper-ties, but not in any way which can be summed up in generalisations. Rather the total *tableau* of these other properties in the particular case has a certain shape or *Gestalt* which determines its moral property.[22]

I accept the first statement. I believe the second statement to be somewhat over-stated in a way which I will shortly explain, but I accept it for the time being. Does the conclusion really follow? Or is there a way in which a gen-eralist can also account for defeasibility and holism?

Consider the following. If some action is right for being A, and an-other action wrong in spite of (or even for) being A, this has to be explained by pointing to some other property which the second action has, which is lacking in the first, or *vice versa*. Therefore, the original norm identifying A as a right-making characteristic has to be qualified. As the particularist will be quick to point out, this is not the end of the matter: for similar reasons, the qualification has to be qualified itself etc., *ad infinitum*. But that doesn't exclude that, each time a qualification is added, it covers *a class of* possible cases. So any statement of a general consideration has a clause for exceptions or default assumption built into it: 'when C you should do A, except when also C-a...n'. Some of these exceptions can, with some thought, be stated in advance by anyone with sufficient moral competence and experience, but nevertheless, this rider is always an open one. Fact or fiction may always confront us with a situation we had not thought of before and which forces us to recognise a new exception to the rule.

Of course, these exception-clauses have exception-clauses built into them as well, and these have the same open-ended character. By means of these exception-clauses, all principles, as I suggested in the first section, are related to each other in a network of belief, some relations already being established, others remaining to be discovered. To have any moral judgement conclusively established, we would have to go through the entire chain from exception-clauses to exception-clauses, which we can never do exhaustively.

(Why not? It seems to me that the limitations of our understanding are only part of the explanation. The other part is that morality, to some extent, is 'invented' by the community of moral agents.[23] In any new situation we are sufficiently constrained by the relevant considerations to be warranted in believing that our conclusion is a discovery and not an invention. But nevertheless, when this conclusion is added to the relevant considerations for the next problem, we start a cumulative process of constructive thinking which inevitably results in the network of moral beliefs being revised, and this not only by our mistakes.)

It follows that our conclusions are always provisional and open to challenge. That is true to our experience: so they are. But it also follows that rationalising judgements are general ones: they always rationalise classes of cases. And this is true of our experience as well. It makes sense to refer to other cases, and to explain their relevance in terms of a *ratio decidendi*, a norm with it's chain of exceptions, exceptions to exceptions etc., truncated of at some point, and for that reason open to further challenge. It is also never true that all the actual properties of a token-context are relevant to determining its moral character. If the situation requires a certain judgement on account of a certain constellation of its properties, we can always imagine the same constellation requiring the same judgement in other cases. Most of the time we are actually acquainted with such cases, sometimes routinely.

The idea of open-ended chains of exception-clauses to exception-clauses may seem very discouraging. In going through the chain, how can our rational confidence in any conclusion ever *grow*? And this seems to be a minimal requirement, even if we are already accustomed to the idea that our confidence will seldom approach certainty. Should we not rather conclude that a *ceteris paribus* clause to a rule undermines its claim to being a rule at all? Things are never equal. And we cannot decide whether the dissimilarities are relevant by reference to the rule. So how do we decide whether we are within the domain of the 'rule' or of its exceptions otherwise than by 'looking at the particular case'?

To give my generalist account some initial plausibility, I need a 'ripples-in-the-pond postulate'. The postulate says that in going through the chain, our chances of meeting any unforeseen exception will normally be reduced substantially. For the entire network of relevant considerations to be applicable by us with any degree of confidence, the complexity of its relations to the world has to be finite.

This constraint on holism explains how W.D. Ross could say that the validity of a principle, notwithstanding its defeasibility, implies a 'tendency' to fix the moral property of cases to which it applies.[24] This way of putting it can be misleading. For we shouldn't exclude, for any individual valid norm, the possibility that its exceptions are more numerous than its valid applications.[25] But such cases have to be rather exceptional themselves, and if they exist, the exceptions will normally (!) be relatively simple, low-level, and familiar. Otherwise, the holistic system can't be handled.[26]

Statements of general considerations in practical arguments will show their character as default-assumptions by the form 'normally if c, then p'. And the conclusion which they allow us to draw, will therefore have the form 'presumably p'. The applicability of these concepts presupposes a certain distribution of the burden of proof: we will only be fully satisfied by a denial of p, if some relevant defeating consideration is adduced.

Suppose you have been told that a person did something morally wrong, you ask what made his action wrong, and the answer is that he lied (intentionally led another person to believe a falsehood). The answer, if a bit short, is satisfactory. Now suppose that you have been told that another person did something morally laudable, you again ask what about his action made it so, and the answer is again that he lied. This, in order to be intelligible at all, requires elucidation. Default rules reflect this a-symmetry in their ordering of the relevant features.

If you hold that, normally, human beings are one-legged, you will not only have many exceptions to explain, but, more basically, it will be very hard to explain them (Veltman 1989, 215).[27]

This means that, even if it is true that the moral character of an action or a person (or a society) results from the relevant properties of the action, the person or society as a whole, it is also true that this moral shape can be analysed, or broken down. Each relevant feature makes a difference, but the difference has to be explained against the background of other features. With a constant background, the significance of the feature is the same. If we have been informed that the action has the property a, we conclude that it is right (courageous etc.). If we now learn that it is also b, we consider it wrong (foolhardy etc.). With every new property the moral meaning, and even what Dancy calls the 'polarity' of the old ones may change, but it does so in a universally valid way. At every particular point we may stop this process, and then we know the moral truth for all cases in which it is proper to stop at this point. The moral 'shape' of a case is built up stepwise from the differences each of its salient features *generally* makes at some particular point in the building process. There may be several routes to the same final holistic conclusion, each with a different starting point, e.g. either one of the sets of properties which invoke two conflicting 'principles'. But not every possible ordering of the relevant properties is equally acceptable. That is why the a-symmetrical idea of specification is appropriate. Exceptions to a principle belong to the logical level of its specification.

Default-generalism, as we might call it, is a modest doctrine: it only asserts that moral shapes are analysable in this way. There are only certain ways of telling the story which make sense, and there is a certain matter of fact which, at this particular point of the story, *always* adds its weight to the same scale. But that need not be the end of the story. Default-generalism accepts the holistic idea that a salient feature doesn't make the same difference everywhere, but it doesn't accept that if a feature makes the same difference here and elsewhere, that is entirely accidental. But this is precisely what particularism has to affirm: 'atomistic' considerations can, by themselves, not only create no certainty, but no 'tendency', and therefore, not even a presumption of relevance either.[28] This brings me back to a point I made in the last section, which I can make more forcefully now: particularists cannot even justify their talk about norms being rules of thumb or summaries, or even checklists or aide-memoires. If we 'look at the case', as they require us to do, and believe that we see something, this belief cannot be reinforced by anything which we have seen before. For even the weakest form of the transfer of probability from one case to another is incompatible with particularism.

My conclusion is reinforced by another observation I made before. The list of qualifications is open-ended, and we discover the need for adding another qualification by being confronted with a particular case. It is not necessary, however, that we are confronted by this case in reality: a description of it might do the job. At this point, the usual particularist metaphor of 'perception' is seriously misleading. The description may refer to the past or the future, to fictional or hypothetical cases (perhaps under some constraints concerning their 'realism').[29] Such descriptions, however, in abstracting from some of the properties of any actual case, in effect cover classes of cases. (Of course, any of the properties abstracted from may introduce another qualification, but that is besides the point.) So what we 'discover' by 'looking' is really the validity of a general, albeit defeasible, consideration.

My analysis confirms the suspicion that particularism is entirely unhelpful for deliberation about hard cases. Particularists recommend heuristics (comparison with other cases, appeal to summary rules), but they cannot explain the value of the heuristics. They are not entitled to any resource for moral thinking beyond 'perception'. Therefore, they cannot explain how people learn to 'perceive' either. Even their fallibilism causes problems, for they cannot give any account of the correction of mistakes. 'Look more carefully', they repeat saying, but they have no criterion of carefulness in looking. All these things depend on the existence of structural connections between ranges of cases, which only generalist forms of holism can account for.

So what is it that drives particularism, what explains its undeniable attraction? Its willingness to attend to the details of the particular case, of course, but this it shares with default-generalism. But there may also be a moral aspect to the initial appeal of particularism. If someone is in need and you are the only one who can help, the right reason for your action seems to be the particular fact that this person needs help now. If you explain your action by saying that people generally have a duty to help needy people, we may suspect you to have, in Williams' memorable phrase, 'one thought too many'. Now I believe that this important insight is in danger of being solidified into a new dogma. For there are such things as duties and obligations deriving their moral force from standing patterns of mutual expectations. If you explain repaying money you borrowed, or keeping to the right side of the road even in a suicidal mood, you may without any impropriety explain your behaviour by saying that people have legitimate expectations for cases like this. To my mind duty can also be a proper additional motive for helping a person in need, even if it shouldn't be the only motive. It is clear that, at least for such motives, particularism cannot be the true account. And because reasons derived from such social norms have a holistic character – as is generally recognised in recent accounts of legal reasoning, it cannot be true either that holism requires particularism.

But let me grant the point that your basic reason should be the need of the needy and not your duty to help them. The idea that this discredits generalism reveals the basic misunderstanding of the nature of rules I discussed. The generalist does not claim that you should help this particular needy person because of the further fact that a valid rule prescribes you to help needy persons in general. There is no such *further* fact. Rather, you should help this needy person, and (other things being equal) the next one, and so on. That is what the rule amounts to.[30]

Conclusion

It is often suggested that applied ethics is in a state of deep methodological crisis, deriving from opposing views concerning the proper way of proceeding. To my mind these suggestions are highly misleading. If we have reason to worry about the state of applied ethics, this is because of the average quality of its productions, not because of any methodological crisis. Its outstanding contributions more or less exemplify the same method, and this method is *endorsed* by both camps which usually are supposed, and usually suppose themselves, to be totally at odds with each other as regards their view on 'methods'. The method essentially involves reference both to cases and to general considerations, and both to principles and to specifying 'maxims'. The knowledge of principles and maxims implies the ability to handle cases, and the appeal to cases is mostly an implicit appeal to principles and maxims.

This is also the method used in all actual moral thinking; whatever it is we call 'moral theory' is fully continuous with reflective moral practice. It is also very similar to the method used in sound legal thinking, which only allows more space to appeals to authority (or 'formal rules').

Really controversial is only the explanation of the appropriateness of this accepted method. I have argued for a view which is both (moderately) holist and generalist in its conception of rationalisation, and which accepts the relevance of both general and particular judgements to the justification of belief. Most of the time a judgement on particular case will consist in a directive or evaluative, *together with* the grounds which rationalise the judgement, but sometimes only of a directive or evaluative, still in search of its *ratio*.

I reject so-called 'deductivism'[31] and atomism on the one hand, particularism on rationalisation and epistemology on the other, but neither principlism nor casuistry.

Principlists acknowledge or should acknowledge that the firm grasp of the meaning of principles only comes from the exposure to cases. They also are able to acknowledge that principles are part of a network of general considerations which can only be applied holistically. Such applications can never be mechanical, but require judgement, and the exercise of judgement may either defeat or override any principle. Even in such cases the ratio for the final decision derives from general considerations specifying the application of principles. The proper subsection of the network of general considerations is often suggested by the careful study of (actual or hypothetical) cases. And this is not merely a matter of heuristics, for the warrant of any particular judgement may consist in a combination of general considerations and particular judgements, in reflective equilibrium.

The proponents of casuistry should acknowledge that the choice of cases as either 'paradigmatic' or 'problematic' is guided by an explicit or implicit reference to relevant basic principles, and that the identification of similarities and differences and the evaluation of their importance rely on implicit or explicit general considerations as well. They should also acknowledge that an appeal to an analogous case is usually, though not necessarily, more convincing if the *ratio decidendi* is made explicit. Cases invite us to re-consider and to re-organize our network of beliefs in such a way that the connectivity is increased, which generates more discursive support for particular options. This may not always result in a neat 'solution' of the moral problem we are considering. But that is a worthwhile insight in its own right.

It is true that such a network of beliefs will have a richness and complexity far beyond any simple list of principles. But it doesn't follow that principles are irrelevant. On the contrary, they structure the system.

If both camps make these possible and laudable adjustments, they will end up being indistinguishable.

Notes

1   I wish to thank the editors and Jurriaan de Haan for useful comments on a draft of this paper, and Jonathan Dancy, Theo van Willigenburg, Henri Wijsbek and other participants to the Summer School on Ethical Theory and Practice (Woudschoten 1996) for discussion of the issues.
2   This is a description of Walzer's practice, not of his theoretical account of justice as 'complex equality', cf. Den Hartogh (forthcoming).
3   Though it is illegal to treat a competent patient without his consent, in the USA as well as in the Netherlands.
4   It may be objected that it is only a particular fact about the second case that we have reason to respect the patient's autonomy in that case. Thus, autonomy would not be the *kind* of thing which (normally) requires respect. I will discuss this particularist construal of the relevant reasons in a later section.
5   Kant, for example, is in some sense a 'deductivist' concerning rationalisation, but he emphatically places the 'locus of certitude' in low-level moral judgements. From the *Critique of Practical Reason* onwards, he even rejects any 'deduction' of the moral law which doesn't start from the fact of our actual low-level moral knowledge. A coherentist epistemology does not in itself refute the possibility of an axiomatic structure of ethics. Similarly, a theonomous morality which regards actions as wrong if God forbids them, is not committed to agree they would be right if God would be found (how?) to command them. On this view God's command rationalises the wrongness of the actions of which we are sure in some other way, e.g. by consulting our conscience.
6   I owe this illuminating term to an unpublished paper of Onora O'Neill, presented in Rotterdam in 1996.

7   I don't want to suggest that all conflicts can be solved by specification. Due to incommensurability and, perhaps, other factors, including unavoidable epistemic deficiencies, a category of genuine dilemma's will remain. Note, however, that on the 'design'-conception even the justified judgement that a dilemma exists may be revisable.

8   'Bread is the staff of life, the body of Christ, the symbol of the Sabbath, the means of hospitality, and so on' Walzer (1983: 8).

9   Green (1990) argues that principlism, by abstracting from theory, has insufficient resources to solve conflicts. He believes that applied ethicists tend to pay insufficient attention to theoretical questions, partly because practitioners tend to be impatient with them. He may have a point. But if the proposed remedy is to start all discussions in applied ethics from one of the textbook-'theories' (rule-utilitarianism, pluralistic deontology or intuitionism, virtue ethics, some brand of contractualism), the remedy is worse than the disease. Besides, one should also be sensitive to the mirror deficiency in ethical theory: lack of awareness of possible contexts of application.

10   The point is only a critical one, if we presuppose all ethical theory to have reductionistic aims, as Williams seems to do.

11   For that reason DeGrazia (1992, 519, 524, 528) is too dismissive of theory.

12   As DeGrazia (1992, 522, 533) suggests, albeit only tentatively, this surely is also the correct interpretation of the way Beauchamp & Childress always intended to use rules for solving conflicts between principles, as for instance in their rejection of strong paternalism. Beauchamp & Childress (1983, 219-220) state that the rule is not 'derived' from the principle, but is (in the epistemological sense) justified by its own intuitive appeal, its coherence with the principle and the intuitive appeal of some of its applications. Beauchamp & Childress (1994, ch. 1), explicitly subscribe to the epistemic reciprocity of general and particular judgements and to the need for specification of principles.

13   For that reason 'reflective equilibrium' should not only or mainly be sought between general considerations on the one hand and judgments of concrete cases on the other, but rather, as Rawls (1993) keeps saying, between considered convictions at all levels of generality. Cf. Beauchamp & Childress (1994, 21).

14   Van Willigenburg, this volume, points to the example of people finding the solution to a pure coordination problem by converging on the salient outcome which may be identified by precedent. But people aim at the salient outcome because they mutually expect each other to do so: it is a social rule or convention. That is confirmed by the fact that the relevant notion of 'salience' in this context is: whatever we mutually know to be salient to each other. See Mehta et al. (1994).

15   That is worth observing because critics of principlism sometimes reject what they call the 'legal' model of moral thinking. This rejection mainly rests on a mistaken 'deductivist' conception of legal reasoning, cf. the Introduction.

16   Like the analogous positions of formalism (legism) and rule-scepticism (legal realism) in jurisprudence. See Hart (1961, ch. 7).

17   Van Willigenburg, this volume, concedes that it is a mystery how probability can be transferred from one case to the other, but resists explaining this by what he believes to be a greater mystery of a rule determining its own future application. Even if we grant him the second mystery (but see note 20), that position is untenable. We don't have two mysteries here, one for the generalist and one for the particularist, but only one: the mystery of how the correct continuation of a series can be identified, whether the series is given by extension (casuistry) or by intension (principlism). Any position invoking this mystery is incompatible with particularism.

18   'Whatever we learn from a case and then transport to another case cannot be entirely specific to the first case; some degree of generality must be present in order to lead us to the next case' (Beauchamp, 1996: 89).

19   He actually says: particular kinds of human situations! Note that this observation, if valid, would only tell us something about warrants: the 'locus of certitude' would be found in lower level general considerations, rather than higher level ones. Higher level considerations could still provide the true rationalisations of the lower level ones. In my own experience, however, it is equally possible that a committee agrees on principles (e.g. the harm principle), but disagrees about 'applications' to classes of cases (cf. Lustig 1992: 498). Privileged or 'core' intuitions within the method of reflective equilibrium can be at every level of generality. Locally they may tend to cluster on some particular level (lower or higher), but that doesn't change the basic point.

20   This leaves us with Kripke's famous problem to explain how a rule can fix its own future application. (For an exhaustive discussion, see Stein (1997)) That problem cannot motivate us to prefer casuistry, however, because casuistry is confronted with exactly the same problem (cf. note 17). Besides, as Kripke (1982) recognises, any thorough scepticism concerning the very possibility of rule-following (expressed in general terms!) would be obviously absurd. Hence Kripke's problem has an answer, even if we don't know it yet.

Here is one answer. How do we know that 'plus' means addition, and not: addition until time t, and always summing to 5 after t? Kripke himself suggests that this is a matter of the convergence of blind inclinations of people forming a linguistic community. But that doesn't explain why a person who says 68+57=5 is 'mistaken', rather than only deviant. However, people are not only blindly inclined to act in certain ways, they also (blindly) expect each other to be so inclined, and adjust their own actions to their expectations. If I get only fl. 5.- instead of the fl. 125.- I expect, I will be angry. Normative language expresses mutually adjusted reactions to successes and failures in co-ordination.

How is it possible for our reactions to be so adjusted? Take two computing machines, one with the function 'plus'=addition, the other with the time-index at t. The second clearly is dysfunctional for co-ordination-purposes (as the so-called millennium-problem illustrates). So there may be a functional (evolutionary) explanation for 'the convergence of blind inclinations'.

21 Some die-hard generalists deny the distinction between overriding and defeating considerations. They want to say that the duty not to lie to the persecutor is only overridden by the need to protect his victim. On my view there is no such duty at all to begin with.

22 Platts (1979, ch. 10).

23 O'Neill's concept of 'design', see note 6, illuminates the point. Cf. Beauchamp (1996, 90-91).

24 Van Willigenburg, this volume objects, that in appealing to a moral consideration ('that would be lying'), we don't claim that there is certain probability of, say, 95%, of the property referred to being determinative of rightness or wrongness (cf. Dancy, 1993, 99-100). Indeed, we don't, because in such statements we imply that – as far as we know – there are no defeating considerations. They are to be understood in a holistic, not in an atomistic way.

25 Such statistical considerations are one reason for preferring either the 'no, unless', or the 'yes, provided that' format for the wording of any norm, but not necessarily the only reason.

26 I agreed with Williams (cf. note 10) that we have no reason to expect the system to be simple. But if it is to be action-guiding, there is a threshold to its possible complexity. That is particularly true to the extent that the actions it is supposed to guide should be adjusted to each other.

27 On default-rules cf. Wijsbek, this volume.

28 Particularism cannot explain moral conflict either. For if one feature of the situation, taken on its own, would justify one moral judgement, and another feature its opposite, we have to remind ourselves that we are not entitled to any such judgement before we have seen the shape of all relevant features, including those two. (Particularism can account for moral dilemma's, however, for it need not assume that we can always rationally choose between two possible 'shapes'.) For a particularist account of conflict see Dancy (1993, ch. 7).

29 'An imaginary case might be an abbreviated sketch of a situation where ...the importance it (a property) can have is revealed' (Dancy 1993, 69). Why should that be of any interest, if we are not entitled to expect it to have this importance in any other case as well?

30   The misunderstanding may be partly due to a tendency to conceive of all rules on the model of legal rules. Legal rules mostly derive their validity from being prescribed by authority, and this prescription is a 'further fact' indeed. Authority provides us with content-independent reasons. So, in a legal context, does precedent (cf. note 14). Moral principles and moral 'precedents' do not.

31   I.e. the idea that the order of justification (warrant) is always from the general rule to the particular case (subsumption-model).

References

Beauchamp, T.L. (1996), 'The Role of Principles in Practical Ethics', in: L.W. Sumner, Joseph Boyle eds., *Philosophical Perspectives on Bioethics*, University of Toronto Press, Toronto, pp. 79-95.

Beauchamp, T.L., Childress, J.F. (1979, 1983, 1989, 1994), *Principles of Biomedical Ethics*, Oxford University Press, New York.

Brody, B. (1988), *Life and Death Decisionmaking*, Oxford University Press, New York.

Dancy, J. (1993), *Moral Reasons*, Blackwell, Oxford.

DeGrazia, D. (1992), 'Moving Forward in Bioethical Theory: Theories, Cases and Specified Principlism', *Journal of Medicine and Philosophy* 17, pp. 511-539.

Green, R.M. (1990), 'Method in Bioethics: A Troubled Assessment', *Journal of Medicine and Philosophy* 15, pp. 179-197.

Hart, H.L.A. (1961), *The Concept of Law*, Oxford University Press.

Hartogh, G. den (forthcoming), The Architectonic of Michael Walzer's Theory of Justice, *Political Theory*.

Jonsen, A., Toulmin, S. (1988), *The Abuse of Casuistry*, University of California Press, Berkeley.

Kripke, S. (1982), *Wittgenstein on Rules and Private Language*, Blackwell Oxford.

Lustig, A. (1992), 'The Method of 'Principlism': a Critique of the Critique', *Journal of Medicine and Philosophy* 17, pp. 487-510.

McDowell, J. (1979), 'Virtue and Reason', *The Monist* 62, pp. 331-350.

Mehta, J., Starmer, C. & Sugden, R. (1994), 'Focal Points in Pure Coordination Games: An Experimental Investigation', *Theory and Decision* 36, 163-185.

Nozick, R. (1968), 'Moral Complications and Moral Structures', *Natural Law Forum* 13, pp. 1-50.

Platts, M. (1979), *Ways of meaning*, Routledge and Kegan Paul, London.

Rawls, J. (1993), *Political Liberalism*, Columbia University Press, New York.

Richardson, H. (1990), 'Specifying Norms as a Way to Resolve Concrete Ethical Problems', *Philosophy and Public Affairs* 19, pp. 279-310.

Richardson, H. (1994), *Practical Reasoning about Final Ends*, Cambridge University Press.

Stein, H.P. (1997), *The Fiber and the Fabric, An Inquiry into Wittgenstein's Views on Rule-Following and Linguistic Normativity*, ILLC Dissertation Series.

Toulmin, S.E. (1981), 'The Tyranny of Principles', *Hastings Center Report* December 1981, pp. 31-39.

Veltman, F. (1989), 'Redelijkheid in het Redeneren', in: Parret, H., ed., *In Alle Redelijkheid*, Boom, Meppel/Amsterdam.

Walzer, M. (1983), *Spheres of Justice*, Martin Robertson, Oxford.

Williams, B. (1985), *Ethics and the Limits of Philosophy*, Fontana Press/Collins.

Willigenburg, T. van (1991), *Inside the Ethical Expert, Problem Solving in Applied Ethics*, Kok Pharos, Kampen.

Winkler, E.R. (1993), 'From Kantianism to Contextualism: The Rise and Fall of the Paradigm Theory in Bioethics', in: Winkler, E.R., Coombs, J.R., *Applied Ethics, A Reader*, Blackwell, Oxford, pp. 366-389.

2 Guidance by Moral Rules, Guidance by Moral Precedents

THEO VAN WILLIGENBURG

Introduction

The rise of so-called applied ethics, like bioethics and business ethics, has evoked a new interest in the methods of moral reflection: how may one reach a structured, ethical survey of a particular problem, leading to a practical decision or a piece of theory with clear practical relevance? Roughly, two approaches of moral reflection can be distinguished. *1*. 'Top-down' approaches,[1] such as principlism, specificism, and deductivism, which tell us that in order to find out what is the right thing to do in a particular case, one should take some fundamental moral principle(s), or a specified principle, or some set of balanced mid-level principles, or a list of moral rules as one's guide. *2*. 'Bottom up' approaches,[2] such as casuistry, which, in a more inductive mode, start from the rich details and the contingent circumstances of real life cases and try to sort out what is morally at stake by comparing the problem case with various precedent cases in the same field.

All these approaches are meant to aid us in our quest for the morally good and right in concrete situations. In addition to telling us how we could justify a moral decision once it has been taken, they also claim to provide *guidance in that they help us reach a justifiable decision*. Methods of moral reflection are meant to help us attain true beliefs about what would be morally appropriate to do or to be. These approaches, therefore, presuppose some idea of what it means to follow a rule, or to follow a precedent in one's search for a moral solution to a problem case.

My purpose in this contribution is to articulate this idea. What does being guided by a moral rule or by a moral precedent amount to? Some theorists do not see much difference between these two forms of guidance, but this is only because they favour a generalist account of guidance-by-precedent. I will defend a particularist account, according to which precedents may be guiding because they play an important role in education toward proper moral judgement. Precedents help the agent to perceive case-features with *sui generis* moral salience, that is salience not explicable in terms of rules.

Guidance by Moral Rules

If a moral rule is to provide guidance it must be understood as some sort of precept which constrains decision options. In a problem case, usually there will be more than one decision option. Take the following case,

> *The perfect donor*
> The medical examination of a man whose daughter needs renal transplantation shows that he is a 'perfect' donor. When the father is informed about this he changes his mind and does not want to donate a kidney. The father asks the physician not to tell the family about his refusal, because he fears their reaction. Perhaps the physician could just say that he is not histocompatible. When the family would ask the physician, should he tell the truth about the father's suitability as a donor?

In this case the doctor could tell the truth, or only part of the truth, or he could avoid telling what is true or simply lie. A moral rule or principle is meant to help us identify the option which is morally more appropriate than others. Now, moral rules only make sense if they provide this guidance also in situations which cannot be specified in advance. If the rule would be: 'In situation A it is morally wrong not to tell the truth and in situation B it is morally right not to tell the truth', where A and B are particular types of real life situations, the rule would be of no help in any situation which is not A or B. Usually, such a rule is therefore read as 'In situation A, and in all situations which are relevantly similar to A, it is morally wrong not to speak the truth, and in situation B, and in all situations which are relevantly similar to B, it is morally right not to speak the truth'. According to this reading, the rule does not only apply to situations which are fully specified in advance but also to relevantly similar situations not necessarily specified in advance. This reading strongly enhances the relevance of the rule. However, the increase in relevance leads to a decrease in guiding power. For, how do we know whether a new situation is sufficiently similarly to A or B for the rule to apply? The rule itself does not tell us. We need other guiding information to determine whether a new situation is really covered by the rule. Would it be possible for a rule or set of rules to include all this information so that we can take it as our guide and trust that it yields the right decision in a new case? That is implausible. Such a rule should list all situations relevantly similar to A or B, or all situations not relevantly similar to A or B (that is, a complete list of exceptions to the rule). Thus, it would have to be infinitely long. As there is no way to represent such infinitely long rules, they cannot be taken as guides. Representation is essential for guidance. Being guided by a rule does not just mean acting in accordance with it (perhaps without knowing it), but also *intentionally* trying to conform to it. Mere dispositions toward particular patterns of behaviour would not suffice. The patterns should derive from the rule. But the rule can only tell me what to do if I can represent it to myself. Since comprehensive representation is impossible, rules fail to provide full guidance.

Default Rules

But perhaps the idea of full guidance is too ambitious. One could argue that moral rules are only meant to provide guidance in *default* situations, that is situations without visible exceptions. We do not think of the rule of truth-telling as an infinitely long description of circumstances requiring that the truth be told. Rules offer fairly general precepts which tell us what to do in 'normal' circumstances. 'Always tell the truth' is a default rule.[3] Wouldn't such a rule provide enough moral guidance? It is true that the default rule itself does not distinguish between situations where it applies and exceptions. But why would that be a problem? Because of it's default character, we know that the rule applies to, say, 95 % of all cases. So, the chances are that it will apply in a new situation in which we ask ourselves whether we should speak the truth. Does that not provide enough guidance?

The answer here depends on our conception of guidance. Moral rules are meant to guide us toward true moral beliefs. I assume that it would be odd to understand guiding strength as statistical power. Moral rules are not 'good guides' because in 95% of the cases they put us on the track of moral truth. A guide to moral thinking is reliable only if it generates justifiable conclusions. In cases where the rule appears not to apply, we cannot justify it's implications by saying: 'But in 95% of the cases the rule does apply!'. The decision to tell the truth about the suitability of the father as donor is definitely not justified by the mere consideration that one generally has to speak the truth. Guiding strength is not a statistical category. If a moral rule can add credibility to a decision taken – and therefore can provide guidance to moral thinking – this is not because in 95% of the cases it leads me to the morally correct answer. In the case at hand it may lead me to a morally wrong answer! If we really think that a default rule puts us in a good position to attain true moral beliefs about a particular case, this is because we have *other* reasons for following the rule in this case, and for thinking that this case is not an exceptional one. These other reasons are, of course, to be found in the circumstances of the case. The rule itself does not tell us why it applies in particular circumstances. Perhaps another rule does tell us but, again, how do we know that this other rule is applicable?[4]

At this point the notion of being guided by a moral rule becomes pretty mysterious. Default rules anyhow offer incomplete guidance, and because of that they may provide no guidance at all. One might think that adding a *ceteris paribus* clause to a rule (making it a default rule) does not prevent the rule from having constraining power, for instance because it gives anyone who thinks that the rule does not apply the *burden of proof*.[5] This is misconceived, however. No one would think that, when the Nazi knocks on the door, the agent who believes that in this case the rule about truth-telling does *not* apply has the burden of proof. But – some will argue – there are cases in which the rule about truth-telling surely constrains our behaviour! Yes, but only if we already know that the rule applies. Before we know *that*, the rule does not exert guiding influence. But how do we know *that*?

The problematic character of the concept of rule-guidance is nicely illustrated by the 'ripples-in-the-pond postulate' which Govert den Hartogh introduces.[6] Den Hartogh acknowledges that moral rules have an open-ended character. They have exception-clauses built into them, and these exception-clauses may have their own exception-clauses etc. According to the 'ripples-in-the-pond postulate', however, going through the chain of exceptions will substantially reduce the chances of meeting any unforeseen exception. So, the more we have worked through the network of exception-clauses, the more rational confidence we may have in the conclusion reached. But, still, at any moment this 'rational confidence' may be seriously mistaken. The uniqueness of case-circumstances allows so many exceptions that the rational confidence Den Hartogh is speaking of easily invites self-deception. The chances are that a full specification of exception-clauses would amount to the description of a particular unique situation, so that the rule would apply to one situation only. Indeed, this would dissolve the rule since rules must be general. Thus, the notion of being guided by a rule becomes deeply problematic.[7]

Guidance by Precedents

In order to be guided by a precedent one has, first of all, to identify its salient features, as one can only follow a precedent under a specific description. The idea of salience is crucial here. What features of the precedent situation catch the eye? What *salient* points in that situation called for particular actions? Following a precedent, secondly, means that one is able to identify a new case as of the same type as the precedent. That is, the precedent helps us solve a new problem by the recognition of salient features shared by the two cases, and by following the precedent on these prominent points.

Pure Precedents

At first sight, guidance by moral precedents meets the same problems as guidance by rules. For, how does one identify the salient features of a precedent case and how does one identify a new case as of the same type as the precedent? On the face of it, identification requires some implicit moral rule. After all, one has to justify the description which makes a precedent relevant for a new case, and the *ratio* for this description appears to rely on some moral rule. Yet, this is not necessarily so. There are problem cases where precedents provide a solution and where the identification of salient features is clearly not rule-guided. I am thinking here of so-called co-ordination problems, which provide for a paradigmatic example of the 'pure' role of precedents. These cases uncover a sort of *sui generis salience* of case-features.

Say that I travel to London to meet an English colleague, and that we agreed to meet each other in the main hall of Waterloo Station. However, we have forgotten to mention a meeting point, so we don't know were to find each other at Waterloo. We are now in the middle of a pure co-ordination problem. It is entirely unimportant where we will meet, as long as we do meet is some place. My only reason to go to a particular place is my suspicion that my colleague might be going there too, and his only reason for going there is his suspicion that I might be going there to find him, perhaps because he has a hunch that I expect him to be going there. No general rule tells us where to go, mutual expectation only may provide us with a reason to go to a particular place.

Suppose, that a couple of years ago when this colleague was in The Netherlands we were in fairly the same situation. We missed each other in the large central railway station in Utrecht. By accident we found each other after half an hour at the entrance of the Pizza Express restaurant in the main hall. Now there is precedent. The point where we once found each other by chance is salient, not because of some specific characteristic of the entrance of the restaurant (such as a nearby sign: meeting point), but rather because we happened to meet there by chance. There is no general reason why the entrance of a Pizza Express restaurant may be a good place to look for my colleague, apart from the contingent fact that I once found him in a similar place. Following the precedent means that I search for a similar prominent location at Waterloo. I may discover that there is no Pizza restaurant but only a large Burger King snack bar there. Should I wait then at the entrance of this snack bar or should I concentrate on other features of the Utrecht-location? Another salient feature of the Utrecht restaurant was its being the most flashy and trendy building in the station hall. Should I be looking, then, for the most eye-catching shop or restaurant at Waterloo? Following the precedent requires an identification of salient features but the choice of a particular feature is arbitrary, apart from the fact that it immediately catches the eye. The only thing I can do is try to imagine what my colleague would consider to be a salient feature of the spot in Utrecht in view of the new situation here at Waterloo station. And of course I could also try to imagine conjectures by my colleague about my choice of a salient feature. Etc.

Things would probably be easier after having this experience two or three times. Say, we miss each other a year later at Amsterdam railway-station, and say that in two or three similar situations in the past we did find each other at the entrance of a fast food restaurant or snack bar. This would be reason enough for me to go to the only snack bar in the main entrance hall of Amsterdam railway station. Following a precedent results now in guarantees that we will easily find each other even without explicit arrangements, because we have developed a pattern of mutual expectations. But this does not make the identification of the salient feature of the place where we meet less accidental. The history of development of the pattern of mutual expectations is the only reason for having these expectations ('I expect him to be at the snack bar, as we always find each other at the entrance of some restaurant'.) There is no other *ratio* for explaining this salience. The selection of a feature as being salient is purely accidental.

Following a Moral Precedent as Following a Background Moral Rule?

However, unlike this pure precedent case with purely accidental salience, precedents in moral reasoning usually involve substantial reasons for the selection of specific features as salient. In moral precedent cases there is usually a background reason for the moral salience of some feature (the fact that it was salient in a former case is not the only reason for its salience). A *ratio decidendi* independent from the history of choice explains why a specific feature is salient. Now, if this *ratio decidendi* were a *general* reason, it would be a rule. Does this mean that following a moral precedent always comes down to following a general background rule with the precedent as an *exemplifying instantiation*?

Some argue that this is indeed the case. According to Govert den Hartogh, for instance, following a rule means that one is able to continue the series of precedents which exemplify this rule.[8] Therefore, according to Den Hartogh, there is not much difference between being guided by a precedent or being guided by a rule. Both involve the ability to continue a series of cases which are tokens of a type of rule. This is in line with Philip Pettit's proposal to solve the rule-following problem by analysing the role of a set of precedent cases in exemplifying an underlying rule.[9] Precedents set us on the track of extrapolation to other cases. This inclination to extrapolate may prompt our responses in new cases. According to Pettit, such an inclination does not only provide for a disposition to respond to new cases in a certain way, but also gets me in touch with a *rule* that guides me.

I do not agree with this way of explaining the ability to continue a series of precedents as tacid rule-following. I will show, that, at a crucial point, Pettit's argument runs into serious trouble. Pettit's main move is to distinguish *exemplification* from *instantiation*. Precedents that – via my inclination to extrapolate them in a certain way – exemplify a rule should *not* be understood as an *instantiation* of this rule. This is exactly what the classical rule-following problem is all about. Any finite set of examples instantiates an infinite number of rules, because a finite set can be extrapolated in an infinite number of ways. Only an infinite list of examples can instantiate *one* rule.[10] A finite set of examples may guide us in finding what is morally required in some new case, because it creates in us the inclination to respond to the new case in a certain way – as Pettit formulates it – but it is difficult to conceptualise this as 'following a rule', as rules cannot be identified on the basis of finite sets of examples alone. Strictly speaking we cannot even say that we are guided by *examples*, as it is ambiguous what the cases involved are examples *of*.

Still, says Pettit, for *some* agent at *some* moment these cases may be examples of a rule. A set of precedents can function for someone as *exemplifications* of the rule, which means, according to Pettit, that one sees a particular rule 'manifested' in these examples.

Exemplification is a three-place-relationship. It involves a set of precedent *examples*, a *person* who regards the examples as meaningful and action-guiding, and a *rule* that the examples are supposed to exemplify.

If a series of precedents exemplifies for some agent a particular rule, does that mean that by continuing the series of precedents the agent is *following* this rule? I think this is the crucial question. I would answer it with a clear 'no'. Following a rule means that one is guided by this rule. That is, because of the rule one has the inclination to respond in a typical way to a new case, and the rule is an *independent* item which steers my inclination or counts against it when my response is incorrect. But this is not what Pettit is arguing for. His argument is that a precedent example may prompt a response in a new case. That is, I have an inclination to extrapolate the precedent in a certain way, and this inclination serves like a description of a rule, 'so far as it gives putative information about the rule: the putative information that the rule requires those responses, those ways of going on, which the inclination supports.'[11] Rule-following is identified here with the typical continuation of precedent examples. To be a rule-follower, says

Pettit, '[A]ll I need to be aware of is that there are some examples that, so far as I am concerned, exemplify a particular rule. Which rule? That rule, I say, gesturing at the original examples and perhaps some others.'[12]

But gesturing at some rule seems to me a far cry from identification. For, what if I have the impression that my inclination goes awry, because it dictates different responses on different occasions? Does this inclination still describe and thereby fix a rule? No, says Pettit, '[T]he rule is fixed by what goes in favourable conditions with my inclination', which means that the rule I am following is the rule 'with which the inclination corresponds under favourable circumstances in the actual world'.[13] Only a standardised or corrected inclination will identify a rule. This means that the agent should be able to explain discrepancies in spontaneous applications by appeal to perturbing factors. But how could the agent identify a discrepancy? He cannot call upon a rule to locate incorrect responses, for the responses themselves may be the result of an inclination which identifies a rule.

A standardised inclination is not an inclination corrected by a guiding rule, but an inclination under optimal epistemic circumstances for the agent. Why, then, do we need this talk about rules, and rule-following? 'That the agent follows such and such a rule will be supervenient in a suitable way on the facts about her inclination and context but it will not be identifiable with any such fact', says Pettit.[14] But why think that such a supervenient rule should exist? The only factors that count in a case are the contextual circumstances and the agent who reacts to them. Why postulate a three-place relationship of exemplification (which relates precedents, agents and rules)? Shouldn't we be content with a two-place relationship of responsiveness in which only agents and circumstances figure?

A Particularistic Account of Precedent-Guidance

In particularistic terms, the problem is that Den Hartogh, Pettit and others want to give a generalist account of what it means to follow a precedent. Guidance by precedents then becomes a disguised form of rule-following. The miracle that case-examples may engender an inclination in the agent to respond in a certain way to a new case is analysed by identifying it with another miracle: that the agent is following a rule that remains to be articulated.

However, neither the fact that I correctly continue a series of precedents nor the fact that I may have reasons to continue the series in a certain way (by judging a case in a particular way), *necessarily* means that I am following a rule. Generalists, however, assume that moral reasons have a rule-like character, because a *ratio decidendi* in a particular case can only be a *general* reason, instead of, say, a particularistic judgement on the balance of reasons. Particularism comes in stronger and weaker forms, but generalism always amounts to a strong stance, because generalists regard features as morally relevant if and only they are covered by a moral rule.[15] But if this is so, morally salient features will always be *invariably* morally relevant, that is they will always in the same way make a contribution to the moral assessment of a case. According to particularism, however, some morally salient features cannot be captured by moral rules. Their moral relevance may vary from one case to another. A feature (say generosity) may even create a positive moral presumption ('morally right') in one case and a negative presumption ('morally wrong') in another case. The strong particularist thinks that the moral salience of features always depends on the circumstances, which implies that morally relevant features cannot be identified by rules.[16] The moderate particularist allows the latter possibility, but denies that moral rules can identify every moral feature. According to the moderate particularist, some features will have *sui generis salience* and others will be relevant because they are universally and uniformly relevant and, therefore, can be identified by a rule. The *sui generis salience* of features which the particularist acknowledges need not be a purely *accidental* salience (as in the pure precedent case). There may be a good reason to think that no other feature than the one selected could have moral salience. But this reason need not be a general one. It may be based on a holistic view of the highly specific case.

How could precedents inform one's judgement in a new case, if the precedents are not to be understood as examples which help one identify and follow a rule? Precedents, says the particularist, help us sharpen our imagination and sensitivity such that we are aware of the *sui generis salience* of a particular feature. This is actually the classical idea of casuistry as a form of *education of the moral judgement*. Working through the taxomonies of cases discussed by the casuists was meant as a training in moral judgement, not as a lesson in moral rules and their exceptions (exemplified by sophisticated examples).

So, the fact that I correctly continue a series of precedents does not necessarily mean that I am following a rule. It may mean that I am educated so as to experience salient features as salient. This salience need not be explicable in more general terms. The fact that a particular feature has impressive power need not be generally explained or justified. The guidance of precedents may be explained in terms of my inclination, after thinking over the precedents, to respond in a certain way to a new case. This inclination is explained by the agents character formed by his history of being challenged to think about what would be morally appropriate to do or to be. Of course, the idea of moral *responsiveness,* which is crucial to this explanation of the guiding role of precedents has a lot of mystery in it. Only if one could argue that the idea of rule-guidance is a lesser mystery, one would have reason to explain precedent-guidance as a three-place relationship. That is, as a relationship in which not only cases and agents figure, but also background rules the following of which is 'supervenient' upon the inclination to continue the series of precedents in a certain way. If rule-following is highly mysterious, then generalist explanations of guidance by moral precedents are highly unsatisfactory.

According to a particularistic account of precedence-guidance case-features may posses *sui generis salience*, but this salience need not be purely accidental, because of the non-accidentiality of the inclination-to-respond of any agent embedded in a form of life. I believe that this reference to life-form ('the-way-it-is-for-us') constitutes a proper explanation.[17] Claiming that this explanation is not enough,[18] is expecting too much. In any case, the appeal to a 'supervenient' rule which is followed in some mysterious way, does not provide for *more* or better explanation.[19]

Notes

1   See for instance M.D. Bayles (1994, pp. 97-112),. Tom L. Beauchamp, J.F. Childress (1994[4]), Tom L. Beauchamp, R. Gillon (1994, pp. 3-12), Henri S. Richardson (1990, pp. 279-31), David Degrazia, (1992, pp. 511-539), Kenneth D. Clouser, (1990, pp. 219-236), Kenneth D. Clouser (1995, pp. 219-236), B.A. Lustig, (1992, pp. 487-510).
2   See for instance Albert R. Jonsen, Stephen Toulmin (1988), Albert R. Jonsen (1991 pp. 295-307), Albert R. Jonsen, (1995, pp. 237-251), John D. Arras,

(1991, pp. 29-51), B. Carney (1993), Gerald Dworking (1995, pp. 224-239), Richard B. Miller (1996).

3   Default rules state what Govert den Hartogh calls 'default assumptions': 'normally if c, than p'. Conclusions drawn from these rules will have the form 'presumably p' etc. See Govert den Hartogh, this volume.

Richardson argues that norms hold 'generally' or 'for the most part', see Henri S. Richardson (1990, pp. 279-310, p. 292). McNaughton and Rawling introduce a so called pro tanto operator 'xS' which abbreviates, 'x should ensure, to best of x's abilities, and insofar as there is not a conflicting duty of greater weight, that...', see David McNaughton and Piers Rawling (1995, pp. 31-47).

4   The additional information we need in order to know whether a rule applies cannot be presented in terms of the *rule* itself (or another rule), unless one has some conception of grasping an infinitely long rule (the rule-in-extension) or an infinitely expanding set of rules. It is curious, therefore, that Barbara Herman introduces so called *rules-of-salience* that enable the agent to pick out those features of circumstances or actions that require moral attention, and which may legitimately be included in a maxim (i.e. the *moral rule* that needs to be tested by the procedure as prescribed by Kant's Categorical Imperative – CI). According to Herman, the Kantian system is in need of some kind of independent 'moral knowledge': 'An agent who came to the CI procedure with no knowledge of the moral characteristics of actions would be very unlikely to describe his action in a morally appropriate way', i.e. in a way to be captured by some moral rule (viz. maxim). 'It is', Herman continues, 'useful to think of the moral knowledge needed by Kantian agents (prior to making moral judgements) as knowledge of a kind of moral rule. Let us call them 'rules of salience'.' These rules, she says, 'constitute the structure of moral salience'. But why would an agent need rules-of-salience to pick out the features of circumstances or action that fit into the moral rules that will be tested by the CI-procedure? And if there are such rules-of-salience, how does the agent know that they apply in a certain case? Are there other rules telling him that particular rules-of-saliece apply? Etc. It is peculiar that Herman thinks of judgments-of-salience in terms of rules. It is surely also very unkantian. See Barbara Herman (1993, p.75 ff).

5   See for instance Govert den Hartogh, General and particular considerations in applied ethics, this volume, note 26.

6   Govert den Hartogh, General and particular considerations in applied ethics, this volume, p.33.

7   Usually the 'gap' here is filled by introducing the concept of *moral judgement*, but this is, of course, just a way of shifting the problem. For, now, one needs to explain what this mysterious ability of moral judgment involves. Is it a form of intuition, or a 'peculiar talent' as Kant thought, or can it be analysed in

terms of complex deliberation within some institutional context as Onora O'-Neill suggests in an unpublished paper ('Principles, Judgment and Institutions')?

8   Govert den Hartogh (1994, pp. 50-58).
9   Philip Pettit (1990, pp. 1-21).
10   About the rule-following problem see Saul Kripke's by now classical *Wittgenstein on Rules and Private Language* (1982).
11   Philip Pettit (1990, pp. 1-2, esp. p.11).
12   Philip Pettit (1990, pp. 1-21, esp. p. 12).
13   Philip Pettit (1990, pp. 1-21, esp. p. 12-13).
14   Philip Pettit (1990, pp. 1-21, esp. p. 16).
15   This is called by Russ Shafer-Landau the *delimiting thesis*: the set of morally relevant feautures is delimited by (the set of prima facie) moral rules. See Russ Schafer-Landau (1997, pp. 584-611).
16   This is -roughly- Jonathan Dancy's position, see his *Moral Reasons*, Oxford, Blackwell, p. 193, especially chapter 4 'Why particularism?'.
17   E.g. John McDowell (1985, pp. 110-129).
18   'The problem is that the particularist seems to replace one non-explanation (which refers to a list of principles) with another (which refers to a form of life)' (Soran Reader, 1997, pp. 269-292, p. 275).
19   I would like to thank Wim van der Steen for his numerous helpful textual comments.

References

Arras, J.D. (1991), 'Getting Down to Cases: The Revival of Casuistry', *Bioethics, The Journal of Medicine and Philosophy* 16, pp. 29-51.

Bayles, M.D. (1994), Moral Theory and Application, *Social Theory and Practice* 10, pp. 97-112.

Beauchamp, T.L. (1994), 'The Four-principles Approach', in R. Gillon, *Principles of Health Care Ethics*, John Wiley, London, pp. 3-12.

Beauchamp, T.L., J.F. Childress (1994[4]), *Principles of Biomedical Ethics*, Oxford University Press, New York.

Carney, B. (1993), *Modern Casuistry: An Essential but Incomplete Method for Clinical Ethical Decision Making*, dissertation, Graduate Theological Union, Berkeley.

Clouser, K.D. (1990), 'A Critique of Principlism', *Journal of Medicine and Philosophy* 15, pp. 219-236.

Clouser, K.D. (1995), 'Common Morality as an Alternative to Principlism', *Kennedy Institute of Ethics Journal* 5, pp. 219-236.

Degrazia, D. (1992), 'Moving Forward in Bioethical Theory: Theories, Cases, and Specified Principlism', *The Journal of Medicine and Philosophy* 17, pp. 511-539.

Dworking, G. (1995), 'Unprincipled Ethics', *Midwest Studies in Philosophy* XX, pp. 224-239.

Hartogh, G. den (1994), 'De rol van regels in praktische argumentatie', in: E.T. Feteris e.a., red., *Met Redenen Omkleed*, Ars Aequi Libri, pp. 50-58.

Herman, B. (1993), *The Practice of Moral Judgment*, Harvard University Press, Cambridge, p.75 ff.

Jonsen, A.R. (1991), 'Casuistry as methodology in clinical ethics', *Theoretical Medicine* 12, pp. 295-307.

Jonsen, A.R. (1995), 'Casuistry: An Alternative or Complement to Principles?', *Kennedy Institute of Ethics Journal* 5, pp. 237-251.

Jonsen, A.R., Toulmin, S. (1988), *The Abuse of Casuistry*, University of California Press, Berkeley.

Kripke, S. (1982), *Wittgenstein on Rules and Private Language*, Blackwell, Oxford.

Lustig, B.A. (1992), 'The Method of Principlism: A Critique of the Critique', *The Journal of Medicine and Philosophy* 17, pp. 487-510.

McDowell, J. (1985), 'Values and Secondary Qualities', in: T. Honderich (ed.), *Morality and Objectivity*, Routledge London, pp. 110-129.

McNaughton, D., Rawling P. (1995), 'Value and Agent-Relative Reason', *Utilitas* 7, pp. 31-47.

Miller, R.B. (1996), *Casuistry and Modern Ethics*, The University of Chicago Press, Chicago.

Pettit, P. (1990), 'The Reality of Rule-Following', *Mind* 99, pp. 1-21.

Reader, S. (1997), 'Principle Ethics, Particularism and Another Possibility', *Philosophy* 72, pp. 269-292.

Richardson, H.S. (1990), 'Specifying Norms as a Way to Resolve Concrete Ethical Problems', *Philosophy and Public Affairs* 19, pp. 279-310.

Schafer-Landau, R. (1997), 'Moral Rules', *Ethics* 107, pp. 584-611.

3 Set a Sprat to Catch a Whale

The Structure, Strength and Function of Analogical Inferences

HENRI WIJSBEK

Introduction[1]

Analogies hinge on similarity-relations. Unfortunately, the only thing that is clear about similarity is what it is not. It is not what 'egalitarians' like John Stuart Mill take it to be. They simply construct the degree of similarity between two objects as a function of the number of shared and non-shared features. The problems with this theory are well-known and need not be rehearsed here. Any two objects have indefinitely many features in common, and indefinitely many features in which they differ. Bare similarity is too unconstrained to be of any use; we need a criterion for *relevant* similarity.

A prima facie promising way to deal with relevant similarity is to treat it as an extension of identity, because inferentially interesting properties of 'identity' can be formalised.[2] If two objects are identical the same set of predicates applies to both of them. This axiom, also known as Leibniz' law, can be used in deductively valid inference schema's like the following:

1 Leibniz' Law
2 P(a)
3 a=b
4 P(b)

This schema indicates that if a certain predicate P holds for an object referred to by the term 'a', and a is identical to b, then P holds for b as well. That might seem trivial, but sometimes it can provide new information, because what is known about an object under one description, 'a', need not be known about that object under another description, 'b'. Let 'a' be shorthand for 'the queen of Thebes', 'b' for 'the mother of Oedipus', and let 'P' stand for the property of being married. Then the schema reads as follows:

1 Identical objects have the same properties.
2 Oedipus is married to the queen of Thebes.
3 The queen of Thebes is identical to the mother of Oedipus.
4 Therefore, Oedipus is married to his own mother.

This is a logically valid deduction. Oedipus was aware of the second premise of course. When he realised that the third was true as well, he correctly applied Leibniz' law and inferred that he had married his own mother. Logic is full of surprises, but luckily few are as dramatic as this one.

The most straightforward way to deal with similarity is to treat it along the same lines. If two objects are similar, they have similar properties.[3] This axiom can then be used in a schema like the one used for the identity-axiom, with '$\approx$' standing for 'is similar to':

1 Leibniz' Similarity Law
2 P(a)
3 a$\approx$b
4 P=(b)

Here is an instantiation of this schema:

1 Similar objects have similar properties.
2 Bob has blue eyes.
3 Tim is Bob's monozygotic twin.
4 Tim has bluish eyes.

This is a rather satisfying piece of reasoning, so perhaps the similarity-axiom works out well. Now consider the following example:

1 Similar objects have similar properties.
2' Bob is married to Lizzy.
3 Tim and Bob are monozygotic twins.
4' Tim is married to Lizzy, or Liza, or Elisabeth.

If we learn that Bob has blue eyes, this justifies the inference that his twin-brother Tim's eyes are bluish as well, but the additional piece of information that Bob is married to Lizzy, definitely does not justify the inference that Tim is also married to Lizzy, not even to Liza or Elisabeth. Substitution of 'has blue eyes' for P, yields a strong argument; whereas if 'is married to Lizzy' is plugged in, the argument becomes pathetically weak by any standard. Here we have two inferences with exactly the same form, one reasonable, the other ridiculous. To aggravate the case, they are based on the same set of similarities, summed up in the premise that Bob and Tim are monozygotic twins. Something has gone badly wrong in this formalisation of similarity.

Wrong in what sense? A formalisation is meant to capture inferentially important properties. The formalisation of similarity based on strict identity failed, because it sanctioned intuitively strong as well as intuitively disastrous inferences. At this stage, two possibilities open up. One possibility is that more sophisticated theories of similarity can do better, another that the effort at formalising similarity was misguided from the beginning. After all, a not uncommon view on analogies is that they belong to the context of discovery rather than to the context of justification and of course standards of validity devised for deductive inferences do not apply to heuristic arguments. The purpose of an analogy, this line of reasoning continues, is to suggest that an explanation or justification that works in one case could also work in another. But only *suggest*; you have to check it by further investigations. On this view, any logical theory of analogies has to be flawed, because of the heuristic nature of analogies.

In this paper I explore both these possibilities. In the next section I outline in a non-technical fashion a more promising theory of similarity based on structural identity rather than on identity per se. In the third section I discuss the proper standard for assessing the strength of analogies. I also explain how such an oblique pattern of reasoning as an analogy can ever be of any use. The proof of the pudding is in the final section in which I illustrate the theory with an extended example.

Structural Similarity

Quite a few cognitive psychologists and computer scientists have tried their hand at analogies (Gentner 1983, 1989; Gick and Holyoak 1980; Holland et al. 1986; Holyoak and Thagard 1989a, 1989b, 1995; Keane et al. 1994). In outlining a structural theory, I draw heavily on their work, without trying to be faithful to any of them.[4] I shall skip all technicalities and concentrate on the underlying basic idea.

To begin with, let's consider the elements of an analogy that should find a place in a structural model. In a typical analogy, we have a situation or event – usually called the target – which is problematic in some way. Either because it is new and we are at a loss for what to say, or because our audience disagrees with us about its proper characterisation. Second, we need a so-called base, a familiar situation or event which invites us to look at the target in a particular way. Finally, what is already accepted about the base must be transferred to the target. If the analogy works, we find out something or convince someone by establishing some kind of similarity between the problematic target and the more familiar base. So a structural model of an analogy should at least contain a base, a target and a similarity function that maps elements from the base to their counterparts in the target.

But more structure than that is needed. I have misleadingly described the base and the target as a situation or event; it would have been more accurate to say that they consist of *descriptions* of salient objects, properties and relations making up a situation or event. The descriptions serve as premises in an argumentative pattern that is mapped from the base onto the target. The overall mapping in turn consists of submappings from the elements in the base to the corresponding elements in the target. In that way, a problematic or contested global similarity is broken down into a set of accepted local similarities. The submappings are subsequently used to set up a corresponding argumentative pattern in the base.

So analogies do not have one definite structure, they have as many structures as there are argumentative patterns. At a more general level however, all analogies have a tripartite structure consisting of an inference in the base, a mapping from the base to the target, and finally a *Doppelgänger* inference in the target. But these parts must be connected in a certain way to make an analogy. The similarities must play a double role. First, 'horizontally' in the mapping connecting target and base, and second, 'vertically' as premises in the target inference.

The double-role-condition explains what went wrong in the example with the twins in the introduction. If we want to find out Tim's eye colour, his twin brother Bob is an appropriate base. Since the colour of Tim's eyes can be explained by referring to the same property that was used in selecting his twin brother as a base – their identical genetic make-up – the double-role-condition is fulfilled. In contrast, if we want to find out the name of Tim's wife, the similarity that makes the base and the target similar is not involved in any inference that explains why Bob's wife has the name she has.

So far the presentation has been excessively abstract. To get an idea of how the theory works, a concrete example will do it no harm.

The second book of Samuel is a collection of rather cruel feats performed during King David's reign, most of them by David himself. One particular story relates how David takes a fancy to Uriah's wife Bathsheba and seduces her while her husband is fighting the Ammonites at Rabbah. Then he sends for Uriah and tells him to deliver a letter to Joab, the commander in chief. In the letter, David orders Joab to 'Put Uriah out in front where the fighting is fiercest and then fall back, so that he gets wounded and killed.' Joab does what his king has ordered him and Uriah is killed. At this point, the prophet Nathan comes to David and tells him the following parable:

> In the same town were two men, one rich, the other poor. The rich man had flocks and herds in great abundance; the poor man had nothing but an ewe lamb, only a single little one which he had bought. He fostered it and it grew up with him and his children, eating his bread, drinking from his cup, sleeping in his arms; it was like a daughter to him. When a traveller came to stay, the rich man would not take anything from his own flock or herd to provide for the wayfarer who had come to him. Instead, he stole the poor man's lamb and prepared that for his guest.
>
> David flew into great rage with the man. 'As Yahweh lives', he said to Nathan, 'the man who did this deserves to die. For doing such a thing and for having shown no pity, he shall make fourfold restitution for the lamb.'
>
> Nathan then said to David, 'You are the man!' (2 Sam. 12, 1-7).

Let's consider the elements in the story about David and Bathsheba. According to David, 'the man who did this deserves to die. For doing such a thing and for having shown no pity, he shall make fourfold restitution for the lamb.' The order of the punishments is somewhat counterintuitive and, legally speaking, it is also very harsh. The Mosaic ordinances prescribed that if a man steals a sheep, he shall repay with four sheep, and a sheep is all the rich man has stolen. (It is remarkable that the killing of Uriah does not play any role in the parable.) Apparently, this particular theft and the subsequent eating of the lamb are morally so appalling, that according to David the offender deserves to be put to death. What properties do these acts have that make them so appalling? Two I think. In the first place, the theft betrays extreme 'graspiness'.[5] The rich man has 'flocks and herds in great abundance' but nevertheless he steals the poor man's only lamb. Secondly, the eating of the lamb is extremely callous. The poor man is deeply attached to his lamb, whereas the rich man does not care a straw about it. David apparently holds the moral principle that such grasping and callous acts constitute a capital crime and consequently that the man who performed them deserves to die.

So upon hearing the parable, David first reasons as follows:

1 The poor man owns one lamb.
2 The poor man is very fond of his lamb.
3 The rich man owns many sheep.
4 The rich man steals the poor man's lamb.
5 The rich man feeds the lamb to the traveller.
6 To steal and eat a pet lamb is grasping and callous.
7 Such grasping and callous conduct is a capital crime.
8 Therefore, the rich man should die.

So far, this is an ordinary piece of moral reasoning with no analogy involved as yet. In the second step, the parable is mapped onto the story about David, Bathsheba, and Uriah. Objects are to be matched if and only if they play a similar role in the base and the target, where 'similar' is to be cashed out in terms of the properties and relations that hold for those objects. Obviously, the rich man is matched with king David, and the poor man with the king's subject, Uriah. Given these mappings, the less obvious correspondence between Bathsheba and the ewe lamb is straightforward. This mapping yields new information about the target as well. As Bathsheba is matched with the ewe lamb, we are supposed to map the properties of the ewe lamb, its innocence and helplessness, onto Bathsheba. Beforehand, nothing had been said about her character.

The base also contains an 'object' without an obvious counterpart in the target, the traveller. What could possibly correspond to him? He visits the rich man and the rich man prepares a lamb for him. One possibility is to think of the traveller as a personification of David's desire. Just as the rich man gives the traveller a lamb which he eats to satisfy his hunger, David has intercourse with Bathsheba to gratify his own horniness. This possibility suggests something about the nature of desires as well: they just visit their subjects, as unexpected and uninvited guests.

In setting up the object correspondences, I used properties only. I could just as well have started with the relations. The order is arbitrary; you begin with whatever strikes you as the most plausible mapping. A salient relation in the base is that between the rich man and the lamb–the rich man steals the poor man's only lamb. A corresponding relation should hold between the corresponding objects in the target–David seduces Uriah's only wife. And just as the traveller eats the stolen lamb, David has intercourse with Bathsheba. The parable also stresses the intimate relationship between the poor man and the ewe lamb. 'He fostered it, and it grew up with him and with his children, eating his bread, drinking from his cup, sleeping in his arms; it was like a daughter to him.' Given the object correspondences, we can transfer this to the target–Uriah loves Bathsheba. We were told nothing explicitly about their relationship, it is something we learn by transferring information from the base. I have listed the relevant similarities in the schema below:

BASE	TARGET	SIMILARITY
OBJECTS		
the rich man	David	
the poor man	Uriah	
the ewe lamb	Bathsheba	
the traveller	David's desire	
PROPERTIES		
rich	king	powerful
poor	subject	powerless

| innocent | pure | blameless |
| hungry | horny | craving satisfaction |

RELATIONS

poor man owns one lamb	Uriah has one wife	scarcity
rich man owns many sheep	David has many wives	abundance
poor man is fond of lamb	Uriah loves Bathsheba	cares deeply for
rich man steals lamb	David seduces Bathsheba	appropriates
traveller eats lamb	David 'consumes' Bathsheba	violates

When Nathan exclaims: 'You are the man!', David's verdict that the man who stole the lamb deserves to die, reflects dramatically upon himself. And David realises it does when he concedes: 'I have sinned against Yahweh'. If it is grasping to steal a lamb when you have countless lambs yourself, then it is even more grasping to seduce somebody else's wife when you have plenty of wives yourself.[6] Both are cases of immoral appropriation, but the latter is more grasping than the former. And if it is callous to eat a pet lamb for dinner, then it is even more callous to have intercourse with someone else's beloved wife. Both acts constitute a violation and again, the latter is more callous than the former, because to love a human being is a deeper relationship than to care for an animal. Therefore, if the principle holds for the rich man, it certainly holds for David. David deserves to die then, but Yahweh does not kill him; he kills his son that Bathsheba gave birth to instead. This, however, belongs to the mysteries of divine justice rather than to the theory of analogical inferences.

The *Doppelgänger*-argument can also be represented schematically:

1' Uriah has one wife, Bathsheba.
2' Uriah loves Bathsheba.
3' David has many wives.
4' David seduces Bathsheba.
5' David has intercourse with Bathsheba.
6' To seduce and have intercourse with another's wife is grasping and callous.
7' Such grasping and callous conduct is a capital crime.
8' Therefore, David should die.

The three steps of the analogy can be represented in one schema:

1 BASE	2 SIMILARITY	3 TARGET
1 Poor man owns one lamb.	–	1' Uriah has one wife, Bathsheba.
2 Poor man is fond of his lamb.	–	2' Uriah loves Bathsheba.
3 Rich man owns many sheep.	–	3' David has many wives.
4 Rich man steals lamb.	–	4' David seduces Bathsheba.
5 Traveller eats lamb.	–	5' David 'consumes' Bathsheba.
6 Such acts are grasping and callous.		6' Such acts are grasping and callous.
7 *Such conduct is a capital crime.*		7' *Such conduct is a capital crime.*
8 Therefore, rich man should die.		8' Therefore, David should die.

This schema concerns one particular analogy only. It can be generalised simply by replacing the particular sentences in the example by the sentence-symbols. The replacement yields the general structure of this analogical argument. Of course, the possibility of constructing a *Doppelgänger* inference is not confined to inferences involving a modus ponens as this schema does. Any pattern has a *Doppelgänger*. In the fourth section I give an example involving a reductio ad absurdum.

Function and Strength

So far I have only discussed structure, I now turn to strength and function. Is Nathan's analogy strong? The answer depends on two factors: Is the base argument strong? And second: Does the transfer preserve the strength? As to the first question, the answer is an unqualified 'yes'. David holds a moral principle that says that anyone who performs very grasping and callous acts should be put to death. The rich man performs such acts; therefore, he should be put to death. This part of the argument is an application of a norm to a non-controversial case. The second question also merits an unqualified 'yes'. The properties in virtue of which the rich man's behaviour is a capital crime are its graspiness and callousness. David's behaviour is, if anything, more grasping and callous than the rich man's. So, if the rich man deserves death because of his behaviour, then David certainly does. I conclude that this analogy is airtight.

This conclusion is inescapable, but there is a catch in the reasoning that leads up to it that has to do with what Hempel calls the redundancy problem (Hempel, 1965). If David subscribes to the moral principle he uses in drawing the conclusion about the base, then why does he not apply it to the target right away? In this particular analogy, the answer is obvious:

Nathan tells David the parable to make him judge himself in judging the rich man. The detour via the base is necessary to make David aware of what he has actually done.

At first sight it might seem rather silly that David does not notice that the parable is about himself – it strikes us immediately – but recent research testifies to the plausibility of David's ignorance. In fact it is very easy to overlook a potential analogy (Gentner, Ratterman & Forbus 1993; Gick & Holyoak 1980; Novick 1988). One of the reasons it is so obvious to us, is that we have the story about David, Uriah and Bathsheba vividly before us, since we have just read it. (An effect referred to as 'priming' in psychology.) And one of the reasons that it passes unnoticed to David is that self-knowledge is hard to come by, the more so when the information is unwelcome. We are not very prone to accept painful truths about ourselves.

All right, Hempel would retort, the analogy is psychologically required and rhetorically effective, but logically speaking the base is a cog that is unconnected to the rest of the machinery. Real analogies are heuristic at best and therefore never valid. Let's take Hempel's objections one by one.

To answer the redundancy-charge it is necessary to make some distinctions. To know the meaning of a concept is to know its extension in all possible worlds. Or, what comes to the same, to be able to tell in any given situation whether an object falls under the concept or not. If this is an adequate characterisation, we have only partial knowledge of the meaning of most, if not all, empirical, moral and legal concepts. By the same token, we have only partial knowledge of the applicability of rules, since all rules contain concepts. David for one has only partial knowledge of the meaning of 'callous' and 'grasping'. He believes that they apply to the rich man's behaviour, but he does not realise that they apply to his own behaviour as well. The parable gives him a reason to conceptualise his own behaviour as callous and grasping. *Given* this conceptualisation of the target, the rule can be applied directly as Hempel claims it always can. But only because the mapping from the base has already forced David to accept this conceptualisation of the target. Even if the base is not *logically* indispensable, it is at least *epistemically* indispensable in that it prepares the ground for applying an argument to the target. Hempel's redundancy-thesis ignores an essential part of the analogy that is effected by the mapping: the conceptualisation or reconceptualisation of the target.

A second remark is pertinent to Hempel's complaint. Nathan wants to convince David of something about his behaviour he does not as yet accept. If the analogy is to work, the conditions for applying the rule used in the inference should be more readily acceptable to the addressee in the base than they are in the target. Better acceptable, yet less well satisfied. The initial unacceptability of the target inference is the reason for introducing a base in the first place. The fact that the conditions for satisfying the rule are less well satisfied in the base, gives the analogy its persuasive force. If the addressee accepts the argument for the base, he certainly has to accept it for the target where the conditions of satisfaction are better fulfilled, or fulfilled at least as well as they are in the base.

But how is it possible for someone to accept an inference in the more dubious base, while not accepting it in the more obvious target? In the introduction I said the target had to be problematic in some sense. It is problematic in the sense that it is not accepted by the addressee, either because he is not aware that it applies because the target is new in some sense, or because he perceives the target in a distorted fashion due to personal bias or common prejudice. The fact that the conditions for applying the rule are actually better – or at least as well – satisfied in the target than they are in the base, suggests that the addressee's initial non-acceptance is due to special circumstances concerning *him*, to *his* bias or ignorance. Analogies can also be used to make decisions about the extension of predicates and the applicability of rules in hitherto undecided cases or in cases where the distortion is common. In the next section I give an example where an analogy is not aimed at curing the idiosyncracies of one addressee, but rather to correct received opinion.

The base then, is not redundant, it's a sprat. In an effective analogy, the analogy-inventor sets a sprat to catch a whale. That is the essential function of analogies. David is made to condemn the rich man because of his callous and grasping acts – a small concession to make. But as his own acts are even more callous and grasping, the rule applies to his own behaviour *a fortiori* – a bitter truth to swallow.

What about Hempel's second charge that analogies are heuristic at best and therefore never valid? 'Validity' is a logical concept, and as we saw, the mapping part of analogies is epistemic rather than logical. A mapping is a matter of conceptualisation, of extending or narrowing down the extension of concepts, and validity does not set any standards for that process. A conceptualisation is consistent, reasonable, semantically justified, but not valid.

Objects, properties and relations can be conceptualised relatively concretely so as to fit either the base or the target, or more abstractly, so as to fit both. For example, the relationship between the poor man and the ewe lamb can be described aptly as 'fondness', whereas 'love' fits its counterpart between Uriah and Bathsheba. 'Love' as I use it is only possible between humans, not between man and beast. But fondness and love share an important core of attention, intimacy, and concern. On a more abstract level, therefore, both relations can be characterised equally well by the predicate 'care'. This shared core is the semantic justification of the transfer. The same principle holds for the other relations. The stealing of a lamb and the seduction of somebody else's wife can both be characterised more abstractly as cases of immoral appropriation. And eating a stolen lamb and having intercourse with somebody else's wife are from a more abstract point of view both cases of some kind of immoral 'consummation' or violation.

Similarity-mappings are only possible because the particular properties and relations of base and target can be represented as belonging to the same type at a more abstract level, because they play the same conceptual role in the analogy.

So the question whether an analogy can be valid does not apply to the mapping, it must be restricted to the constitutive inferences. Well, can they ever be valid? Sure they can. In so far as they instantiate a valid pattern, they are valid. But I should say something more about the kind of validity inferences in analogies usually have.

Classically, an argument is valid if and only if the conclusion is true whenever all the premises are true. Classical validity has a logical property called monotonicity. This means that if a conclusion follows from a set of premises, it follows from every extension of that set as well. Consequently, extra premises, new information, cannot alter the truth-value of the conclusion. If a conclusion is true whenever all the premises in the argument are, it is certainly true when all the premises *and* some additional premises are.

The argument with the identity-axiom from the introduction is monotonic in this sense. If Oedipus married the queen of Thebes and the queen of Thebes is one and the same person as Oedipus mother, Oedipus married his mother. Given the truth of those premises, additional premises can never alter the truth-value of the conclusion.

It is important to keep in mind that neither causal regularities nor norms should be read as logical implications or universally quantified sentences. One pair of twins with different eye-colour does not make us retract our belief in the causal regularity between genetic make-up and eye colour. 'Twins have similar eye-colour' should not be read as 'All twins have similar eye-colour', but rather as the default-rule 'Normally twins have similar eye-colour'. The latter is not falsified by one pair of twins with different eye colours, whereas its universal counterpart would be. Causal regularities and norms can absorb exceptions where their universal counterparts would succumb to them. The same holds for the more general similarity-rule. 'Similar objects have similar properties' should not be read as 'All similar objects have similar properties', but rather as 'Normally similar objects have similar properties'.

Arguments depending on default-rules are non-monotonic. They can guarantee provisional certainty at best. It is not impossible that a pair of twins has different eye-colour, due to a mutation, a disease, laser therapy or whatever. In that case, the three premises in the inference about the twins from the introduction would all be true, yet, the conclusion would be false – Tim does not have bluish eyes. The conclusion followed from the first three premises, but it does not follow from the extended set. The additional information that Tim has had laser therapy cancels the inferential power of the default similarity-rule. Specific knowledge about a particular object overrules general assumptions about the class of objects as a whole.

So, whereas the inference from the introduction was valid, the following is not:

1 Similar objects have similar properties.
2 Bob has blue eyes.
3 Tim is Bob's monozygotic twin.
4 Tim has had laser therapy.
5 Tim has bluish eyes.

Likewise, it is not true that if the rich man and David have both been callous and grasping, the latter should be put to death if and only if the former should. It is possible that further information about David or the circumstances pertaining to his offence makes us withdraw our judgement about him, without changing our beliefs about any of the premises. That is actually what happened. As we saw, Yahweh did not kill David, although David committed the same crime as the rich man did. I did not pursue the matter and referred it to the mysteries of divine justice. But we can give a more rational account of Yahweh's judgement if we attribute a non-monotonic concept of validity to him. Further relevant circumstances can be adduced in favour of David that did not hold for the rich man. After hearing the parable, David exclaims: 'I have sinned against Yahweh'. David's repentance wins him Yahweh's forgiveness. Both subscribe to the norm that very callous and grasping deeds merit death, but that does not exclude the possibility of exonerating facts. Causal regularities as well as norms are default-rules that allow of exceptions without losing their status as rules.

What is the use of having default-rules? If I had to put my money on one answer to the question 'Do twins have the same eye-colour, yes or no?', I would quite confidently put it on 'yes' unless I knew of some very special circumstances. And other things equal, David deserves the same punishment as the rich man. But additional information can block the possibility of drawing a conclusion from a default-rule that can be drawn from the same rule and less information. To mark their provisional character, we could add 'presumably' to conclusions that are drawn from default-rules, rather than render them as purely descriptive sentences.[7]

With the refinements from this paragraph in mind, the inference from the introduction should be written as follows:

1 Normally similar objects have similar properties.
2 Bob has blue eyes.
3 Tim is Bob's monozygotic twin.
4 Presumably Tim has bluish eyes.

To return to Hempel's indictment, analogies are neither redundant nor just heuristic. If the conditions of application are fulfilled, they can be the best way to persuade someone who is inclined – for 'improper' reasons – not to be persuaded by the target-inference taken on its own. And they can be used to incorporate a new phenomenon in our conceptual framework. In both cases they are heuristic and in both cases the base plays an indispensable role. The conceptualisation of the target would be a shot in the dark if it were not moored to the familiar, accepted base and fixed in an inferential schema. So analogies can be both heuristic and well justified, without being classically valid.

The Theory at Work in Defence of Abortion

So far, I have outlined a structural theory of analogies and indicated the kind of validity they are capable of. I have also tried to explain how such a devious way of reasoning as analogies can serve a legitimate purpose. Nathan's parable was meant to prevent the outline to become too abstract. But one example is not enough to figure out what features belong to this one example only, and what features have a general character. This paragraph is meant to facilitate the separation of the particular and the general. In Nathan's parable, a rule that applied in the base was extended to cover the target as well. My next example involves a rule that supposedly holds for the target, but is shown by analogy not really to hold. Nathan's analogy was very strong, this example is more dubious in some interesting ways. And Nathan's parable was directed at David's idiosyncratic bias, while this example is meant to challenge received opinion.

A second reason for getting down to details is that general theories should make us understand concrete phenomena better. In my opinion, the best justification for a general theory about analogies is that it enables us to understand and evaluate particular analogies better. To see if this theory does, I shall now put it to test on a famous analogy invented by Judith Jarvis Thomson as a refutation of a seemingly obvious argument to the effect that abortion is always immoral.

Thomson's argument proceeds from the intuitively plausible principle that a person's right to life is always stricter and stronger than some other person's right to decide what happens in and to her body. In the case of abortion it is unclear whether the principle holds, because personhood is a predicate that admits of borderline cases and whether or not it applies to foetuses is at the centre of the dispute. So she grants her opponents that the foetus is a person. At this point in her article, a by now notorious violinist enters the stage:

It sounds plausible. But now let me ask you to imagine this. You wake up in the morning and find yourself back to back in bed with an unconscious violinist. A famous unconscious violinist. He has been found to have a fatal kidney ailment, and the Society of Music Lovers has canvassed all the available medical records and found that you alone have the right blood type to help. They have therefore kidnapped you, and last night the violinist's circulatory system was plugged into yours, so that your kidneys can be used to extract poison from his blood as well as your own. The director of the hospital now tells you, 'Look, we're sorry the Society of Musical Lovers did this to you – we would never have permitted it if we had known. But still, they did it, and the violinist now is plugged into you. To unplug you would be to kill him. But never mind, it's only for nine months. By then he will have recovered from his ailment, and can safely be unplugged from you.' Is it morally incumbent on you to accede to this situation? No doubt it would be very nice of you if you did, a great kindness. But do you *have* to accede to it? What if it were not nine months, but nine years? Or longer still? What if the director of the hospital says, 'Tough luck, I agree, but you've now got to stay in bed, with the violinist plugged into you, for the rest of your life. Because remember this. All persons have a right to life, and violinists are persons. Granted you have a right to decide what happens in and to your body, but a person's right to life outweighs your right to decide what happens in and to your body. So you cannot ever be unplugged from him.' I imagine you would regard this as outrageous, which suggests that something really is wrong with the plausible-sounding argument I mentioned a moment ago. (Thomson 1971, 48f)

In the story about the violinist the principle that the right to life always outweighs the right to decide yields an outrageous result. But under certain circumstances, abortion is similar in all relevant respects to the story Thomson used as a counterexample to the principle. Therefore, if it is outrageous to force you to stay in bed with the violinist for nine months, it is equally outrageous to force a pregnant woman to carry the foetus to term under those circumstances. Let's look at the details of this argument.

Thomson assumes the principle that the right to life outweighs the right to decide what happens in and to your body (1); then she states the principle that you have a right to decide (2) and the fact that the Society of Music Lovers has kidnapped you (3). The kidnapping violates your right to decide (4); and there is a more or less direct causal chain linking the kidnapping with your being plugged into the violinist (5); therefore, the latter event violates your right to decide as well (6). In the next premise she states the principle that the violinist has a right to life (7) and that unplugging yourself from him would violate this right (8). Now there is a tie, because whatever is decided, one right is going to be violated: if the violinist is unplugged, his right to life (6); if you have to stay plugged in, your right to decide (8). At this point, the principle stated in the first premise is invoked: as the violinist's right to life outweighs your right to decide, you ought to stay plugged in (9). But intuitively, to force you to stay plugged in would be outrageous! (10); and therefore, the principle that yields such an outrageous conclusion cannot be sound after all (11). Schematically:

1 The right to life outweighs the right to decide.
2 You have a right to decide.
3 The Society of music lovers has kidnapped you.
4 Kidnapping violates your right to decide.
5 The kidnapping led up to the plugging.
6 Therefore, the plugging violates your right to decide as well.[4,5]
7 The violinist has a right to life.
8 Unplugging the violinist violates his right to life.
9 Therefore, you have to stay plugged in.[1,6,8]
10 But surely you do not have to stay plugged in!
11 The violinist's right to life does not outweigh your right to decide.[1,9,10]

The elements of the violinist story can be transferred, one to one, to a case of abortion. We must introduce someone corresponding to the Society of Music Lovers; let's call him Jack the Raper. This leads up to the following correspondences:

BASE	TARGET	SIMILARITY
OBJECTS		
violinist	foetus	
you	woman	
Society of music lovers	Jack	
PROPERTIES		
plugged in	carried	receiving sustenance
bound up with	carrying	providing sustenance
kidnapper	raper	offending

RELATIONS

Society kidnapped you	Jack raped woman	violates right to decide
kidnap leads to plugging	rape leads to pregnancy	violates right to decide
you unplug violinist	woman aborts foetus	violates right to life

How come these mappings are so obvious? Nothing forces you, logically speaking, to pair off things in this way. The answer is: you apply the principle of semantic justification automatically. For instance, the story about the violinist tells us that if he is not plugged into your system, he will not survive. We all know that a foetus depends in a similar way on the bodily functions of the pregnant woman. Both violinist and foetus depend for their lives on a third person, neither will survive being severed from that person. Or take the kidnapping. That feature of the story can only be transferred if we know that rape can result in pregnancy. The nine months is also a clue that is not likely to be overlooked. It immediately reminds us of childbearing and suggests a mapping between first, the violinist and the foetus and second, you and the woman.

We all have this background knowledge of course, but we are not always aware of all the subtle and often tacit knowledge needed to make all the right connections. That is the reason why it is generally hard to find an analogous base. If Thomson's article were not called *A Defence of Abortion*, but *A Defence of Classical Music*, the bare story about the violinist would probably not make us think of abortion. The title and introduction prepare the ground for that. (The priming-effect again.)

The same argument as the one just outlined can now be applied to the target, yielding a *Doppelgänger*-pattern about abortion with the conclusion that the foetus' right to life does not outweigh the woman's right to decide to have an abortion if her pregnancy results from rape.

1' The right to life outweighs the right to decide.
2' The woman has a right to decide.
3' Jack raped the woman.
4' Rape violates the woman's right to decide.
5' The rape led up to the pregnancy.
6' Therefore, the pregnancy violates the woman's right to decide as well.[4',5']
7' The foetus has a right to life.
8' Abortion violates the foetus' right to life.

9' Therefore, the woman should carry the foetus to term.[1',6',8']
10' But surely the woman does not have to carry the foetus!
11' The foetus' right to life does not outweigh the woman's right to decide.[1', 9',10']

To summarise the three interconnected steps of this analogy: It begins with an argument that proceeds from a principle in the first premise to a contradiction in the ninth and tenth, which, by means of the reductio-ad-absurdum-rule, sanctions the conclusion that the principle does not hold in the base. In the second step a mapping function connects the elements from the base with the elements from the target. Finally, the results of the mapping serve as building blocks for a *Doppelgänger*-argument in the target. Below, the structure is represented schematically: (I have abbreviated 'the right to decide': RD and 'the right to life': RL.)

1 BASE	2 SIMILARITY	3 TARGET
1 RL outweighs RD.		1' RL outweighs RD.
2 You have RD.		2' Woman has RD.
3 Society kidnapped you.	–	3' Jack raped the woman.
4 Kidnapping violates RD.		4' Rape violates RD.
5 Kidnapping led to plugging.	–	5' Rape led to pregnancy.
6 Plugging violates RD.		6' Pregnancy violates RD.
7 The violinist has RL.		7' The foetus has RL.
8 Unplugging violates RL.	–	8' Abortion violates RL.
9 You ought to stay plugged in.		9' Woman ought to carry foetus.
10 That is outrageous!		*10' That is outrageous!*
11 RL does not outweigh RD.		11' RL does not outweigh RD.

By now it should be obvious that the strength of an analogy depends on two factors: the strength of the base argument and the strength of the mapping. Thomson introduces the violinist in order to arouse a sense of outrage. *Of course* you do not have to accede to the situation described in the base. And if that is so, then *of course* neither does a woman have to carry a foetus to term if her pregnancy is due to rape. I shall evaluate the two *of courses* one by one.

The conclusion Thomson arrives at is based on (among others) two intuitively plausible premises: a general principle (1) and a particular judgement (10). Because a contradiction can be derived from them, they cannot both be true an consequently one has to go. To make sure we drop the right one, we have to investigate the grounds for both. If the grounds for the particular judgement are weaker than the grounds for the principle, we should keep the principle and revise our judgement rather than as Thomson does, reject the principle and stick to the particular judgement.

The initial plausibility of the principle appears to rest on safe grounds. It reflects the relative importance of two goods, life and autonomy. At first sight, it would be outrageous to force you to stay in bed plugged into the violinist for nine months. But what exactly causes the sense of outrage? The amount of harm involved. To make sure the reader accepts her argument, Thomson steadily increases the time you have to spend in bed, and consequently the harm you are caused to suffer, from nine months, to nine years, to a whole lifetime. At a given point the harm caused is certain to make the intuitive balance tip over in favour of unplugging.

Her story focuses on the harm you have to suffer, thereby ignoring the perspective of the other protagonist. Let's fiddle around with the circumstances of the violinist a little and see what happens. I agree that the situation is outrageous, but as things stand, his life actually depends on you. These unfortunate facts being as they are, would you unplug the poor violinist and watch him slowly poison himself to death? A 55 year old world-famous violinist? What if he is 33, and has a loving wife and a piano playing daughter? Could you unplug yourself and look them in the eye? What if he were an 11 year old prodigy, a twentieth-century Mozart? What would you say to his parents? What are nine months of harm to you compared to his whole life? And of course the time you have to spend in bed can be shortened rather than increased, from nine months to say nine weeks or nine hours.

The sense of outrage is not only a function of the amount of harm you are caused to suffer, but it also depends on the amount of harm you cause to suffer if you unplug yourself. As that amount can be both increased and diminished, the 'direction' of outrage can be made to shift from outrage at having to stay plugged in for nine years to a total stranger, to outrage at not staying plugged in for nine hours to a 11 year old Mozart. But then the whole argument rests on a floating sense of outrage; a rather shaky ground indeed.

A second consideration points in the same direction.[8] Why is it that the story is about a violinist? Thomson emphatically draws our attention to this feature: '...an unconscious violinist. A famous unconscious violinist.' Why not just any odd person? Because she takes for granted that even if you were to be plugged into a famous violinist, into someone that is who is capable of bringing enjoyment to millions of people, even then it would be outrageous to force you to stay plugged in. And if that is outrageous, how much more so would it be to force a woman to carry a foetus to term that is unlikely to bring any enjoyment to anyone and very likely to bring misery to at least one. If the sense of outrage at having to stay plugged in prevails in the full knowledge of the enjoyment the violinist will probably provide, Thomson has made her case for abortion much stronger.

But another reaction seems available to people with consequentialist sympathies. If this is what is at stake – a human life *and* the enjoyment of millions of people on the one hand, and a few months of moderate suffering on the other – the outcome will unequivocally be in favour of staying plugged in. As Godwin said, if you have to choose between saving archbishop Fénélon and your mother from a burning house, pure, unadulterated justice requires you to choose the archbishop. Perhaps the sense of outrage at being forced to stay plugged in turns out to be rash if you consider things impartially.

Thomson's analogy strongly suggests that rights depend on costs, and if they do, *all* costs should be taken into account: yours, the violinist's and those of the general public. But Thomson rejects this account of rights explicitly. In fact she argues that no clash ever occurs between the right to life and the right to decide in the example.[9] That somebody has a right to life, so Thomson continues her argument, does not mean that he should be guaranteed the means to exist; it only means that he should not be killed unjustly. It would never be unjust to unplug yourself, but it could be very egoistic and callous. These complaints are no less grave than being unjust, Thomson continues, they are just different. If you were to consent to stay plugged into the violinist, thereby giving him the right to use your body, that would be very *kind* of you. But unless you consent explicitly, he does not have a *right* to the use of your body. His right to life cannot imply that you have the duty to provide the necessary means for his existence. Precisely that assumption led up to the unpalatable conclusion.

I am not sure what to make of this move. Perhaps it would not be only extremely callous and egoistic and unkind to unplug yourself, but actually unjust. Article 450 in the Dutch penal code requires everybody to be what Thomson calls a Minimally Decent Samaritan. If someone happens to be in a life-threatening situation and you can help him out without serious risk or harm to yourself, you have the duty to provide the help. Is this not a case in point? If so, does not that duty outweigh the right to decide what happens in and to your body? Whatever the answer, I will not pursue the issue here. It belongs to the philosophy of rights rather than to the theory of analogical inferences.

The second *of course*, the actual mapping from the violinist to the foetus, has been heavily criticised by feminists. The relationship between a woman and a total stranger is completely different from that between a pregnant woman and the foetus. Dworkin (1995) cites some of the relevant literature in *Life's Dominion*. Catherine MacKinnon for one insists on the difference between women-foetus relationships on the one hand and on the other hand relationships like that between a tenant and his landlord or between the violinist and you in Thomson's example. In the latter kind two separate individuals have become connected either deliberately or accidentally and one of the partners has a sovereign right to sever the connection if he wishes. 'In my opinion and in the experience of many pregnant women, the foetus is a human form of life. It is alive.[...] More than a body part but less than a person, where it is, is largely what it is. From the standpoint of the pregnant woman, it is both me and not me. It 'is' the pregnant woman in the sense that it is in her and is hers more than anyone's. It 'is not' her in the sense that she is not all there is.' [...] 'Her foetus is not merely 'in her' as an inanimate object might be,' MacKinnon continues, 'or something alive but alien that has been transplanted into her body [...] She already has an intense physical and emotional investment in it unlike that which any other person, including its father, has; because of these physical and emotional connections it is as wrong to say that the foetus is separate from her as to say that it is not.' (MacKinnon, cited in Dworkin 1995, 54f.).

In my opinion, this critique is off the mark. Thomson's example is about pregnancy due to rape, a fact that must increase the sense of separateness dramatically. I have the intuition – not backed up by any research – that a woman pregnant after rape does not think of the foetus in terms of 'me' at all, nor in terms of a neutral stranger, but rather as an horrific intruder.[10] And if that is true, the analogy only wins in strength because the dependency relation in the target between the foetus and the raped woman is morally more blemished than that in the base and consequently less wrong to sever. In that case, the conditions of application of the *reductio ad absurdum* would be better fulfilled in the target than they are in the base –

the sense of outrage at having to carry the foetus to term would be stronger than the outrage at having to stay in bed with a stranger – and consequently, anyone who accepts the base-inference should certainly accept the target-inference.

But perhaps the mapping is not very strong for another reason. If it is the amount of harm that causes the outrage, then the amount of harm the pregnancy causes you to suffer is crucial. Is being pregnant more costly to you than staying in bed with the violinist? In very rare cases perhaps it is, but a run-of-the-mill pregnancy certainly compares favourably to being tied down for nine months in bed with a total stranger. Except for cigarette-smoking and one or two other bad habits you'd better quit anyway, you can go on doing whatever you did before for the better part of the nine months. In that case, the conditions of application would be better satisfied in the base than in the target, so acceptance of the base-inference would not give the addressee any reason to accept the target-inference. Or more precisely, the addressee's outrage at the fact that you would have to stay in bed for nine months, would not force him to feel outrage at the much less harmful pregnancy.

In what way has the theory shed light on Thomson's argument? First, it enabled us (or at least me) to see its structure more clearly, and subsequently, to evaluate its strength better. The inference was based on a reductio that required us to drop one of the intuitively acceptable premises. But a reductio does not tell which of two contradictory premises to drop. Thomson trusted the particular judgement better than the general principle and consequently the principle had to go. But an investigation of the grounds for holding the principle and the particular judgement respectively, provided some reasons to drop the judgement instead. So even if the base argument instantiates a valid pattern, it does not force you to draw the conclusion Thomson draws.

The mapping was not flawless either. At least on one reading, the grounds for feeling outrage at the fact that you would have to stay tied down in bed to a total stranger are more compelling than the grounds for feeling outrage at the fact that a woman would have to carry a fetus to term. On that reading, the acceptance of the base-inference does not provide the addressee with a good reason to accept the target-inference as well.

As it is so easy to find fault with the strength of the analogy, it is unlikely that it can fulfil its purpose – to catch the whale of received opinion.

Concluding Remarks

Analogies have an interconnected, tripartite structure, consisting of a base inference, a similarity mapping and a *Doppelgänger*-inference in the target. It is crucial that the mapped sub-parts play a double role, one in the mapping and one in the inference. As far as the inferences instantiate a valid pattern, they are valid. Usually, the inferences are non-monotonic in the sense that the conclusions they sanction are defeasible. However, an analogy as a whole cannot even be non-monotonically valid, because validity does not set a standard for mappings. Nevertheless, the overall mapping can be reasonable in so far as it is based on reasonable, connected sub-mappings.

Analogies provide a method for incorporating new or contested phenomena consistently into an existing conceptual framework. So apart from their heuristic function, they have a justificatory role to play as well. Their devious nature suggest that they will find employment principally when the target-inference cannot be applied directly due to ignorance or bias on the part of the addressee.

Knowledge is useful because it enables us to find our way in the natural and social world. If we can gain genuinely new knowledge by satisfying ourselves with something less than absolute certainty, then that is a price we should gladly pay. It's the kind of knowledge we always had about the world anyway. For a large part, it is gained through analogies.

Notes

1 I wish to thank Svend Andersen, Nils Holtug, Peter Rijpkema, Theo Rosier, Klaas Rozemond and Arend Soeteman for many useful comments on earlier drafts. Thanks are also due to Wim van der Steen for spending a lot of time and patience on improving my English of sorts. My greatest debt however is to Frank Veltman. But for his help, this paper would have been *a lot* worse.

2 Formally $\forall X \forall x \forall y((x{=}y \rightarrow (X(x) \leftrightarrow X(y)))$.

3 Formally $\forall X \forall X' \forall x \forall y((x{\approx}y) \rightarrow (X(x) \leftrightarrow X'(y)))$.

4 The structural theory has been effectively criticised by Hofstadter (1995, especially 155-193) in his beautifully clear and amusing book.

5   'Grasping' is a translation of the Greek 'pleonexia': the desire to have more than you are entitled to. Aristotle classifies it as a form of injustice in the fifth book of his Nichomachean Ethics. It is sometimes translated with 'greed', but The Revised Oxford Translation renders it as 'grasping'. I think graspiness is exactly the vice David exhibits here.

6   The story does not tell exactly how many wives David has. It gives up counting after seven.

7   What I say about defaults derives from Veltman. An easily accessible introduction can be found in Veltman (1998). Those interested in the technical details are referred to Veltman (1996).

8   Klaas Rozemond drew my attention to this problem.

9   But if that is so, the analogy is misleading.

10   Suzanne van de Vathorst pointed out two examples to me that vindicate this intuition; one from the brothers Taviani's movie *Chaos* and one from Toni Morrison's novel *Beloved*. In the former a mother feels nothing but despise for a son she gave birth to after she had been raped. In the latter female slaves terminate their pregnancy when slaveholders have raped them.

References

Aristotle (1984), *The complete works of Aristotle*, J. Barnes (ed), Princeton University Press, Princeton.

Davies, T.R. (1988), 'Determination, uniformity and relevance: normative criteria for generalization and reasoning by analogy', in D.H. Helman, *op.cit.*, pp. 227-50.

Dworkin, R. (1995), *Life's Dominion. An argument about abortion and euthanasia*, Harper Collins, London.

Gentner, D. (1983), 'Structure-mapping: a theoretical framework for analogy', *Cognitive Science* 7, pp. 155-170.

Gentner, D. (1989), 'The mechanisms of analogical learning', in S. Vosniadou and A. Ortony, pp. 199-241.

Gentner, D., Ratterman, M.J. and Forbus, K.D. (1993), 'The roles of similarity in transfer: separating retrievability from inferential soundness', *Cognitive Psychology*, vol. 25, pp. 524-575.

Gick, M. and Holyoak, K. (1980), 'Analogical problem solving', *Cognitive Psychology*, vol. 12, pp. 306-355.

Gick, M. and Holyoak, K. (1983), 'Schema induction and analogical transfer', *Cognitive Psychology*, vol. 15, pp. 1-38.

88 Reasoning in Ethics and Law

Helman, D.H. (ed)(1988), *Analogical Reasoning*, Kluwer, Dordrecht.
Hempel, C.G. (1965), 'Models and analogies in scientific explanation', in C.G. Hempel, *op.cit.*, pp. 433-447.
Hempel, C.G. (1965), *Aspects of scientific explanation*, Free Press, New York.
Hofstadter, D. (1995), *Fluid Concepts and Creative Analogies*, BasicBooks, New York.
Holland, J.H., Holyoak, K.J., Nisbett, R.E. and Thagard, P.R. (1986), *Induction. Processes of inference, learning, and discovery*, Bradford books/MIT, Cambridge, Mass.
Holyoak, K.J. and Thagard, P. (1989a), 'Analogical mapping by constraint satisfaction', *Cognitive Science*, vol. 13, pp. 295-355.
Holyoak, K.J. and Thagard, P. (1989b), 'A computational model of analogical problem solving', in S. Vosniadou and A. Ortony, *op. cit.*, pp. 242-266.
Holyoak, K.J. and Thagard, P. (1995), *Mental leaps: analogy in creative thought*, The MIT press, Cambridge, Mass.
Keane, M., Ledgeway, T. and Duff, S. (1994), 'Constraints on analogical mapping: a comparison of three models', *Cognitive Science*, vol. 18, pp. 387-438.
Novick, L. (1988), 'Analogical transfer, problem similarity, and expertise', *Journal of experimental Psychology: learning, memory and cognition,* vol. 14, pp. 510-520.
Thomson, J.J. (1971), 'A Defence of Abortion', *Philosophy and Public Affairs*, vol. 1, pp. 47-66.
Veltman, F. (1996), 'Defaults in Update Semantics', *Journal of Philosophical Logic*, vol. 25, pp. 221-261.
Veltman, F. (1998), 'Een zogenaamde denkfout', *Algemeen Nederlands Tijdschrift voor Wijsbegeerte*, vol. 90, pp. 11-25.
Vosniadou, S. and Ortony, A. (eds) (1989), *Similarity and analogical reasoning*, Cambridge University Press.

4 The Reconstruction of Legal Analogy-Argumentation
Monological and Dialogical Approaches

HARM KLOOSTERHUIS

Introduction

In 1951 Hubertus te Poel has two houses built by contractor Quint on land which Te Poel rents from his brother Heinrich. When construction is under way, Hubertus is unable to pay and Heinrich, the owner of the land, by right of accession becomes the owner of the houses built thereon. In a lawsuit which eventually comes before the Supreme Court, Quint demands payment for his activities by Heinrich. After all, Heinrich would have been 'unjustifiably enriched' at the expense of Quint. Since there was no explicit statutory rule for this legal claim, the Supreme Court had to fill a gap in the law. In the important judgement, in Dutch jurisprudence known as 'Quint v. Te Poel', the Supreme Court considers, among other things:

> ... that (...) according to art. 658 and 1603 of the Civil Code, the landlord cannot be expected, by paying a certain amount of money, to annul the enrichment enjoyed by him because of the works constructed by the holder or tenant of the land on which the works have been constructed;
> that it is implausible that a claim which the law withholds the holder and the tenant, would befall the contractor who has constructed these works under agreement with the tenant, and who suffered damage because his co-contractor is unable to make payments;...

Here the Supreme Court uses an analogy-argumentation: the gap in the law is filled by analogical application of two existing of legal standards (art. 658 and 1603 of the Civil Code) which were meant for different (yet similar) cases, to a case for which no legal rules had been laid down. The judicial gap is filled by means of a construction of a new legal norm: he who constructs works (Quint), contracted to do so by the tenant (Hubertus), and who suffers damage because his co-contractor appears to be unable to make payments, does not have a case from unjustified enrichment.

Both in legal theory and in legal practice traditionally quite a lot of attention is paid to the use of analogy-argumentation and other 'specifically legal argumentation forms' such as *a contrario* and *a fortiori* argumentation. There are two explanations for this.

First, the very use of analogy-argumentation raises a number of questions. Analogy-argumentation is used - as is apparent from the judgement 'Quint v. Te Poel' - to solve legal questions whenever there is a gap in the legal system. The judge construes a legal norm and, as such, acts as a 'substitute-legislator'. This often invites the question whether analogy-argumentation is allowable, and in case there are no objections, whether the judge has used the correct analogy-argumentation.[1]

Second, the *reconstruction* of analogy-argumentation raises a number of problems. The acceptability of analogy-argumentation can only be assessed if it has been construed in an adequate fashion. The argumentation must be identified as such, unexpressed elements must be made explicit and the structure of the argumentation, which is often complex, needs to be analysed. This *rational reconstruction* of analogy argumentation – which aims at the assessment of its quality – is a difficult task that has been approached by legal theorists from different angles.

I discuss here two of these approaches, the traditional, monological approach of analogy-argumentation and the dialogical approach. My aim is to assess these approaches as instruments for the rational reconstruction of analogy-argumentation. First I outline the traditional monological approach. Then I discuss the dialogical approach developed as a reaction to the traditional approach. Lastly I indicate how these approaches may be used to develop a more comprehensive and systematic method of reconstruction. My starting-point is the pragma-dialectical argumentation theory.

The Monological Analysis of Analogy-Argumentation

Within the framework of legal theory, analogy-argumentation is tradition-ally reconstructed mainly from a logical perspective, with the aim to check whether the conclusion is justified on formal grounds. Authors such as Tammelo (1969) and Klug (1982) consider analogy-argumentation as a specifically legal argumentation form, which on the face of it does not meet the requirements of logical validity, but which can be reconstructed as a logically valid argumentation. This approach of analogy-argumentation can be characterised as *monological* and *product-oriented*. It is monological because the reconstruction abstracts from the discussion context of the ar-gumentation. It is product-oriented or individualised because the recon-struction aims at the final product of the discussion process. Let me discuss Tammelo's analysis as a significant exponent of this traditional approach.

Tammelo's Analysis of Analogy-Argumentation

In *Outlines of Modern Legal Logic* (1969) Tammelo discusses the logical aspects of the *a simili* argumentation which he considers to be a specifically legal argument, together with *a contrario* argumentation and *a fortiori* ar-gumentation. Tammelo's definition of analogy-argumentation runs as follows: '*Argumentum a simile* proceeds from the idea that if a certain legal consequence is attached to certain legally relevant facts, one is entitled to attach the same legal consequence to essentially similar legally relevant facts' (Tammelo 1969, 129).

Tammelo argues that analogy-argumentation should be considered as invalid argumentation with legally binding conclusions. By supplementing the unexpressed argument, the argumentation can be reconstructed as valid. The following illustrates this:

1 If complex of facts F occurs, it is called theft.
2 *A complex of facts F', similar to F, occurs.*
3 F' must be treated as theft.

When Tammelo supplements and reconstructs this argumentation, he uses the following example. Suppose complex of facts F means: illegally taking away a good with the intention of appropriating it. A person illegally takes away electricity from the electricity company. Although electricity cannot be regarded as a 'good', taking it away is in essence similar to taking away a good. The social and economical consequences are, after all, the same. For that reason the same sanctions should be imposed on taking away electricity as on taking away a good. To this conclusion Tammelo adds: 'However sound this conclusion may be from the viewpoint of morals or social policy, it is unsound from the logical viewpoint.'

According to Tammelo the invalid argumentation can be turned into a valid one by adapting the first premise. The reconstructed analogy-argumentation runs like this:

> 1 *If* this action involves taking away a good unlawfully or if this action is considered by an authorised legal authority to be similar to taking away a good, *then* this action should be considered as theft.
> 2 This action is considered to be an *action similar to theft* by an authorised legal authority.
> 3 This action must be considered as theft.

To this reconstruction Tammelo adds that it is only justified to accept the changed first premise if there are sufficient grounds for applying the same legal consequences to cases which are not laid down as to cases which do fall within the range of the legal standard. He concludes that the analogy-argumentation should be considered as a *modus deficiens*: no logically necessary conclusions follow from the premises as put forward. But at the same time Tammelo states, that if a premise is changed, as in the reconstruction above, to turn the argumentation into a logically valid one, the argumentation is, strictly speaking, no longer an analogy-argumentation. Therefore his reconstruction is an abstraction of the idiosyncratic character of the analogy-argumentation. No conclusion is drawn on the basis of a comparison. Instead, the comparison has 'shifted' to the antecedent of the reconstructed, new first premise, thus reconstructing the analogy-argumentation as a *modes ponens* argumentation.

Tammelo considers the new first premise in the argumentation as 'readily available' ('sure to be understood and accepted in the given legal community'). True as this may be, it is mainly due to the extremely general character of this premise. The main objection to this reconstruction is that a new legal standard is formulated which does not fit in with the actual practice of applying analogy-argumentation. Tammelo's own example makes this clear. The standard constructed on the basis of analogy-argumentation which is the foundation for the final decision reads: 'If this action involves taking away a good unlawfully then this action must be considered as theft' and not the much broader premise as formulated by Tammelo. Tammelo does not specify why it would be necessary to take as a starting-point this much broader premise.

More general objections concerning monological reconstructions of analogy-argumentation may be added to this critical comment on Tammelo's analysis.

Characteristic of this approach is the complete abstraction from the communicative and interactional context in which the analogy-argumentation is used. The *identity* of the person putting forward the analogy-argumentation is ignored and so is the *phase* of the legal proceedings in which analogy-argumentation is employed. Instead, the argumentation is reconstructed as an abstract argumentative product of just one language user, usually a judge.

The fact that no justice is done to the functional character of analogy-argumentation is yet another consequence of this abstract approach. It is also unclear what sort of interpretative problems the analogy-argumentation may solve. The different rules applying to the use of analogy-argumentation in various areas of law are likewise ignored.

These objections have implications for the reconstruction of analogy-argumentation. In *analysis* of argumentation the interaction between the judge and his explicit or implicit antagonists is not taken into account. As a consequence this approach cannot adequately describe and explain the structural complexity of analogy-argumentation. Most logical reconstructions of analogy-argumentation amount to a simple argumentation with two premises and a conclusion. This approach lacks a systematic description of how to arrive at a reconstruction.[2] Analogy-argumentation is analysed as an incomplete argumentation form made logically valid by adding an element. As my comments on Tammelo show, this reconstruction is an abstraction of its idiosyncratic character.[3]

Concerning the *evaluation* of the analogy-argumentation, the monological approach restricts assessment to logical validity and is not systematically related to the legal discussion rules bearing on the argumentation. The abstraction from the discussion situation in the logical approach raises yet another problem. Attention is paid to the legitimizing pro-argumentation only, whereas the negating counter-argumentation is ignored. The result is that forms of complex argumentation cannot be related to the critical reactions which are characteristic of analogy-argumentation. More specifically, this approach does not analyse the relation between analogy-argumentation and *a contrario* argumentation.

Because of the abstract nature of this approach, moreover, the reconstruction does neither do justice to the fact that analogy-argumentation can be employed to solve various types of interpretation problems, nor to its various assessment criteria. Precisely because of this disregard of the various uses of analogy-argumentation, the logical approach fails to clarify its 'specific judicial nature'.

The Dialogical Approach of the Analogy-argumentation

In order to overcome the disadvantages of the monological approach, authors such as Alexy (1983), Aarnio (1988) and Peczenik (1989) (see also Aarnio, Alexi and Peczenik 1981) have analysed judicial argumentation from a *dialogical* perspective. This approach regards argumentation as part of a discussion. The acceptability of the argumentation is made to depend on formal and procedural requirements applying to the discussion process in which a standpoint is defended.[4] Since Peczenik gives the most elaborate analysis of analogy-argumentation, his findings will serve as a starting-point for the discussion of the dialogical approach.[5]

Peczenik's Analysis of Analogy-Argumentation

When analysing judicial argumentation, Peczenik distinguishes two forms of justifications: a *legal* justification ('contextually sufficient legal justification') which justifies a judgement on the grounds of legal discussion rules and principles, and a *deep* justification in which these rules and principles are justified.[6]

Both forms of justification, according to Peczenik, imply the use of 'transformations', which involve an argumentative 'jump', resulting in a non-deductive step. Legal justification involves transformations *in the law*, whereas deep justification implies transformations *towards the law*.

Peczenik regards the *decision transformation,* executed to decide what legal decision is justified in a particular case, as a transformation in the law. When a specific legal judgement is the result, when the premises consist of a least one legal standard and when, moreover, this judgement cannot be deduced from the legal standard or the account of the facts, it is considered to be a decision transformation.[7] In Peczenik's analysis analogy-argumentation is a decision transformation creating a new legal standard.[8] He distinguishes between statutory analogy and legal analogy.[9] I first describe Peczenik's definition as well as his analysis of these two forms of analogy-argumentation. Then I discuss the standards he proposes for the assessment of analogy-argumentation.

Peczenik's definition of statutory analogy reads as follows: 'One applies a statutory rule to a case which, viewed from the ordinary linguistic angle, is included in neither the core nor the periphery of the application area of the statute in question, but resembles the cases covered by this statute in essential respects' (Peczenik 1989, 392). The application of statutory analogy is needed as a result of a gap in the law.[10]

This is Peczenik's reconstruction of statutory analogy:

1 If the fact F or another fact, relevantly similar to F, occurs, then obtaining of G is obligatory.
2 *H is relevantly similar to F.*
3 If H occurs, then obtaining of G is obligatory.

In this analysis the analogy-argumentation has been reconstructed as a logically valid argumentation, as it is done in Tammelo's reconstruction. The relevant similarities between F and H are crucial in this argumentation. Apart from statutory analogy, Peczenik distinguishes legal analogy. Legal analogy should meet the following requirements:

1 A general norm, G, is justifiable on the basis of the resemblance between a number of established rules, r1 - rn, thus regarded as special cases of G.
2 A case, C, lies outside of the linguistically natural area of application of these rules, r1 - rn.
3 On the other hand, the general norm, G, covers C; in other words, C shows relevant similarities to cases regulated by the less general rules, r1 - rn.
4 One adjudicates case C in accordance with G.

The principle of equality is the foundation for the application of both statutory analogy and legal analogy. The assessment of the similarity between cases is crucial for the evaluation of the analogy-argumentation. A sound assessment, according to Peczenik, must therefore weigh various types of arguments. To this end Peczenik proposes standards for the assessment of analogy-argumentation, by contrasting the use of analogy-argumentation with the use of *a contrario* argumentation. He introduces the following structure of an *a contrario* argumentation:

> Obtaining of the situation G is obligatory only if the fact C takes place (*premise*).
> The fact C does not occur, obtaining of G is not obligatory (*conclusion*).

We have seen that the use of analogy-argumentation is justified by the principle of similar cases being treated in similar ways. The use of *a contrario* argumentation is justified on the grounds that the law must be obeyed. Peczenik argues that the choice between analogy and *a contrario* is decided by weighing two aspects of legal certainty: predictability and other moral considerations.

To facilitate the process of weighing, Peczenik proposes ten *reasoning norms* as a guideline for choosing between analogy and *a contrario* argumentation.

> 1 If an action is not explicitly forbidden by a statute or another established source of law, one should consider it as permitted by the interpreted valid law, unless strong reasons for assuming the opposite exist. In other words, one should, as a rule, interpret prohibitions *a contrario*, not by analogy.[11]
> 2 Only relevant similarities between cases constitute a sufficient reason for conclusion by analogy.
> 3 One should not construe provisions establishing time limits by analogy. Neither should one construe them extensively, unless particularly strong reasons for assuming the opposite exist.(...) *Ratio legis* of the time limits is to assure fixity of the law, whereas analogy and extensive interpretation tend to lower fixity.
> 4 One should not construe provisions establishing sufficient conditions for not following a general norm extensively or by analogy, unless strong reasons for assuming the opposite exist.
> 5 Only very strong reasons can justify a use of analogy, leading to the conclusion that an error exists in the text of the statute.

6   One should not construe provisions constituting exceptions from a general norm extensively or by analogy, unless strong reasons for the opposite exist.[12]

7   Not all reasons justifying extensive interpretation of a statute are strong enough to also justify reasoning by analogy.

8   One should not construe provisions imposing burdens or restrictions on a person, unless very strong reasons for assuming the opposite exist.(...) Consequently, one should not construe such provisions extensively or by analogy.

9   A statutory provision should be applied analogously to cases not covered by its literal content, if another provision states that they relevantly resemble those which are thus covered.

10 One may utilise *argumentum a contrario* only in exceptional cases, when interpreting rule based on precedents.

These ten norms, according to Peczenik, will help us choose between the use of analogy-argumentation and *a contrario* argumentation, by balancing justice and legal certainty in judicial decisions.

Peczenik's approach offers advantages over Tammelo's reconstruction since it puts analogy-argumentation in the context of a problem solving process. In Peczenik's method, analogy-argumentation is characterised as an argumentation scheme in a discussion meeting dialogical requirements. He emphasises, more comprehensively than other authors, the standards for the correct use of analogy-argumentation and in this respect his approach of analogy-argumentation may be regarded as the most complete.

Nevertheless, Peczenik's method too has considerable drawbacks. By emphasizing the dialogical character of judicial argumentation as well as the judge's role in the discussion, analogy-argumentation is indeed related to its underlying norms. In the reconstruction of analogy-argumentation, however, he hardly elaborates this point of view and he falls back on the analysis of a judge's abstract product of argumentation. The analysis and assessment of (complex) analogy-argumentation, therefore, suffers from the same disadvantages as the monological approach.

Because Peczenik describes analogy-argumentation as a decision transformation and because he distinguishes between two forms of analogy-argumentation, he does account for the functional character of this argumentation. He ignores, however, the relation between different interpretative problems as well as the various functions of analogy-argumentation in different contexts.

As we saw before, Peczenik's analysis of discussion rules is the most elaborate. The ten norms he proposes offer a survey of considerations we should weigh when evaluating the use of analogy-argumentation. Thus he offers, more so than others, a starting-point for a fruitful assessment of analogy-argumentation. Peczenik himself grants that his norms are provisional. The system underlying these norms too, leaves something to be desired. Some norms relate to the correct choice of analogy-argumentation, others to its correct application. Some norms are related to areas of law, others to legal principles, without any clarification of the connection between the two. Some of Peczenik's norms seem to indicate that he distinguishes between different applications of analogy-argumentation, but his analysis of the argumentation disregards this distinction. Finally, his norms are at no point incorporated in a method for the reconstruction of the analogy-argumentation.

Despite the fact that analogy-argumentation is analysed in the context of a discussion, one last critical remark must be made. In Peczenik's dialogical approach too all attention is fixed on justifying pro-argumentation whereas negating counter-argumentation is ignored completely. In his analysis too forms of complex argumentation are never related to specific critical reactions one may expect when analogy-argumentation is used, nor does Peczenik clarify to the interrelationship between analogy-argumentation and *a contrario* argumentation.

Starting-points for a Pragma-Dialectical Reconstruction of Analogy-Argumentation

How can we develop Tammelo and Peczenik's insights into a more comprehensive and systematic method for the reconstruction of analogy-argumentation? I will answer this question by appealing to the pragma-dialectical argumentation theory. This theory reconstructs analogy-argumentation as part of a discussion subject to dialectical rules. I will use the argumentation in the judgement 'Quint v. Te Poel' to illustrate how insights from the pragma-dialectical argumentation theory and insights from legal theory can be combined in a productive way. I focus on how the complex argumentation of this judgement can be regarded as a reflection of the critical reactions evoked by analogy-argumentation.

In the pragma-dialectical approach, argumentation schemes such as analogy-argumentation are analysed as dialectical procedures in a critical discussion. An argumentation scheme is 'a more or less conventionalized way of representing the argumentative relationship between the arguments and the standpoint being defended in a discourse procedure aimed at attempting to convince somebody who doubts the acceptability of the standpoint' (Van Eemeren en Grootendorst 1992). A critical evaluation of argumentation schemes involves, at some point, the use of an *intersubjective evaluation procedure* to test the argumentation for compatibility with the following two criteria:

1 Is the analogy-argumentation an acceptable argumentation scheme?
2 Has the analogy-argumentation been used in a correct way?

When evaluating argumentation, one first has to establish whether the *correct* argumentation scheme *has been chosen*. A scheme is correct if it belongs to the argumentation schemes which are allowable, in principle, in a given discussion context in defense of a particular standpoint. Only if a scheme is recognised as correct, we can find out whether the analogy-argumentation was *used in the correct way*, the second criterion. This procedure involves, among other things, the evaluation of the analogy criterion itself as well as an assessment of the cases which are compared on the assumption of similarity. Little systematic research has been devoted to standards needed to know whether a judge may use analogy-argumentation to solve a particular interpretative problem, and to factors that determine whether this kind of argumentation is acceptable. As far as I know, there is no detailed survey of standards to evaluate the correct use of analogy-argumentation as an argumentation scheme. Occasional standards have been suggested to ascertain whether, in a given case, it is appropriate to use either analogy-argumentation or *a contrario* argumentation. As we saw in the previous section, Peczenik has offered the most elaborate survey. Let us now systemise these standards in order to arrive at a method for the reconstruction of analogy-argumentation.

The first class of standards concerns the question how the *area of law* bears on analogical or *a contrario* application of legal standards. Legal theory, as a rule, has it that the area of law to which the legal standard belongs, determines the possibilities of using that standard analogically or *a contrario*. The most telling example of this rule is the ban on analogy in criminal law: 'stretching penalisation' on the basis of analogy-argumentation is contrary to the very nature of criminal law. Tax law is yet another area of law that limits the possibilities to apply legal rules analogically. It is generally assumed that analogical application is admissible only if advantageous to the taxpayer. Finally, as we will see later, civil law too limits the possibilities of applying analogy-argumentation to legal rules.

The second class of standards deals with the *type of standards* to which the legal norm is taken to belong: the type of standard affects the admissability of analogical or *a contrario* application. Aarnio (1987, 106), for instance, distinguishes between material and procedural standards. According to him, the principle of legal certainty should prevail in the interpretation of procedural standards and therefore the use of analogical application is limited. Another important distinction is between standards that oblige, standards that permit, standards that confer authority and assessment standards. Peczenik (1989: 396), for instance, indicates that binding standards must be interpreted restrictively and can only be applied analogically in exceptional cases.

The third class of standards concerns the *structure* of the legal standard that is applied either analogically or *a contrario*. The character of the conditional link between the terms of application and legal consequence determines the structure of the legal standard. If a legal standard expresses necessary or necessary and sufficient conditions for the legal consequence, analogy-argumentation is not admissible whereas *a contrario* is. If the legal standard expresses sufficient conditions, analogy-argumentation may be admissible.

The fourth class of standards relates to *constituents* of the legal standard. In addition to terms of application and legal consequence, the following normative elements are distinguished: norm-subject, norm-object, deontological modality and indications as to time and place. These elements likewise affect the admissibility of analogy-argumentation or *a contrario* argumentation. Peczenik points out that stipulations as to time in legal standards should not be applied analogically.

If these norms are accepted as a starting-point and are integrated into the pragma-dialectic standards for the evaluation of analogy-argumentation, it is possible to draw up the following assessment standards.

Checklist for the evaluation of analogy-argumentation

1   Is the analogy-argumentation a suitable argumentation scheme?

      A   Is it a matter of a gap in the judicial system?
          - Is it a matter of a normative gap?
          - Is it a matter of an axiological gap?

      B   Can the gap be filled by means of an analogy-argumentation?
          - What judicial field does the analogical legal standard belong to?
          - What type of norms does the analogical legal standard belong to?
          - What type of conditional link is expressed by the analogical legal standard?
          - To what normative element does the analogical legal standard apply?

2   Has the analogy-argumentation been applied correctly?

      a   Is the existing legal norm which served as a starting-point valid?
      b   Is this particular case, as far as the relevant points are concerned, indeed similar to the description of juristic facts in the existing legal standard?
      c   Is this particular case, as far as the relevant points are concerned, not essentially different from the description of juristic facts in the existing legal standard?
      d   Wouldn't it be advisable to compare this particular case with the description of juristic facts of different legal standards?

Taking these standards as a starting-point, it is possible to arrive at a more systematic, complete reconstruction of analogy-argumentation in judicial decisions. More systematic since there is a clear interdependency between the assessment-standards at hand. If a judge is confronted, for instance, with a gap which cannot be filled by analogy-argumentation, he need not consider possible similarities between existing and construed legal standards. The reconstruction is more complete because it does not only focus on the formal validity of the argumentation and the acceptability of the premises but also on standards that indicate whether or not an analogy-argumentation was called for in the first place and whether it was applied correctly. Rather than reducing the analogy-argumentation to a simple argumentation structure, this enables us to reconstruct it as argumentation with a complex structure. The elements of this structure may be regarded as reflections of the different judging-standards. To illustrate this, let us have a closer look at the case 'Quint v. Te Poel'. Apart from the arguments quoted at the beginning of this contribution, the Supreme Court put forward a number of considerations to accompany the analogy-argumentation:

Quint v. Te Poel (Supreme Court 30-1-1959, NJ 1959, No. 548)

Considering that the argument also addresses the Court's interpretation of art. 1269 ('All obligations proceed from either agreement, or from the law')
Considering:
(1) that the Court is right in stating that the regulation of art. 1269 does not allow the assumption that an obligation between two persons arises in all cases in which a judge is of the opinion that the rules of reasonableness and fairness dictate that one person carries out a certain performance for the other;
(2) that the Court, however, having found that Quint's assumed claim is not supported by any specific section of the law, and therefore concluding that Quint is not entitled to his claim, has given too limited an interpretation of the words "from the law";
(3) that, after all, from these words it does by no means follow that all obligations should be directly supported by some section of the law, but from these can only be inferred that in cases not specifically laid down in the law, that the solution has to be accepted which fits within the system of the law and is in keeping with cases that are laid down in the law;
(4) that now it has to be investigated whether, in the present case, an obligation within the meaning of the law can be assumed to have been created between parties;
Considering:
(5) that in this context the question arises whether the owner of a property who, because of the fact that the accession rule applies here, is obliged to

compensate him who has constructed the works to the amount of his enrichment;

(6) that the law does provide for cases when works have been constructed by someone with only limited legal authorisation (art. 762, 772 and 826 of the Civil Code); that these – mutually divergent – regulations, however, which are connected with the special nature of the commercial claims to which they refer, cannot, in this context, be of decisive significance;

(7) that, however, according to art. 658 and 1603 of the Civil Code, the landlord cannot be expected, by paying a certain amount of money, to annul the enrichment enjoyed by him because of the works constructed by the holder or tenant of the land on which the works have been constructed;

(8) that it is implausible that a claim which the law withholds the holder and the tenant, would befall the contractor who has constructed these works under agreement with the tenant, and who suffered damage because his co-contractor is unable to make payments;

(9) that what is stipulated in art. 659 of the Civil Code does not alter this since a special provision, equal to that of the bona fide owner, does not befall Quint, who could have known the works would be constructed on land which did not belong to the client by consulting the public registers, doing so, in Quints own words, only after the construction had been completed.

Reflecting on these considerations in the light of the judging-standards I mentioned earlier, one can determine how decisive a role these considerations play in judging analogy-argumentation.

The first consideration can be viewed in the light of the question whether analogy-argumentation is an appropriate argumentation scheme to fill up a gap. The Supreme Court, in this respect, holds that an alternative solution – a direct appeal to 'reasonableness and fairness' as a source of the agreement – has been rejected by the Court.

The second and third consideration of the Supreme Court likewise concerns the adequacy of analogy-argumentation. The Court's answer was negative and the Supreme Court agreed. The Supreme Court, in these considerations, judges that a statement of law – 'All obligations proceed from either agreement, or from the law' – does not imply that all obligations should be directly supported by some section of the law. Instead we can only infer that in cases not specifically laid down in the law, the solution has to be accepted which meets two requirements: it should fit within the system of the law and it should be in keeping with cases that are laid down in the law. These considerations reflect the fundamental character of this case. The Supreme Court, in this judgement, admits the possibility to employ analogy-argumentation in cases like these for filling up gaps and, at the same time, formulates two general requirements which have to be met in analogy-argumentation.

After arguing that analogy-argumentation is a suitable argumentation scheme, the Supreme Court confronts the question what analogical application is the most acceptable. Considerations 6 through 9 deal with this question. Considerations 6 and 9 can be regarded as negative answers to question 2b: someone with only limited legal authorisation as well as the bona fide owner do have a case from unjustified enrichment, the point being that the case of Quint, the person who is personally authorized, though not *bona fide*, is in fact *dissimilar*. The negative answers to question 2b could be regarded as examples of *a contrario* argumentation.

Finally, considerations 7 and 8 contain the core of the analogy-argumentation: the holder and the tenant do not have a case resulting from unjustified enrichment and, therefore, neither has the person acting on behalf of the tenant.

Conclusion

I have shown how analogy-argumentation is reconstructed by legal theoreticians who assume either a monological or a dialogical perspective. I have tried to indicate along which lines the dialogical perspective may be developed to arrive at a more complete reconstruction. The standards for judging as formulated may serve as a starting point. A careful analysis of case law in which analogy-argumentation plays an important role would make clear in how far these standards need to be made more specific.

Notes

1   Alexy (1978) quite rightly points out that analogy-argumentation would never have attracted so much attention if it would have dealt with a simple logical deduction rule. See also Wróblewski (1974) for the difference between simple deduction rules and systematic legal inference rules such as the analogy-

argumentation. Wróblewski assumes that the application of simple deduction rules is not regulated by legal standards, whereas the application of systematic legal inference rules is.

2   Van Eemeren and Grootendorst (1978) discuss the differences between an argumentation-theoretical approach of argumentation on the one hand and a purely logical approach on the other. They present a summary of the abstraction steps to be taken to arrive at a logical analysis.

3   Compare, in this context, J.C. Hage in: Feteris et al. (1994, 91).

4   Compare for an analysis of the various approaches within the legal argumentation theory Feteris (1994).

5   Compare Aarnio, Alexy and Peczenik (1981) who, in a collection of three articles, develop a theory on legal argumentation.

6   Compare Feteris (1994) for an extensive discussion of Peczenik's theory.

7   The legal standard is determined by the sources of law, and may be the result of deductive inference or of a general transformation of a standard.

8   The other decision transformations distinguished by Peczenik are: precise interpretation and subsumption, reduction and elimination and solving a conflict between legal standards.

9   Other authors call statutory analogy 'singular analogy' or *'analogia legis'*; legal analogy is called 'generic analogy' or *'analogia juris'*. Compare, among others, Nieuwenhuis (1976).

10 Peczenik distinguishes two types of gaps. There are gaps which are determined in a non-normative way; in cases like these the law is not sufficiently normative. Then there are gaps determined on the grounds of evaluation. This sort of considerations leads to the conclusion that the law does not meet requirements of rationality. This distinction amounts to the difference between normative and axiological gaps.

11 In reference to norm 1 Peczenik distinguishes between weak and strong authority: weak if there is no standard prohibiting a certain action; strong if there is a certain standard that does confer authority.

12 This standard – *exceptiones non sunt extendendae* – is considered by Peczenik as more general than the fourth norm.

References

Aarnio, A. (1988), *The Rational as Reasonable. A Treatise on Legal Justification*, Reidel, Dordrecht.

Aarnio, A., Alexy, R. and Peczenik, A. (1981), 'The foundation of legal reasoning', *Rechtstheorie*, vol. 21, Nr. 2, pp. 133-58, Nr. 3, pp. 257-79, Nr. 4, pp. 423-48.

Alexy, R. (1983), *Theorie der juristischen Argumentation. Die Theorie des rationalen Diskurses als Theorie der juristischen Begründung*, Suhrkamp, Frankfurt.

Eemeren, F.H. van and Grootendorst, R. (1982), *Regels voor redelijke discussies*, Proefschrift UvA, Foris Publications, Dordrecht.

Eemeren, F.H. van and Grootendorst, R. (1987), 'Het analyseren en beoordelen van betogende teksten', *Tijdschrift voor Taalbeheersing*, 9-1, pp. 48-66.

Eemeren, F.H. van and Grootendorst, R. (1992), *Argumentation, Communication and Fallacies*, Erlbaum, Hillsdale.

Feteris, E.T. (1994), *Redelijkheid in juridische argumentatie. Een overzicht van theorieën over het rechtvaardigen van juridische beslissingen*, W.E.J. Tjeenk Willink, Zwolle.

Hage, J.C. (1994), 'Reden gebaseerde logica: een speciale logica voor het recht', in E.T. Feteris et al., *Met redenen omkleed. Bijdragen aan het symposium juridische argumentatie 1993*, Ars Aequi Libri, Nijmegen, pp. 90-8.

Klug, U. (1982), *Juristische Logik*, (4th edition), Springer-Verlag, Berlin/ Heidelberg/New York.

Nieuwenhuis, J.H. (1976), 'Legitimatie en heuristiek van het rechterlijk oordeel', in R.M. Themis, pp. 494-515.

Peczenik, A. (1989), *On Law and Reason*, Kluwer, Dordrecht/Boston/London.

Tammelo, I. (1969), *Outlines of modern legal logic*, Franz Steiner Verlag, Wiesbaden.

Wróblewski, J. (1974), 'Legal Syllogism and Rationality of Judicial Decision', *Rechtstheorie*, pp. 33-46.

Part II:
Facts, Judgements, Theories

5 The Role of Facts in Legal Reasoning

H.J.M. BOUKEMA

Introduction

Legal reasoning is actually the kind employed by lawyers. That is why Ilmar Tammelo and Julius Stone chose 'Legal Systems and Lawyers' Reasonings' as the title of their treatise on legal reasoning.[1]

Lawyers have an ingrained respect for facts and only a subordinate interest in truth. At trial level, they strive to select and establish relevant facts in order to construe the applicable applicability of rules of law which secure a desired conclusion. They follow generally accepted lines of argumentation, including logically flawed ones such as the *argumentum analogium* and the *argumentum a contrario*. They are interested in presenting the relevant facts so that the conclusions, as prescribed by the legal system, will follow. Obviously, this *modus operandi* may have little to do with the truth, which is neither the concern of the lawyers for the defence nor that of the lawyers for the plaintiff. Public prosecutors, though, must bear in mind that theirs is a public responsibility and that it ill befits them or the Crown to present falsehoods to the courts. The judge is much more interested in the truth and in all the facts, but civil (and criminal) procedure determines his access to the facts and, hence, the truth. In giving legal advice, lawyers try in fact to predict the outcome of a case if the matter were brought to trial.[2] A prophecy of what the court will do relies heavily on the proper gauging of all relevant facts and the assessment of applicable legal rules.

It is because of the aforesaid practice and constrictions of criminal procedure that lawyers can defend the ugliest customers and yet have a clear conscience. They are solely concerned with the facts as adjudged in court and the proper conclusions accordant with the legal system. Trial lawyers are not responsible for the legal system, which belongs to the lawgivers' domain of responsibility.

Lawgivers, just like judges, have respect for the facts. The concept of 'acquired rights' does reflect a respect for the *'fait accompli'*.[3] The Dutch Civil Code expressly grants legal status to *faits accomplis*.[4]

At appellate level before the Supreme Court, the facts cease to be a matter of discussion, for, by statute, the Dutch Supreme Court's only interest is to ascertain whether the law has been properly applied. Therefore, blunders concerning facts at trial level may have disastrous consequences . A Dutch sociologist, F. Bruinsma, after selecting some recent landmark cases, interviewed the litigants and discovered that, in quite a number of cases, the litigants were at a loss to understand the Supreme Court's reasoning – an excusable failure when one bears in mind the court's predilection for abstruse and tortuous constructions. Worse still, the court's decision in many cases was based on wrong facts.[5]

Facts

I take the concept of 'fact' in its everyday meaning: an actually occurring event, quality, relation, state of affairs; that which is actual, real; a thing certainly known to have occurred or to be true; a datum of experience; a thing assumed as basis for inference.[6]

Lawyers distinguish between facts on the one hand and rules, standards, norms etc. on the other and, more precisely, between statements on facts and statements on the law. In legal theory and legislation, this distinction is usually regarded as perspicuous.

In practice, however, lawyers do not always stick to this neat distinction. Statements on facts can be presented as statements on law or *vice versa*. This does not imply that the average lawyer has a penchant for twisted reasoning. Indeed, some statements on fact are also statements on law. Statements concerning 'possession' by a pawnbroker refer to facts, but also to his prima facie legal position, and may have implications for the burden of proof. So may the registration of a mortgage. Moreover, statements on fact necessarily presuppose a normative setting. The decision to select one fact above the other is a normative one. So is the decision regarding the way in which facts are to be presented. The phrasing of statements on facts and the argumentation about the applicable rules of law are all normative, but of different normative categories. The selection and phrasing of facts may betray the court's selection *and evaluation* of the facts. Both selection and wording of the facts are a preamble of the way in which the court explains its decision. An experienced trial lawyer senses already whether the court is about to 'find' for plaintiff or defendant when the court is merely summing up the facts.

At trial level, the selection of relevant facts usually dictates the outcome of the case. At the Supreme Court's level, the facts are no longer subject to scrutiny; they are given data. But the Supreme Court can criticise the lower courts' handling of the case, their choice of argument etc. Occasionally, the Supreme Court uses its power to quash a lower court's judgement on the ground that the facts have been misrepresented. Facts and their relevance are determined by their context, the role they serve in argumentation, and the way in which they are viewed by the observer.

An example from the medical profession may serve to clarify my statement. If I look at an X-ray photograph of my left leg, I perceive a conglomeration of black, white and grey dots and lines. To my surgeon, it is evidence of a complicated fracture of the tibia which has been mended with the help of osteosynthetic material. To my health insurance company, it merely validates the payment of expenses. The knowledge of the observer – or lack of it – enables him to attach meaning to the facts.

From legal practice similar examples can be drawn. Suppose for a fact that one person regularly pays an amount of money to another one. Depending on other circumstances and facts, lawyers construct out of some regular payments a lease contract and thereby ascribe the protection of rent control to a party. In this way, they determine the value of property. Depending on the circumstances such payments may be proof for constructing a labour agreement.

To be relevant for lawyers' reasonings, facts, if contested, need to be proven in a court of law. Thus, what counts as a relevant fact depends on the rules of civil (or criminal) procedure. Some facts may be inadmissible for presentation in court because of civil (or criminal) procedure. This aspect of legal practice underscores once more that getting to the truth is not a primary objective in lawyers' reasoning. On the contrary, lawyers' reasoning is first aimed at the selection and establishment of relevant facts, both with the desired outcome of the case in mind whereas, at a further stage of the litigation, lawyers' reasoning is aimed at an outcome based on the established facts and a selection of applicable rules. The court at trial level argues in a similar vein as the trial lawyers, but the court is regarding the facts limited by the facts as presented in court. The Supreme Court has no discretion as to facts: it must take the facts as they are established at trial or appeal level. Again, the facts may not reflect the truth, let alone the entire truth.

A fairly recent example from Dutch legal history illustrates what I have just said. Until a fundamental change in divorce law took place at the end of the swinging sixties, grounds for divorce were restricted and did not include mutual consent. One of these grounds was adultery. Rules of civil procedure prescribe that a plaintiff's statement of fact which is not sufficiently refuted by the defendant, becomes an established fact in the litigation. If one of the partners asserted that adultery had been committed by the other partner and the defendant did not oppose, the courts were satisfied that a ground for annulment of marriage was present and decreed a divorce. Thus, a rule of civil procedure was enforced regardless of the truth. It was a formula commonly known as the Great Lie. Both the courts and the contestants knew how matters stood, but, except for a few conservative Roman Catholic judges, everyone was satisfied. The lawgiver wisely put an end to this inordinate use of civil procedure.

Civil procedure determines which party has to shoulder the burden of proof and is obligated to prove contested facts. (In criminal law, the burden of proof rests on the shoulders of the prosecution.) Allocating the burden of proof can lead to much wrangling, since the impracticability of proving certain facts may be decisive for the outcome of a case. In such a situation, rules of civil procedure take precedence over the facts. It is once again clear that all this has little to do with the truth.

Lawyers

Lawyers' reasonings vary according to their functions and objectives. Lawyers employed by the Ministry of Justice to draft legislation must collect facts and devise legal rules for the sake of the general weal. They must also pay attention to the will and whims of their political masters and the authority of Parliament. Neither Ministers nor Parliament instinctively go for the truth, if the facts which determine the truth are liable to embarrass political expediency.

Legal scholars at universities have the task of scrutinising the legal system and its case-law. They are also expected to create new pathways in case-law or, alternatively, to criticise pathways when necessary. They teach the law as it is, and how the law ought to be.

Judges must deliver judgements which are acceptable for the different parties concerned: for fellow-lawyers who must be satisfied that the judgement falls within the parameters of the legal system and complies with its precepts and principles; for the litigants who need to be reassured that their arguments have been properly listened to and justice has been done; and, lastly, for society at large which expects the judgement to be consistent with fundamental principles of human conduct and prevailing moral standards.[7]

Advocates have different objectives in mind. They try to present facts and make use of applicable rules in a manner most favourable to their clients. Public prosecutors have the same objective, but are limited by being subservient to the Crown. Even so, they must strive to lay bare the truth. They must avoid prosecuting if they believe the defendant to be not guilty. Ministers of Justice may feel an urge to send directives to public prosecutors in an effort to keep abreast of current political opinion, but the prosecutors must remind themselves that the cause they are serving is higher than the momentary triumphs of their political masters. The public weal takes precedence. A built-in problem is, of course, that any determination what the public weal consists of in a particular case may in the end very well amount to a political preference. The Crown is supposed to serve the public good. Ruling politicians tend to adhere to party politics. The result might be differing political views. I readily admit that my pointing at the aforementioned potential political clash seems to be more a matter of theory than of practical prevalence. Still, public prosecutors must not only refrain from presenting falsehoods to the court, they must also refuse to try cases which they know to be unfair.

In view of the different functions of various lawyers, it is hard to make general statements about the role of facts in legal reasoning, but the kind of reasoning which can be heard in a court of law is archetypical of lawyers' reasoning. Ultimately it is the courts that determine the meaning of specific rules of law. Oliver Wendell Holmes has become a somewhat neglected author, but one of the truisms he uttered as a jurist is still substantiated almost daily in our own time:

> The prophecies of what the courts will do in fact, and nothing more preten-
> tious, are what I mean by the law.[8]

The Dutch Supreme Court has persistently shown its allegiance to this *dictum*. Whereas, for example, the lawgiver expressly prohibits compound interest, the Supreme Court has chosen to disregard the interdiction, so that what is unlawful becomes lawful.[9] Apparently, this Court has decided as if it is the ultimate source of law and is not restricted by Constitution, Code, Statute or precedents. In fairness, it should be added that the Dutch Supreme Court habitually and faithfully rules in accordance with recent legislation and precedents, the latter having no formally binding force as in the case in the Anglo-American legal tradition.

Since the main purpose of this chapter is to examine the role of facts in legal reasoning, I must confine myself as far as possible to trial level, but now and then I shall glance upwards to Supreme Court level.

The prophesies of what the courts will do imply predictions of both the courts' dealing with facts and with the law. These prophecies also imply that there are regularities to be detected in the court's handling of facts.

Deductive and Inductive Reasonings

Lawyers' reasoning at trial level is both deductive and inductive. The authentication of facts is more important in the former type of reasoning than in the latter. The legal system ascribes certain consequences to certain facts. The law of property, for instance, consists of a fairly rigid system for determining ownership. Although inductive reasoning may also be employed here, this type of reasoning prevails in the realm of torts. For that matter, deductive reasoning is also employed in this realm, notably in intellectual property cases.

One may query whether the traditional dichotomy of inductive versus inductive reasoning is helpful. A more apposite distinction might be between reasonings serving to find a solution for a case at bar and reasonings serving to explain and justify a decision of the court. The former dichotomy being established and well-known, I propose to continue the use of those terms, but in the sense just explained.

Reasoning at bar requires warranted (or justified) premises and the disposal of all likely relevant information at hand, and must be valid, meaning that correct premises lead to a justified conclusion. The role of facts in such reasoning is not less important, though slightly different. Without certain facts there can be no deduction at all. Certain facts govern, for example, a purchase agreement or a patent registration. If the relevant facts are unavailable, there can be no legal action. In reasoning at bar facts can be used to refute the implied condition that all relevant information has been presented and, therefore, can become weapons for attacking a legal action. The court's reasoning is mainly intended to explain its selection and establishment of facts, the applicability of rules selected and justification of the ensuing conclusion. The court's reasoning is intended for the losing party. He should be persuaded that his point of view has been heard, his arguments have been weighed and justice has been done.

Civil procedure is intended to ensure that the courts are presented with all the relevant facts at hand. In recent years, courts in The Netherlands have tended to assume a more active role in ascertaining the relevant facts than they have in the past. Not only a wish to make the courts work more effectively has caused this improvement, but also the conclusion of sociologists, amongst others, that wrong facts have been instrumental in deciding the outcome of various important cases.[10]

Courts at Work

The trial judge selects, establishes, evaluates, and qualifies the facts just as the police, the prosecution and the defence do in criminal cases and litigants in civil matters.[11] The courts only report the facts which are relevant for the legal evaluation of the case at bar, that is, the facts which can support the court's decision. The facts are put into legal jargon, because they are being processed for judicial consumption. This is an expedient without which the courts would fail to function properly.[12] The selection and presentation of facts plays a dominant role in lawyers' reasoning at trial level. If a defendant who is accused of a robbery has an alibi which proves he was elsewhere at the time of the crime, he is released. If a trademark was registered in bad faith, that is, if the owner of a trademark was an agent for a foreign trademark owner, the latter can claim nullification.

Once again I underscore a vital aspect of legal reasoning. At appellate level and higher, legal questions are always assessed against the background of the relevant facts established at trial level. Section 419,3 of the Dutch Civil Procedure Code rules that the Supreme Court is obliged to accept the facts acknowledged by the lower court, for it is only concerned with the proper application of the law and not with anything else. The reason for this provision is coined in the phrase *litis finire oportet*: all litigation must eventually come to an end.

But even these clear ordinances, which are quite understandable and functional, are sometimes circumvented by inventive higher courts, according to T. Koopmans. He is a former Justice at the European Court of Justice in Luxembourg and at present an Advocate-General at the Dutch Supreme Court. Koopmans points out that the European Court, whose task it is, among others, to answer points of law raised by the national courts of Member States, rephrases the questions which the latter put before it.[13] Koopmans argues that if lawyers have not all the necessary facts at their disposal, they make them up and call it casuistry.[14] The reason for this practice is presumably the traditionally held belief amongst many practitioners of the law that the law simply flows from the facts. Koopmans insists that the courts have discretionary power to evaluate the facts of the case and rule upon its selection of facts.[15] The courts have less freedom as regards facts: they must make do with the facts which are presented to them in a moot trial. But the courts do have discretionary powers in selecting the relevant facts. It should cause no problem if facts are established by one party and not disputed by the other. When facts are in dispute there are rules of civil procedure to determine which facts the courts may consider for its consecutive reasoning. If the courts cannot rule which facts are to be accepted, they rely on procedural rules to shift the burden of proof to a particular side.

In order to achieve a suitable judgement, it is usual for a court to gauge the facts presented to it by comparing them with other well-known facts or rules of experience. The court can evaluate facts by using life experience as a frame of reference in just the same way as any well-informed and educated person would normally view them.[16] On the basis of such precepts constructed by the court itself, it may infer that a certain behaviour of competitors amounts to predatory pricing or was intended to default on contractual obligations etc.

Which are the relevant facts or, rather, which facts will the court consider to be relevant or decisive? Case law is casuistic indeed. Because the answers to these questions are elusive, it is often difficult to foretell the end result or pin one's hope on legal certainty.

An illustration of the roundabout way in which even the Supreme Court treats facts and of the difficulty of predicting its judgements is the case in which the court quashed a lower court's ruling that chances of a 47-year-old man living for 18 years are equal to those of a married couple of 47 years each living for 18 years.[17] The Supreme Court also quashed a lower court's finding that, according to rules of experience, a bulldozer driver may expect a toddler to keep a safe distance from his machine.[18] The Supreme Court declared that rules of experience made it reasonable to expect that work on the country's sea defences would take longer during winter gales than during the summer.[19] That daily use of dangerous welding machines numbs the user's sense of danger is, according to the Supreme Court, a general rule of experience which every educated person is likely to be aware of.[20]

In all these instances, the Supreme Court ruled that the lower court did not adequately gauge facts against generally accepted rules of experience. Thus, in spite of the lawmaker having vetoed rulings on facts, the Supreme Court circumvents the prohibition by challenging a lower court's argumentation and conclusions relating to facts rather than discussing the facts themselves.

Fact and Fiction

Legal systems not only operate with facts but also with fictions. A deed drawn up by a public notary is statutorily accurate, but may be proven wrong by the other side. This is a matter of burden of proof. The accuracy of this deed, then, is a fiction to be used until it is successfully challenged. A conviction for embezzlement by a criminal judge is proof in a civil torts case if an irrevocable judgement was given after a full exchange of argument on both sides. Although the criminal court may have erred, the judgement of guilt stays unless it is challenged in another criminal court of law. (Opportunities of such challenge are all but non-existent. It would me most difficult to prove in a civil court that the criminal court was wrong.) Judgements between parties establishing their respective rights are matters of indisputable facts. Needless to say, all of these facts are not necessarily true, they are fictions.

Some facts are inadmissible as evidence even if they are true. Some functionaries have the right of excusal or exemption, whereas others have a legal privilege. Consequently, the courts do not always deal with the truth or even all relevant facts: some facts may be deliberately hidden before the court and the court operates under the – statutory correct – apprehension that it is trying the real case. According to out-of-court reality the court is juggling with facts and fiction alike. Obviously, the layman's confidence in the course of justice cannot be boosted if the courts are thus inhibited in its perceived duty to dispense justice.

Criminal law has a set of both subtle and strict rules about the inadmissibility of evidence and, hence, of facts. In civil law, the Supreme Court has as yet not ruled any evidence inadmissible. Judges are eager to find the truth, but are limited by the legal system which encourages them to remain passive. They are, by and large, confined to the case as it is presented by the litigants or the prosecutor and the defendant.

In criminal cases, the court appoints a judge to investigate the facts of a matter which the prosecution wishes to bring to trial. In civil cases, the courts have, in recent years, been granted modest means to find the truth.[21] The courts may order the litigants to appear in order to clarify their position and to answer questions. The court may also require certain documents to be presented. But, on the whole, the court has to restrict itself to what is on file, while its scrutiny of the facts is further circumscribed by what it can gather from the file. If it is unaware which relevant documents may exist, the court cannot ask for information. Moreover, if someone files the wrong type of legal action, for example a breach of contract when it should have been a tort, the courts find it difficult to provide help in spite of the abundance of facts which may have been uncovered, or the pure and simple truth which has come to light.

Unlike the British and American legal systems, the Dutch civil law counterpart hardly provides for pre-trial discovery. The only opportunities to establish facts prior to the trial are the judge's pre-trial investigations of an issue which the prosecutor wishes to bring to trial (but these preliminaries are actually a part of the legal proceedings against the defendant). In civil cases, anyone may request a hearing of witnesses (an *enquête valétudinaire*). Such a hearing must not be abusive or a mere fishing expedition. The applicant must have a legitimate interest in establishing facts which may be decisive for the outcome of the litigation and important for the purposes of corroboration or which may be lost if a witness is elderly or has to go abroad. The hearing of witnesses before a judge does not include the possibility of requesting the submission of documents.[22]

Conclusion

Facts are a prerequisite for lawyers' reasonings: without them there can be no law. Once a lawyer is confronted with facts he begins to select and qualify. At trial level, facts determine the outcome of cases. In civil and criminal procedure alike traditions, precedents and chance determine the way in which facts support lawyers' reasonings and the court's findings.

It is hard to draw a clear borderline between statements on facts and statements on law. Perhaps a sharp division is of little consequence, although the Supreme Court's task has been based by the Dutch legal system on precisely this dichotomy. Statutory and even constitutional jurisdiction make the dividing line significant in some situations, but the Supreme Court cannot always be bothered to heed to the lawgiver's neat distinction.

Notes

1   The phrase 'lawyers' reasoning' may not have a euphonious sound, but is definitely more accurate than the usual term 'legal reasoning'. The latter is a wider expression, which can refer, amongst others, to the reasoning undertaken by lawgivers, that is to say, people who may not have studied case-law or are missing a legal background. Lacking these qualifications, they cannot be practitioners of lawyers' reasoning. Nevertheless, the reasoning they use in their lawmaking task may well rank as legal reasoning. The phrase is borrowed from the title of Julius Stone's *Legal Systems and Lawyers' Reasoning* (1964).
2   Cf. Oliver Wendell Holmes (1920, pp. 167-203).
3   B.W.M. Nieskens (1991).
4   Dutch Civil Code. See Sections 3:45,3 (lapse of rights); 3:53,2 (accession); 3:58 (forfeiture of rights); 6:258 (protection of third rights).
5   F. Bruinsma, R. Welbergen (1988).
6   H.W. Fowler, F.G. Fowler (1918, p. 291); J. Coulson (1976, p. 297), Peter A. Angeles (1981). Legal textbooks on civil procedure also take the everyday

meaning of 'fact' for granted. Cf. D.J. Veegens (1989); T. Koopmans (1989, p.89.

7   For an elaboration of the concept of acceptability of judgement see H.J.M. Bou-kema (1980). Recently, the concept of acceptability by the public at large was emphasized in an interview by a retiring Advocate-General to the Supreme Court of the Netherlands. Cf. Caroline Lindo (1996, p. 118). Leijten argued that 'the people would revolt' if the Supreme Court would have acquitted a notorious drugsdealer.

8   Oliver Wendell Holmes (1920, pp. 167-203).

9   Hoge Raad, 1 May 1924, Nederlandse Jurisprudentie 1924, 684.

10 E.g. Bruinsma, see note 5.

11 Cf. Koopmans, 1989, p.80.

12 Cf. Koopmans, 1989, p.83; Veegens, 1989, p.173.

13 Cf. Koopmans, 1989, p.84.

14 Cf. Koopmans, 1989, p.85.

15 Cf. Koopmans, 1989, p.86.

16 Cf. Veegens, 1989, p.211.

17 Hoge Raad 27 March 1953, Nederlandse Jurisprudentie 1953, p. 617. [The Su-preme Court therewith refuted John Allen Paulos' concern about innumeracy. See his *Innumeracy, Mathematical Illiteracy and its Consequences* (1988)] See also Hoge Raad 6 April 1933, Nederlandse Jurisprudentie 1933, p. 881, and Hoge Raad 14 April 1978, Nederlandse Jurisprudentie 1979, p. 245.

18 Hoge Raad 25 September 1981, Nederlandse Jurisprudentie 1982, p. 254, anno-tated by C.J.H.Brunner. Whenever a minor is the subject of a case handled by the Supreme Court, the matter is usually one of extreme tragedy. The Supreme Court has quite often gone out of its way to redress a lower court's callousness. Usually, the former does so by trying to come to grips with the true facts and then to find fault with the lower court's line of reasoning. In like manner, the Su-preme Court found that not only toddlers but also eight-year-olds are impulsive and are more accident-prone in present-day traffic than adults: Hoge Raad 23 May 1986, Nederlandse Jurisprudentie 1987, p. 482, annotated by C.J.H. Brun-ner. See also Veegens, 1989, pp. 212, 213.

19 Hoge Raad 18 June 1926, Nederlandse Jurisprudentie 1926, p. 1121.

20 Hoge Raad 14 April 1978, Nederlandse Jurisprudentie 1979, p. 245.

21 The most recent study of facts in lawyers' reasonings in civil matters is a Dutch publication by an Advocate-General of the Supreme Court, J.B.M. Vranken (1995). A still illuminating survey of the way the Supreme Court may touch facts notwithstanding the lawgiver's prohibition to do so is by J. van Schellen (1981).

22 Two Dutch authors have argued that some documents which are material for the outcome of civil litigation may be claimed by the opposing party. (J.M. Baren-

drecht, W.A.J.P. van den Reek (1994, pp. 739-745.) There is only haphazard case-law in support of this view.

References

Angeles, P.A. (1981), *Dictionary of Philosophy*, Barnes & Noble Books, New York.

Barendrecht, J.M., Reek, W.A.J.P. van den (1994), *Exhibitieplicht en bewijsbeslag*, WPNR No. 6155, pp. 739-745.

Boukema, H.J.M. (1980), *Judging*, Tjeenk Willink, Deventer.

Bruinsma, F., Welbergen, R. (1988), *De Hoge Raad van onderen*, Tjeenk Willink, Zwolle.

Coulson, J. (1976), *The Concise Oxford Dictionary*, Oxford University Press, London, p. 297.

Fowler, H.W., Fowler, F.G. (1918), *The Concise Oxford Dictionary of Current English*, Oxford, p. 291.

Koopmans, T. (1989), *Juridische dialectiek*, in: Mededelingen der Koninklijke Nederlandse Academie van Wetenschappen, Afd. Letterkunde, nieuwe reeks, deel 45, no.3, p.89.

Lindo, C. (1996), 'Jan Leijten, een betrokken buitenstaander', *Nederlands Juristenblad* 71, 4, p. 118.

Nieskens, B.W.M. (1991), *Het fait accompli in het vermogensrecht*, Tjeenk Willink, Deventer.

Paulos, J.A. (1988), *Innumeracy, Mathematical Illiteracy and its Consequences*, Hill and Wang, New York.

Schellen, J. van (1981), *Wat heeft cassatie ons te bieden?*, Kluwer, Deventer.

Stone, J. (1964), *Legal Systems and Lawyers' Reasoning*, Stanford University Press, Stanford.

Veegens, D.J. (1989), *Cassatie in burgerlijke zaken*, derde druk, bewerkt door E. Korthals Altes en H.A. Groen, Tjeenk Willink, Zwolle.

Vranken, J.V.M. (1995), *Algemeen Deel* [Mr C. Asser's *Handleiding tot de beoefening van het Nederlands burgerlijk recht*], Tjeenk Willink, Zwolle.

Wendell Holmes, O. (1920), 'The Path of the Law', in: *Collected Legal Papers*, New York, pp. 167-203.

6 Parallels Between Science and Ethics

WIM J. VAN DER STEEN

Introduction

Considering sources of reliable knowledge, most people nowadays hold science in high esteem. Upon ethics many would pass a less favourable verdict. Ethics says nothing about the world 'out there'; it does not deal with facts but only with things that ought to be; its principles are a matter of opinion rather than knowledge. Derogatory views such as subjectivism, relativism, and scepticism in ethics itself strengthen this attitude among outsiders.

In this chapter, I oppose the view that science and ethics should differ in this way (for more details, see Van der Steen 1995). I argue that, in principle, science and ethics are in the same boat because science is not value-free in any sense, and because ethics analogously is not fact-free. Science cannot be purely empirical and ethics cannot be purely normative.

Thus, I would not equate any difference between science and ethics with differences between empirical statements and normative statements. The two categories of statements are visibly different indeed. On the face of it, we are not at liberty to accept or reject well-confirmed empirical statements according to our preferences, whereas we are at liberty, more so at any rate, to let preferences determine what normative statements we endorse. This perception apparently fuels the derogatory views of ethics I mentioned. As briefly indicated in the next section, I would not agree with this characterisation of the difference, but I would not deny that a clear difference exists. However that may be, my aim is not to characterise empirical *versus* normative matters. The thesis about science *versus* ethics which I defend is robust in that it does not depend on any such characterisation.

How should we characterise theories in science and in ethics? That is apparently a meta-level question in the province of philosophy. Considering science we could search for an answer in philosophy of science. Ethics is not similarly covered by an independent meta-discipline. It belongs to philosophy; so it keeps meta-analyses in its own hands. Meta-ethics is tightly linked to the primary, normative subject matter of ethics.

Philosophy of science and meta-ethics are almost disjunct areas. That is unfortunate because issues in the two areas are similar to a large extent. In this chapter, I put one theme that should figure in both areas at centre stage, the theme of methodological trade-offs (for details, see Van der Steen 1993, 1995).

The basic idea is this. Many methodological criteria are important in science and in ethics. Theories cannot satisfy all the criteria at the same time. Hence, we must face trade-offs among criteria. For example, if a theory can't be general and simple at the same time, we have to decide which criterion, generality or simplicity, should get first priority *in the context of interest*. The context-dependence of trade-offs entails that science cannot be value-free in any sense. Science needs ethics. Ethics likewise needs science.

After some preliminaries in the next section, my points of departure will be examples from science and ethics, in this order. The examples together with theoretical arguments indicate that we should do away with boundaries between science and ethics. The defence of my thesis that science and ethics should not be different does not concern argumentation in a direct way, but it has substantial implications for moral argumentation and, analogously, legal argumentation. Some implications are charted in a separate section.

Preliminaries: Bambrough's Query

Philosophers in the analytical tradition have tended to endorse a subjectivist view of morals. Yet common sense indicates that moral stances can be objective. I agree with Bambrough (1979) that we should take common sense seriously, and that we should distrust the view that morality cannot be objective in any sense.

By way of a starter, Bambrough (p. 15) introduces the common sense view with a telling, simple example:

My proof that we have moral knowledge consists essentially in saying, 'We know that this child, who is about to undergo what would otherwise be painful surgery, should be given an anaesthetic before the operation. Therefore we know at least one moral proposition to be true.'

Next, Bambrough reviews various arguments against the objectivity of morals. First, he considers the argument that 'moral disagreement is more widespread, more radical and more persistent than disagreement about matters of fact' (p. 18). This argument is plainly invalid, Bambrough says. It is not true that controversy is more common in ethics than in science. In both areas consensus and controversy are common. Aside from that, controversy does not imply that no party is right. Objectivity is compatible with controversy.

Second, many scholars have made much of the fact that 'when we express a moral conviction we thereby reveal something of our attitudes and feelings' (p. 21). Those who emphasise this tend to endorse subjectivism in the form of emotivism. Bambrough argues that we should resist emotivism. It is true that we may express attitudes and feelings in utterances conveying moral approval, but that is no less true of factual statements expressing beliefs (p. 22).

The parallel between *approve* and *believe* and between *good* and *true* is so close that it provides a useful test of the paradoxes of subjectivism and emotivism. The emotivist puts the cart before the horse in trying to explain goodness in terms of approval, just as he would if he tried to explain truth in terms of belief. Belief cannot be explained without introducing the notion of truth, and approval cannot be explained without introducing the notion of goodness. To believe is (roughly) to hold to be true, and to approve is (equally roughly) to hold to be good. Hence it is as unsatisfactory to try to reduce goodness to approval, or to approval plus some other component, as it would be to try to reduce truth to belief, or to belief plus some other component.

Third, as Hume noted, in the justification of moral views we sooner or later arrive at principles that do not themselves allow of justification (p. 23). That is true, of course, and it is true no less in the case of empirical theses. Infinite chains of justification are impossible in ethics and science alike.

Fourth, some argue that 'a dispute which is *purely* moral is inconclusive in principle. The specifically *moral* element in moral disputes is one which cannot be resolved by investigation and reflection' (p. 24). Here Bambrough replies that purely moral discussions or arguments do not exist. Empirical issues always play a role as well. Further, the argument is suspect because, if sensible, it should apply to science also. '... if a moral conclusion can be proved only to a man who accepts unprovable moral premises then a physical conclusion can be proved only to a man who accepts unprovable physical premises' (p. 26).

Fifth, one comes across the argument that 'there are recognised methods for settling factual and logical disputes, but there are no recognised methods for settling moral disputes' (p. 26). Bambrough simply dismisses this thesis as false; it should be obvious that he is right in this. Naturally, no recognised methods exist with which one can settle *all* moral disputes. But this is also true of factual disputes.

Sixth, according to a different argument we appear to be free in the choice of a morality, but we have no such freedom vis-a-vis empirical matters. Bambrough (p. 43) denies that such a difference exists.

It is the objective theorist of morals who has the strongest reason to favour freedom of moral inquiry, just as it is the physicist or astronomer, who believes that answers to questions of physics and astronomy are in principle obtainable and establishable, who sees the greatest merit in freedom of scientific inquiry. To claim that there is such a thing as knowledge, or knowledge of such and such a kind, is not to claim to possess such knowledge ... .

Bambrough's arguments appear to have much force, but the last argument is confused. He conflates two different things, the freedom to choose subjects of inquiry, and the freedom to accept or reject results of inquiry. The passage quoted, which pleads for freedom of inquiry, confusingly presupposes an objectivity of morals that should restrict our freedom to accept or reject results of inquiry. That is indeed the point of the arguments preceding the last one.

Apart from this, I disagree with Bambrough that science is value-free (has freedom of scientific inquiry). In the next section, I argue that lack of value-freedom, rather than value-freedom, entails parallels between science and ethics. Also, I argue that substantive connections should exist in addition to methodological parallels as envisaged by Bambrough.

Trade-offs, Facts and Values

If reliable knowledge is to be found anywhere, science will be the place to search for it. That is a common view, which is linked with the thesis that science is value-free.

Proponents of the thesis will not deny that values structure science in many ways. Empirical research concerning values has a legitimate place in science. Further, ethical norms and values constrain research projects, for example, because we are not free to treat experimental subjects – animals or human beings – in any way we please. Next, values co-determine which subjects are studied in science, not least via funding practices. Lastly, science has constitutive values of its own in the form of methodology. Defenders of value-freedom won't deny these things. They merely hold that contextual values do not or should not influence the way subjects of interest are investigated. I argue here that value-freedom does not even exist in this limited sense.

In principle, contextual values could affect science in two different ways that count against the thesis of value-freedom. First, it is conceivable that theories of science contain normative statements expressing such values. Most researchers would militate against this. They would argue that being empirical is a defining feature of scientific theories. I would be willing to agree, but this is to a large extent a matter of definition. On a narrow definition of science it is value-free in the sense that it is empirical; on a broad definition contextual values may well enter the picture. How should we view an article that reviews controlled experiments with a drug, and also recommends particular treatments on the basis of this? We could stipulate that it contains value-free science and in addition to this items that do not belong to science. Or we could take a broader view and locate contextual considerations in science itself. Nothing much hinges on this.

Second, the acceptance or rejection of scientific theories narrowly construed could depend on contextual values. Helen Longino (1990) and John Dupré (1993) have argued that this is indeed a common situation, but in my view they have not provided fundamental arguments showing that contextual values unavoidably have this role. I argue that the issue of methodological trade-offs most clearly shows why it is legitimate for values to affect the acceptance or rejection of scientific theories.

Constitutive values of science in the form of methodology are diverse. We want our theories to be general, universal, coherent, simple, well-confirmed, realistic, precise, and so forth. Now, anyone who bothers to scrutinise some live science cannot fail to observe that theories seldom satisfy all these methodological criteria at the same time. As Levins (1967, 1968) recognised long ago, scientists must face trade-offs among the criteria. For example, in modelling complex phenomena they must often simplify at the cost of realism.

The substance of science does not provide guidelines for the scientist to determine priorities among criteria. Neither does methodology itself. Hence, scientists who aim to justify priorities can but resort to contextual considerations. Thus, if they want a theory to have practical relevance, say for the treatment of patients in medicine, they had better give a high priority to realism rather than generality. If scientists choose to ignore contextual values they are saddled with free-floating methodologies.

Consider the following hypothetical example. We want to find out if a particular drug alleviates symptoms in patients with a nasty disease that can't be cured. So we perform a neat controlled experiment, which indicates that symptoms are alleviated within three weeks (the experimental period) due to the drug's action. Negative side-effects are not observed during this period. For the sake of argument, let's assume that the set-up warrants the general thesis that the drug, within three weeks after being taken, causes alleviation of symptoms without side-effects. Would this thesis, if true, be scientifically acceptable? I would not regard it as acceptable in the context envisaged here, if it would turn out that the drug causes death after four weeks.

I am aware of the objection that scientific truths remain truths, whatever their importance in applications. Shouldn't we say, so the objection goes, that the scientific merits of the thesis must be judged apart from practical merits? Let's go along with the objection, and see where it lands us.

The mere fact that the thesis is true does not make it scientifically acceptable. We could test many thousands of chemicals, each of which affects thousands of physiological processes in human beings and other organisms. Numbers of scientific truths about causation that the tests could provide are virtually boundless. The mere accumulation of such truths would not make sense; it would not represent acceptable science. We must be selective, and aim at *relevant* causal relations. Hence the issue becomes whether we can judge theoretical relevance apart from practical relevance. Theoretical relevance exists if methodological criteria are satisfied. But all criteria can't be satisfied at the same time. So we come back to the trade-off problem, which entails that theoretical relevance can't stand apart.

Some would defend a separate place for theoretical relevance by the following line of reasoning. Existing theory helps us determine, without recourse to practical matters, which effects of chemicals are worthy of investigation. For example, theory says that genes effect protein synthesis, and that some genetic defects cause disease, conceived as biological malfunction, via changes in particular proteins. If we want to know how particular malfunctions due to genetic defects can be restored, then theory helps us concentrate on particular chemicals and particular effects. True, the context determines what causal relations are relevant, but contexts can be purely theoretical.

I would grant that contexts *as presented in scientific texts* can be purely theoretical. They mostly are, but that is misleading. Theories are causally selective. They contain lots of *ceteris paribus* assumptions, implicit ones mostly, to the effect that causes disregarded are inoperative. These assumptions are often violated in natural situations. How should we judge causal selections in theories? The answer should again be that we are forced to rely on external considerations.

A purely genetic theory of particular disorders would have methodological merits, for example the merit of simplicity. But it would be weak methodologically on other counts. Thus, it would not be realistic in that it covers phenomena in a one-sided way. A theory which adds environmental causes to genetic ones would be more realistic, but it would have to be complex. Which kind of theory should we prefer? Some would answer that scientists have a right to settle this trade-off problem according to their tastes. That would amount to putting subjective whim at the heart of science. It would not sit well with a defence of value-freedom, because value-freedom is meant to ensure objectivity. More rational is the stance that we must allow contextual values to help us deal with trade-offs.

My analysis, if correct, should have profound implications for the relations between science and ethics. Let me go back first to Bambrough's views of these relations. Bambrough rightly notes that science and ethics are methodologically similar. But his thesis that both science and ethics can be objective must be amended with the crucial comment that objectivity is highly selective. Selectivity, and trade-offs associated with selectivity, entail that substantive connections exist between science and ethics in addition to methodological parallels.

Bambrough presupposes that science is value-free. However, science is not value-free in any sense. Therefore, ethicists should not simply rely on scientists for the empirical information they need in making normative principles operative. Theories and data of science are intrinsically selective. So ethicists will have to determine whether selections offered to them are adequate for their purposes. The determination of adequacy is not a matter of scientific expertise. Thus, ethicists should have a training in science that allows them to distinguish between adequate and inadequate forms of selectivity.

Scientists, conversely, should recognise values underlying causal selections, and they should acknowledge that it is legitimate for ethics to help determine methodological choices.

The example of genetically determined diseases nicely illustrates these points. It is more fully worked out in the next section, to show that causal attributions can be flawed beyond being merely selective. This should not surprise us, since causal patterns in natural phenomena are extremely complex. It is hard for scientists not to cherish the causal relations they happen to concentrate on. Thus, they are easily tempted to overrate the impact of the causal factors they identify. At times, outsiders are best qualified to recognise this phenomenon. This is an additional reason for ethicists to play an active role in the assessment of empirical matters.

The Riddle of Genetic Determination

In many disciplines, the determination of human behaviour has been a subject of long-lasting controversy. On one extreme view, behaviour is determined by biological features, ultimately genes. On the opposite, equally extreme view, the environment – not least culture – rather than biology shapes behaviour. A continuum of different views exists in between the extremes. For clarity of exposition, I focus on the extremes.

Considering the opposing views – genetic determination *versus* environmental determination – our prime question should not be which view fits the evidence best. Instead, we must realise that the two views are not as clear as their adherents would have it. The concepts of genetic determination and environmental determination are tricky. According to common biological wisdom, all features of organisms are influenced both by genetic and by environmental factors. Eye colour in adults is said to be genetically determined. Yet, many environmental factors – for example, oxygen for breathing – have a causal share in the process that leads to a particular eye colour. The colour of your eyes is due to a sequence of processes, from conception onwards, which involved many factors in the environment (inside and outside the womb) in addition to genetic ones. What, then, does the thesis that eye colour is genetically determined mean?

In brief the answer is as follows. A statement to the effect that some feature of a particular organism is genetically determined is strictly speaking meaningless. Instead we must look at *differences* in features between organisms (see for example Gifford 1990, Voorzanger 1987). Thus, eye colour in adults is genetically determined in the sense that differences between persons in eye colour are *always* due to a genetic difference, and not to any environmental difference. This is a strong form of genetic determination which is aptly covered by the shorthand that suppresses reference to differences. Weaker forms of determination should always be relativised to a particular comparison. Skin colour is an example. The racial difference in skin colour between a white person and a black person reflects a genetic difference. But two white persons ('white' in the racial sense) may differ in skin colour due to a purely environmental difference. If you are at liberty to enjoy protracted holidays with lots of sun-bathing, while your twin is forced to remain in his office, the two of you may exhibit differences in skin colour due to environmental differences. Hence, under some comparisons skin colour is 'genetically determined', under different comparisons it is 'environmentally determined', and in yet other cases we are dealing with a mixture.

Strong genetic determination is rare. So is strong environmental determination. Thus, the controversy over the determination of human behaviour is misguided. Theories which say that behaviour *in general* is genetically determined (or environmentally determined, or determined by genetic *and* environmental factors) must be rejected because they are meaningless. Evidence for or against such theories cannot exist. The reason for rejection is conceptual, not factual. Such theories must be replaced by 'local' theories that specify genetic and environmental influences for particular features in particular situations.

The theories I am envisaging represent an inappropriate form of causal selectivity, and inappropriate methodological trade-offs. Researchers who one-sidedly concentrate on genes as causes of behaviour, tend to come up with overgeneral concepts and theories of genetic determination. Too much emphasis is put on the methodological criterion of generality, with the result that theorising becomes unclear and unrealistic. As an illustration I analyse here genetic determination in biological psychiatry (for details see Van der Steen 1995, Chapter 8).

Methodologically inappropriate usage of the general term 'genetic determination' has fostered the view in psychiatry that major mental disorders are primarily caused by genetic defects. For example, twin studies showing that identical twins are often (in at least 25% of the cases) concordant for schizophrenia, while concordance in non-identical twins is much lower, allegedly demonstrate that schizophrenia is a genetic disorder. This assumes that identical and non-identical twins are exposed to similar correspondences and differences in environmental factors. Evidence indicates that this assumption is reasonable. In line with the emphasis on genetics, the search is primarily for biological treatments. Defective genes are thought to cause anomalies of neurotransmitters in the brain. Neuroleptics constitute the most important treatment since they are thought to correct the anomalies.

In fact, the twin evidence cannot tell us much about aetiology. Let's note first that the existence of discordant identical twins indicates that environmental factors also play a crucial role. A more fundamental point is that twin studies concern the population level, which as such does not allow inferences about individuals. Suppose that persons who often eat a particular species of fish tend to develop schizophrenia more often than persons who dislike the fish. Suppose further that concordance for food preferences is higher in identical twins than in non-identical twins. That could suffice in principle to generate similar differences in concordance for schizophrenia. But it would be odd in this case to regard genetic factors (those involved in food preferences) as a salient cause of schizophrenia in individuals.

Twins are not the only source of evidence. Other studies do point to a role for genetic factors, but the issue is controversial.

Apart from all this, the assumption that genetic factors are causally implicated does not entail that they explain salient symptoms. David Healy (1990) has rightly argued that psychiatric disorders such as schizophrenia in their primary manifestation could well be rather benign. It is conceivable that the social environment, not least in a medical setting, should foster detoriation in patients with relatively mild primary symptoms.

The prominence of treatments with neuroleptics is unfortunate (Breggin 1991). Controlled experiments have not unambiguously shown that commonly used drugs are effective. Moreover, psychotherapy, indeed lay therapies, may well be as beneficial and have less side-effects. Drugs may have serious side-effects. Prolonged usage of (classical) neuroleptics leads to brain damage in a large proportion of the patients. In the US alone about one million persons suffer from an irreversible motor disease called tardive dyskinesia caused by neuroleptics.

What explains the bias in favour of biological approaches in psychiatry? An important factor is presumably the wide-spread influence of the philosophical paradigm of reductionism in current science (there is another form of bias amounting to a gross distortion of biology; see Van der Steen 1995). At least as important is the power of the pharmaceutical industry over medicine including psychiatry. Many psychiatrists with important offices in the profession also hold positions in the industry. Further, links exist between industry and organisations responsible for the regulation of treatments. Many studies have shown that this fosters bias, even fraud (for details, see Abraham 1995, Breggin 1991, Payer 1992, Stelfox, Chua, O'Rourke and Detsky 1998).

How should ethicists react to all this? I have not uncovered any literature in ethics which squarely deals with the situation. Brown (1991) does note that neuroleptics often cause tardive dyskinesia. He is also aware of the fact that the efficacy of the drugs is in doubt, and he knows about the possible efficacy of other therapies. With approval he notes that both intra- and extra-institutional review are now being promoted in psychiatry. His ultimate conclusion is as follows (p. 181). 'These kinds of procedures are timely and desirable. It is to be hoped that psychiatrists will commit themselves to such pursuits, thereby enhancing the ethical foundations of drug treatment.'

Leave it all to the psychiatrists? That appears to be Brown's message. I would favour a different option. Ethicists should be aware of causal selectivity in psychiatry, and science in general. They should know about limitations of general theories of science resulting from methodological trade-offs. They should expose bias due to links between science, industry and regulatory agencies, and think about better forms of democracy that prevent dissemination of harmful treatments (Dutton 1988). They should state that the pervasiveness of drug use is morally wrong. Last but not least, they should chart consequences for cost containment in health care.

Ethicists are often asked to develop models for rationing, which is widely thought to be unavoidable as a form of cost containment. I would hold that any cost containment required can be realised conceivably by dispensing with medical treatments without benefits, and harmful treatments. More than ninety percent of current treatments have not been subjected to controlled trials. Many treatments which have been tested and found wanting are still widely applied. No one is able now to reliably estimate overall benefits and harms in health care.

Ethics will only be able to deal with the problems I discussed if its current research strategies are drastically changed. General models of ethics in which normative aspects predominate, and which rely on the scientist for empirical input, are a poor base for responsible moral decisions.

The Riddle of Egoism and Altruism

Concepts and theories of genetic determination belong to science. My analysis of genetic determination in psychiatry is an example that illustrates why ethics must attend to empirical matters. The point of the example is not merely that science is not pervasively trustworthy, and that ethicists must therefore know about limitations of science. As we saw in previous sections, the issues at stake are more fundamental. Science is causally selective, intrinsically so. Its theories cannot satisfy all methodological criteria. Scientists face methodological trade-offs that are best settled by external considerations. This calls for expertise from outside science. By implication, ethics deserves a place in science proper, and we must aim to break down existing barriers between science and ethics.

We should arrive at similar conclusions, if we take examples from ethics itself as a point of departure. The example in the present section, egoism and altruism in ethics, illustrates this (for details, see Van der Steen, 1995). (I use the terms 'egoism' and 'altruism' for behaviours and also for theories dealing with behaviours; intended meanings should be clear from the context.)

No one will deny that the subject of egoism and altruism belongs to ethics. But it belongs to science also. Let me start with an empirical issue in the domain of science. Is human behaviour exclusively motivated by self-interest? According to the doctrine of universal self-interest, *psychological egoism* for short, it is. This doctrine is popular in many areas of science. Could it possibly be true? As in the case of genetic determination, this question cannot be answered by an appeal to evidence, since the doctrine is problematic for conceptual reasons. Let's look at the concepts of egoism and altruism in some detail.

The classification of behaviours or acts into altruistic and egoistic ones involves various criteria of classification. The non-exhaustive list of criteria below fits in with general views discussed in the literature.

1 Benefits for self *versus* no benefits for self.
2 Benefits for others *versus* no benefits for others.
3 Motivated by benefits involved *versus* not so motivated.

Even this simplistic scheme would lead to a classification with at least 8 fully specified categories of behaviours or acts. This should dispose of any simple dichotomy of egoism *versus* altruism.

The notion of benefit calls for further distinctions. First, we should distinguish between *first-order* benefits and *second-order* benefits, which involve attitudes toward first-order ones. If you come up with constructive criticism of what I am writing here, and feel good about it, you realise a first-order benefit for me and a second-order benefit for yourself.

Second, we should distinguish between *primary* benefits and *secondary* benefits. Writing a book that pleases many people and sells well may lead to a substantial increase in your income. Thus a primary first-order benefit for others would carry a secondary first-order benefit for yourself in its wake.

Considering benefits we will also have to specify a *currency*. For example, evolutionary biologists concerned with altruism and egoism concentrate on reproductive output (numbers of descendants) as an overriding criterion for benefits. Ethicists work with quite different currencies, for example, satisfaction, pleasure, happiness, and various forms of utility.

The core meaning of 'egoism' presumably involves benefits for self and motivation in line with this. Altruism, contrariwise, involves benefits for others and motivation in line with that. In other respects, authors writing about egoism and altruism commonly leave intended meanings unspecified.

Because terms such as 'egoism' and 'altruism' cover so many different meanings, it is unwise to formulate hypotheses about egoism or altruism without qualification. As in the case of genetic determination, we had better prefer 'local' hypotheses and theories about specific forms of behaviour over putatively general ones. Psychological egoism as a general doctrine is anyhow meaningless.

These comments carry over to the domain of ethics. At issue there is ethical egoism, a natural analogue of psychological egoism. The 'egoism' of ethical egoism likewise covers a heterogeneous collection of behaviours. Let's look at a sample of views defended by ethicists.

Gauthier (1987) has argued that self-interest can provide us with reasons to be moral. In a crucial passage (pp. 19-20) he argues as follows. If we accept social requirements as overriding our self-anchored reasons, then others will more easily accept us as a willing partner or participant in mutually advantageous interactions. What kind of person should we wish to be if we are rational? The obvious answer is that it is better not to let self-anchored reasons prevail and not to free-ride on others. Interestingly, Gauthier states that we should act against our self-anchored reasons *for self-anchored reasons.* In other words, it is in our own interest not to let self-interest be our sole guide.

This is enormously confusing. Gauthier is using crucial terms in different senses. In my terminology, he is saying that secondary benefits for self associated with primary benefits for others could justify a particular, broadly defined form of ethical egoism.

Stephen Scott (1988, pp. 479-499) defends ethical egoism in a different way:

> ... I take up a distinction, for which I have coined terms, between *direct* and *reflexive* purposes. An action is directly self-interested if *its purpose* is a good (as a means or as an end) for the agent. It is reflexively self-interested if *his doing it* is a good for him, whether its purpose is or not. ...
>
> The point to which the distinction moves is that a selfless life is one whose direct aim is selfless. If it is also reasonable, its reflexive aim is self-interested. I am not saying that the agent's motive must entirely consist in the reflexive good, but I am saying that a selfless direct motive makes no sense by itself.

Scott appears to defend egoism by appealing to a different distinction. He focuses on second-order benefits rather than secondary ones. Acts which provide first-order benefits for others may be commendable if second-order benefits for ourselves ensue.

At first sight, Gauthier and Scott provide arguments in favour of the same doctrine, ethical egoism. But this is actually a misleading characterisation. Conceptual analysis shows that they are in fact discussing different subjects.

On the view of both authors, ethical egoism is a substantive doctrine. Others have argued that the doctrine, on broad interpretations, easily degenerates into a tautology. If benefits are taken to include secondary and/or second-order ones, every act appears *necessarily* egoistic in the sense that people can but do what they want to do, so that their acts will always be self-serving in some way (see for example Taylor 1975, and Nielson 1984).

Remarkably, ethical egoism has *also* been criticised on the ground that it is contradictory (see for example Lemos 1984, Putnam 1992). This should make us all the more suspicious. For example, inclusive ethical egoism may take the form of high-minded egoism, which incites us to act virtuously and develop a good character because these things are benefits for ourselves. This is conceptually suspect because a selfish motivation to aim at these things is at odds with the very notion of acting virtuously and having a good character.

Let's take stock. Concerning ethical egoism as a general doctrine four views are possible in principle. The doctrine could be (1) valid for substantive reasons, or (2) invalid for substantive reasons, or (3) valid for logical reasons, or (4) invalid for logical reasons. All general options conceivable are continually discussed in the literature (I have not mentioned an example of (1); Nagel 1970 will do). This suggests that the issue is approached in the wrong way because researchers are using the terms 'egoism' and 'altruism' for different concepts. The controversies are generated by different conceptualisations.

Our priority should be to get rid of options (3) and (4) because ethics is first and foremost about substantive issues. Or so it should be. The distinctions introduced in this section should help us achieve this. They indicate that broad definitions are not useful because they lead to tautologies and contradictions. If we opt for narrow definitions, however, a single pair of concepts will not suffice. Instead we need an array of concepts for different forms of behaviour. Likewise, we will presumably need to replace overarching theories of egoism and altruism by more informative, 'local' ones.

Why would ethicists tenaciously cling to overgeneral terms such as 'egoism' and 'altruism'? Part of the answer, I think, is that ethics undervalues the impact of empirical matters. To be useful, concepts of ethics, like those of science, must satisfy two broad methodological criteria, clarity of meaning and *empirical* relevance. To the extent that ethicists overvalues the methodological criterion of generality, they run the risk that the criteria of clarity and empirical relevance are not satisfied to minimally required degrees. As in the example of genetic determination, that would represent an inappropriate response to a methodological trade-off problem.

In ethics, clarity does receive much attention. In spite of this, a satisfactory degree of conceptual clarity has not been forthcoming in the case of 'egoism' and 'altruism'. That is because these terms cover heterogeneous categories. The heterogeneity is at odds with the criterion of empirical relevance, which receives much less attention in ethics.

Empirical relevance is important for ethics since normative discourse needs concepts with empirical *reference*. Thus, concepts of egoism and altruism in ethics should apply to behaviours in the real world. To be relevant empirically, the concepts should exhibit homogeneity of reference to a reasonable degree.

In addition to empirically relevant concepts, normative ethics needs empirical *theses*. We can't formulate sensible guidelines for human behaviour unless we know what human beings are like. Suppose, for example, that psychological egoism were amply confirmed by empirical studies. If so, then ethical egoism would be pointless. Guidelines for behaviours which are performed anyway, are superfluous.

In point of fact, psychological egoism is nowadays defended in many areas of science. Here we find the same confusion due to overgeneral concepts. In a thought-provoking book, Michael Wallach and Lise Wallach (1983), have argued convincingly that psychology and psychotherapies commonly presuppose – wrongly so – that human beings are pervasively selfish. In a wide-ranging analysis, they show that available evidence does not confirm general psychological egoism, however conceived. Scientific research on the subject apparently suffers from pervasive bias.

The example of egoism and altruism in ethics supports the conclusions of the previous analyses, which took science as a point of departure. It is wrong to allot empirical matters to science, and normative matters to ethics. Science can't do without ethics. Conversely, ethics should not simply rely on science for an empirical input into normative work. It should cover empirical issues in addition to normative principles. The existing boundaries between ethics and science are unacceptable.

Methodology and Ethics

The upshot of my analysis so far is that ethics should become more empirical and that science should become more normative. If this would be realised, science and ethics would become much more similar than they are now. Similarities should also be fostered by a common methodology. In this section I briefly indicate how potential similarities are undervalued for lack of a methodological awareness in ethics.

I argued that science is not value-free in any reasonable sense of the term. Likewise, ethics is not fact-free in any corresponding sense. If it is true that ethics needs to address empirical issues, it will necessarily inherit the methodological trade-off problem from science. As briefly indicated in the previous section, the example of egoism and altruism should illustrate this. The trade-off problem should also surface in ethics more narrowly conceived, which does not have a salient focus on empirical matters. High generality is a commendable feature of many normative theories in ethics. But we should not be surprised to learn that such theories do not easily allow of practical application. Thus, it may be wise to opt against generality if we aim at practicality. (Trade-offs and other methodological themes in ethics are discussed in more detail in Van der Steen and Musschenga 1992.)

Ethics, like philosophy of science, has seldom considered the methodological trade-off problem. *Normative* trade-offs concerning principles that pull in different directions are widely discussed, but methodology is taken for granted.

Another symptom of poorly developed methodology in ethics is the enormous confusion over the nature of theorising. On the one hand, highly general theories still have many defenders. On the other hand, many ethicist even hold that ethics must dispense with theories altogether. Neither party pays much attention to the meaning of 'theory', the crucial methodological notion in the disputes. The disputants implicitly use entirely different conceptions of theory. If we want to develop better strategies for theorising in ethics, a dissolution of this sort of controversy is badly needed as a preliminary activity.

Those who oppose general theories in ethics (see for example Clark and Simpson 1989) are envisaging highly abstract theories which allegedly do not allow the derivation of 'moral rules' used in real life. However, we may choose to regard such rules as substantive principles that constitute theories at intermediate levels of generality. The anti-theory movement denies the status of theory to lower level generalities for no obvious reason. The discussion should be about appropriate levels of generality, not about the use of theories in general (for further comments see Van der Steen and Musschenga 1992).

Abstract theorising in ethics is also criticised by those who defend casuistry as an alternative (see for example Jonsen and Toulmin 1988). The same confusion reigns here. Jonsen and Toulmin note that abstract theories do not permit the derivation of particular judgements, that we must decide moral issues in concrete situations on a case-by-case basis. Throughout their book they contrast theories with particulars. However, what they choose to call 'particulars' are actually lower-level generalities which are wrongly denied the status of theory (for more details, see Van der Steen and Musschenga 1992).

The same confusion exists in environmental ethics (Van der Steen 1995). This discipline aims at a normative perspective on a great variety of organisms and more inclusive entities such as species and ecosystems. It would not be easy to elaborate one general theory encompassing all that. In a controversy over the feasibility of such a theory the opposing parties are known – confusingly so – as monists and pluralists. Monists hold that a single theory is possible, pluralists deny this. The entire dispute is spurious since opposing parties endorse different conceptions of theory.

A survey of various meanings of 'theory' is beyond the scope of this chapter. But anyhow one thing is clear on my analysis. It is unwise to reserve the term 'theory' as a honorific label for abstract, general entities.

Implications for Moral Argumentation

The most salient implication of my analysis for moral argumentation is devastatingly simple and far-reaching. Moral argumentation should not exist. Neither should empirical argumentation. If boundaries between science and ethics would dissolve, as they should, then we would not have these separate domains of argumentation.

Arguably, within ethics *cum* science, we could still have (i) arguments which only contain empirical statements, (ii) arguments which only contain normative statements, and (iii) arguments which contain both empirical and normative statements. We could decide to reserve the label of moral argument (or legal argument, as the case may be) for categories (ii) and (iii), if the normative statements would concern morals (or matters of law, in the case of legal argument).

But this classification of arguments is misleading. If my analysis is right, normative considerations (not exclusively methodological ones) should essentially affect the assessment of arguments in domain (i), and empirical matters should affect the assessment of arguments in domain (ii). Thus, we would ultimately be left with argumentation in domain (iii). This would again make the existence of a separate domain of moral (or legal) argumentation problematic.

Furthermore, the classification departs from the problematic assumption that purely normative statements are feasible. As I argued in the analysis of egoism and altruism, moral statements make sense only if they contain concepts with empirical reference. If ethicists advise us to make egoism the standard of our conduct (as some do, unfortunately), they are making sense only if 'egoism' represents behaviours that human beings actually perform or can perform. Also, they should assume that human beings are capable of preferring egoism over altruism, or *vice versa*. As I have argued, 'egoism' and 'altruism' are actually confused notions, but better notions should likewise touch on empirical matters. In brief, purely normative statements cannot exist.

Normative notions of ethics are intrinsically connected to empirical matters. Thus, it would be misleading to construe category (iii) as the set of arguments that move from normative premises plus empirical premises to a normative conclusion. Purely normative statements do not exist, not even in present-day ethics. If we overlook this, then we might be tempted to allow for separate theorising about normative *elements* of ethics. But this kind of theorising cannot sensibly be done. Empirical matters extend all the way in to the core of normative ethics, covertly if not overtly.

I am not sure that empirical statements of science, conversely, contain normative presuppositions. My argument against value-freedom for science places such presuppositions, however essential, at some remove from empirical statements as such. Thus, it may be possible to retain the distinction of categories (i) and (iii), with the understanding that normative components of arguments in (iii) do not come in separate packages.

However, a full-fledged appraisal of arguments in category (i) should ultimately confront us with normative matters in the province of ethics. The example of genetic determination amply illustrates this. Purely scientific arguments in category (i) are possible only to the extent that we care to suppress the normative context.

We can but conclude that fundamental differences between argumentation in science and argumentation in ethics do not exist. *Mutatis mutandis*, what I said about ethics *versus* empirical science should apply with equal force to the domain of law *versus* empirical science.

The case studies in this chapter also affect the pragmatic context of moral (and legal) argumentation. Considering pragmatics, I would argue that we ought to re-evaluate locations of proper expertise. Empirical matters should not be left to the scientist, and normative matters should not be left to the ethicist. Existing divisions of labour are wrong. I am not sure about the best way to actually change them. Educational reforms aiming at bridges between science and ethics are possibly the best option.

Conclusions

What patterns of reasoning are legitimate in ethics? To answer this question we need to know about the role of ethical theory. Unfortunately, the term 'theory' is used in many different senses in ethics. We need to clear up the prevailing confusion before we can even begin to address our question.

We can only come to grips with ethical theories by resorting to methodology, which has the proper tools in its store to analyse theories. Methodology, unfortunately, is poorly developed in ethics.

Application of two important methodological strategies, conceptual analysis and analysis of trade-offs, indicates that the search of highly general theories in science and in ethics is misguided. We should be content mostly with theories at low levels of generality. In this respect, and in other methodological respects, science and ethics are fundamentally similar.

Ethical theories unavoidably have empirical components. The elaboration of these components should not be left to the scientist. Instead, it is desirable that ethics itself pursues the study of empirical matters. It should indeed develop into a critic of science. Science, conversely, cannot do without ethics.

Science and ethics would become much more similar than they are now if they would aim to interconnect empirical and normative matters, as they should.

The analysis in this chapter should have implications for moral (and legal) argumentation. It implies, for example, that there is no place for purely normative statements in moral arguments. Pragmatically, the analysis calls for relocations of expertise in moral and empirical matters.

References

Abraham, J. (1995), *Science, Politics and the Pharmaceutical Industry: Controversy and Bias in Drug Regulation,* UCL Press, London.

Bambrough, R. (1979), *Moral Scepticism and Moral Knowledge,* Routledge & Kegan Paul, London.

Breggin, P. (1991), *Toxic Psychiatry. Drugs and Electroconvulsing Therapy: The Truth and the Better Alternatives,* St. Martin's Press , New York; reprinted 1993, Harper Collins, London.

Brown, P. (1991), 'Ethical aspects of drug treatment', In Bloch, S., and P. Chodoff (eds), *Psychiatric Ethics,* pp. 167-184, Oxford University Press, New York.

Clarke, S.C., and E. Simpson (eds) (1989), *Anti-Theory in Ethics and Moral Conservatism,* Suny Press, Albany.

Dupré, J. (1993), *The Disorder of Things: Metaphysical Foundations of the Disunity of Science,* Harvard University Press, Cambridge, Mass.

Dutton, D.B. (1988), *Worse than the Disease: Pitfalls of Medical Progress.* Cambridge University Press, Cambridge.

Gauthier, D. (1987), 'Reason to be moral?', *Synthese* 72, pp. 5-27.

Gifford, F. (1990), 'Genetic Traits', *Biology and Philosophy* 5, pp. 327-347.

Healy, D. (1990), *The Suspended Revolution: Psychiatry and Psychotherapy Re-examined,* Faber and Faber, London.

Jonsen, A.R., and S. Toulmin (1988), *The Abuse of Casuistry: A History of Moral Reasoning,* University of California Press, Berkeley.

Lemos, N.M. (1984), 'High-minded egoism and the problem of priggishness', *Mind* 93, pp. 542-558.

Levins, R. (1966), 'The strategy of model building in population biology", *American Scientist* 54, pp. 421-31.

Levins, R. (1968), *Evolution in Changing Environments,* Princeton University Press, Princeton.

Longino, H.L. (1990), *Science as Social Knowledge,* Princeton University Press, Princeton.

Nagel, T. (1970), *The Possibility of Altruism,* Princeton University Press, Princeton.

Nielsen, K. (1984), 'The voices of egoism', *Philosophical Studies* (Ireland) 30, pp. 83-107.

Payer, L. (1992), *Disease-Mongers: How Doctors, Drug Companies, and Insurers are Making You Feel Sick,* Wiley, New York.

Putnam, D. (1992), 'Egoism and virtue', *The Journal of Value Inquiry* 26, pp. 117-124.

Stelfox, H.T., G. Chua, K. O'Rourke, and A.S. Detsky (1998), 'Conflict of interest in the debate over calcium-channel antagonists', *New England Journal of Medicine* 338, pp. 101-106.

Stone, C.D. (1987), *Earth and Other Ethics: The Case of Moral Pluralism,* Harper and Row, New York.

Taylor, P.W. (1975), *Principles of Ethics: An Introduction,* Dickenson, Encino California.

Van der Steen, W.J. (1993), *A Practical Philosophy for the Life Sciences,* Suny Press, Albany.

Van der Steen, W.J. (1995), *Facts, Values, and Methodology: A New Approach to Ethics,* Rodopi, Amsterdam and Atlanta.

Van der Steen, W.J., and A.W. Musschenga (1992), 'The issue of generality in ethics', *Journal of Value Inquiry* 26, pp. 511-524.

Voorzanger, B. (1987), *Woorden, Waarden, en de Evolutie van Gedrag: Humane Sociobiologie in Methodologisch Perspectief,* Free University Press, Amsterdam.

Wallach, M.A., and L. Wallach (1983), *Psychology's Sanction of Selfishness: The Error of Egoism in Theory and Therapy,* Freeman and Company, San Francisco.

7 What is Truth?

Incest and Narrative Coherence in Law

CEES W. MARIS[1]

Truth in Law

My Story

My Story (*Mijn Verhaal*) by Yolanda, published in 1994, is the autobiography of an incest victim that ended in a controversial lawsuit. Yolanda tells us that in 1978 she lost her virginity to her eleven-years old brother when she was only eight. Shortly afterwards her father and mother joined in and sexual intercourse became an everyday occurrence in the family. When Yolanda protested she was punished by her mother with sadistic gusto; she forced her daughter to sit on the stove with her buttocks exposed, she rubbed salt in her wounds and pulled out her toenails. This casual cruelty developed into fully-fledged S.M. games, with members of the family and, later on, outsiders as well sticking candles, vibrators, broken bottles, chair legs, pokers and screwdrivers into Yolanda's vagina and other apertures. A pruner was used to cut off pieces of her skin. Her labia and clitoris were cut with razor blades. She was tortured with electric shocks and made to eat faeces. She was also the unwilling victim of strangulation sex and hung by the neck with a nylon stocking till she passed out. After a while the family started holding weekly S.M. parties with many guests, who were later asked to pay.

> Everyone undressed; it usually started with my mother having it away with some bloke. Or else I had to strip naked and give her a body rub, or lick her. My father and brother either watched or else they made out with each other. They'd give each other a blow job, something like that. Afterwards my father and Adriaan would usually tie me to the bed with my arms and legs

spread. Then they'd beat me till I was bleeding. Sometimes there were four men who wanted to have sex with me one after the other; or else they all did it at once. (p. 42)

Among the party-goers were dignitaries from Epe, a provincial town in the east of Holland; they included a local architect and his wife, Yolanda's GP and her dentist, a clergyman, a policeman, a church elder, an engineer and a lawyer. Yolanda's mother started a successful recruiting drive for clients. From the time she was twelve Yolanda serviced five visitors per day; at the weekend the number rose to thirty. She had intercourse with thirty Turkish men one after another. She remains haunted by dim memories of satanic rituals. From the age of fifteen Yolanda also had full-blown relationships with a number of men, all of whom proved to be pimps or sadists. The man whom she married in 1985 was the most vicious of all. Yolanda wrote:

If all the men in Epe who'd had sex with me were to go on holiday together the shops would go bankrupt. The Market Square would be too small for them. (p. 52)

From the time she was ten Yolanda was constantly getting pregnant. She was aborted by her parents sixteen times between the years 1980 and 1990; they used instruments such as pokers, vibrators and barbecue skewers. Six children, including two twins, were murdered at birth in grisly fashion, to the glee of those present.

When its head emerged my mother tried unsuccessfully to grip it with a pair of pliers. So my brother had to bore a hole in its head. My mother tried cutting me open with the pliers till she could get her fingers in; afterwards she pulled or cut it out in pieces. (p. 73)

Yolanda gave names to the murdered babies. In 1989 Patrick was born; he was at once killed, hung, flayed and cut open from top to toe. Yolanda's brother who worked in a butcher's shop cut out a piece of Patrick's flesh and forced her to eat it. Three other children were spared only to be raped later on by their father.

No-one noticed Yolanda's incessant pregnancies; her complaints were ignored. It was not until 1990 that the police first listened to her. Her parents confessed and in 1991, together with her brother and her ex-husband, they were given prison sentences of up to 7 years for offences in the area of assault and sexual abuse. In 1992 Yolanda's account of the murders of her babies was finally taken seriously. A search for their corpses however was to no avail. On the basis of her allegations a second lawsuit was initiated against the accused who had by then withdrawn their original confessions. For lack of evidence the public prosecutor decided not to take the charges of infanticide to court. Sentences of 2 to 5 years were passed down on charges of illegal abortions and grievous bodily harm. All the accused appealed against the sentences.

The appeal in the incest case in Epe was held after Yolanda's book was published. The court hearings pivoted round the veracity of her story. The Public Prosecutor limited the charges against the parents and the ex-husband to those of rape and forcible abortions.[2] Expert witnesses gave conflicting interpretations of the evidence. A gynaecologist stated that the 24 abortions alleged could not possibly have taken place in the given period. Many of the methods of abortion that Yolanda described such as that with a large vibrator could not have led to the alleged result, or would have inflicted such injuries that she would have had to be hospitalized. One psychiatrist stated that Yolanda's parents were so suggestible that little value could be attached to their original confessions. Another psychologist, Nel Draijer, argued for the truth of Yolanda's allegations. She recommended an enquiry as to whether Yolanda suffered from a multiple personality disorder; the different partial personae of individuals with this disorder could account for her contradictory statements, without her basic plausibility being undermined. The court in Arnhem acquitted Yolanda's ex-husband of committing an abortion with a vibrator. It condemned her parents to four years prison for forcible abortions committed in 1982 whereby Yolanda's physical integrity was violated in an abhorrent fashion, causing her permanent psychological harm.

The legal debate about the truth of Yolanda's allegations is typical of the problems of the burden of proof in incest trials. Normally speaking, because incest occurs in the bosom of the family, the only witnesses are the victim and the perpetrator. The truth of allegations in such cases is extraordinarily difficult to substantiate after the fact. On the other hand if the allegations are true, the psychological harm inflicted on the victim is potentially very great precisely because of the close relations between victim and perpetrator. The question then is how the law is supposed to deal with cases of this sort where the seriousness of the offence is in inverse proportion to the weight of evidence. Can suspects appeal to the normal legal principle of the benefit of the doubt? Or do victims deserve extra support with the burden of proof being eased as some feminist lawyers have argued?

The question can just as easily be reversed however; are incest cases with their conflicting narratives where all empirical basis is absent so exceptional? Are they not in fact exemplary for legal cases in general? This is indeed the case, if one subscribes to the *narrative theory of law*. According to this theory all human knowledge consists of stories, narrative constructs that cannot be verified by any independent empirical reality. The same goes for the 'facts' on which the furnishing of proof in legal cases depends: facts in law exist not as objective data, but form part of a narrative about reality. Subscribers to the narrativist theory turn to the notion of *narrative coherence* for establishing convincing legal proof; it is the degree of coherence, they argue, that determines which version of a criminal occurrence is the most plausible.

The purpose of my story on the contrary is to show that this theory of narrative robs criminal law of all its legitimacy; without any anchoring in empirical experience, the whole idea of legal proof becomes subject to reasonable scepticism – as Yolanda's case shows in so exemplary a fashion.

Narrativity and Coherence in the Law

Focqué and 't Hart (1990) develop their theory of narrative law with specific reference to criminal law. By 'narrativity' they mean

> ... the complex totality of knowledge and perceptions as expressed by people about themselves and their culture in the form of stories without there being any claim to the unambiguous certainty that scientific knowledge strives for (...). (p. 271)

They reject the notion of knowledge as providing a 'picture' of reality, by which a subject has a theoretical image of an objective reality. They see this approach as erroneous, because every 'so-called description of reality' is the result of an interpretation in which both object and subject are themselves constructed:

Subject and object, Storyteller and story are not separate positions but configurations of and within a general story, that embraces both the Storyteller and his own tale. (p. 368)

Scientific knowledge too is based on a pre-scientific image of reality. The same is true of law. Focqué and 't Hart see legal dogma as the product of an ideologically biased image of humanity, society and law - as a sort of story in other words. Furthermore the social reality on which the system of legal norms is imposed also has its own story to tell. From these two component parts the judge or magistrate constructs the narrative that will offer the legal solution for a concrete case. A living reality is thus transformed by legal dogma into a new legal reality with its own narrative structure.

The activity of reviewing and classifying, arranging and rearranging, summing up and naming, qualifying and assessing the components of a narrative structure also occurs in fairy stories in much clearer fashion than in the numerous realities of myths or the various roles in a play. ('t Hart, 1983, 425)

Due to the 'picture' model of knowledge however lawyers have mistakenly tended to regard norms and facts as inevitable 'natural' givens. The narrativist perception that what is really involved is social constructs creates space for reappraising the prevailing notions of norms and realities. In criminal law the narrative element should therefore be allowed much more scope – at least this is the conclusion of Focqué and 't Hart. The prevailing rigorous selection on the basis of legal relevance imposes much too rigid a formalist straightjacket on the diversity of human interpretation, creating an unbridgeable gulf between the dogmatic reality of the law and the everyday lives of the parties to a suit.[3] Criminal law should accordingly become less formal, not just confining itself to what is normally counted as legally relevant; it should listen more to what the parties to a suit have to tell. It is a question of whether the justifiable 'can claim social recognition of divergent or different interpretation of one's own experience as a right' (Focqué and 't Hart, 1990, p. 343).[4] In short:

Instead of submitting to a single dominant system of knowledge that is thought of as natural, relational law aims to be an instrument for mediating a pluralism of attributions of meaning. (p. 362)

Which story however should the judge believe where there is so much pluralism of interpretation? In the absence of an objective external reality for controlling conflicting stories, narrative theory cannot appeal to the correspondence criterion of truth.

As an alternative Jackson (1990) proposes a criterion of narrative coherence. Like Focqué and 't Hart, Jackson rejects the prevailing notion that the major and minor premises of the syllogism of the legal norm *refer* to objectively established legal norms or to objective legal facts respectively, and that the conclusion should result from establishing a correspondence between the premises. He advises us

> ... to abandon popular notions of 'reference' (...) both as regards the word of
> the witness in relation to the anterior facts to which he/she claims to refer,
> and to the relationship between the general rule of law (the major premise)
> and the legally determined facts of the case (the minor premise). (p. 380)

According to Jackson the major and minor premises each have their own narrative form and content, and the conclusion is reached by assessing the similarities between these stories. This conclusion must meet with the criterion for plausibility of *narrative coherence*: the syllogism offers a plausible conclusion provided the different stories form a coherent whole, and also provided that they comply with the narrative world view which members of society rely on for meaning. Justification of the minor premise in which the 'facts' are ascertained is a also question of coherence. The story of a witness must first of all be *internally coherent*, that is, it must show a consistency and consonance in its separate elements. It must also comply with the requirement of *external coherence*, that is, it must be plausible in the light of the prevailing stock of social knowledge, consisting of exemplary stories and social constructs that reflect one's everyday experience and culture.

Against this I would argue that the case of Yolanda, exactly because its pronouncedly narrative character, exposes the limitations of the narrativist theory of law, especially when it is a question of ascertaining facts in the minor premise.[5] In the first place, contrary to what Focqué and 't Hart assert, the more open the criminal process becomes for narrative diversity, the smaller the chance is of narrative coherence. Yolanda's case is a paragon of narrativity. Over the conflicting accounts of the concerned parties, legal representatives and legal authorities, psychologists, psychiatrists and sociologists all wove a tissue of conflicting interpretations based on their own disparate theoretical perspectives; each of these perspectives in turn had its impact on the statements of the main protagonists. No trace of Yolanda's controversial claim of incest was to be found outside the stories. The findings of both the initial court and the court of appeal were then not only empirically speaking underdetermined, they also suffered from a far-reaching narrative incoherence. If every criminal suit were as narrative in character as the incest case of Yolanda, the judge would always have to bring a verdict of acquittal and criminal law would lose its meaning (See the next section).

Secondly, contrary to Jackson's assertions, even if despite all this you achieve a narrative coherence there still remains so much room for reasonable doubt that coherence in itself can no longer be seen as being an adequate criterion for legal proof. Coherence does admittedly play an important role in justifying claims to truth in criminal law, but a privileged place for experience is equally necessary. In cases of incest too a similar anchoring in experience is possible (See the third section).

Ascertaining the Truth in Cases of Incest

Witnesses and Experts

So many disparate stories were told by experts and concerned parties during the Yolanda trials that narrative coherence was hard to find.[6] According to Jackson's criterion of external coherence, stories like this involving concrete cases of incest must be shown totally with more general ideas within the prevailing world view, if one is to arrive at a plausible assessment of the incident. Narrative coherence however seems then to retreat ever further beyond the horizon, so violent is the clash between the standpoints of lawyers, psychologists and social scientists about the role of criminal proceedings, the ascertaining of legal truth and the proper psychological method to be used in incest trials.

In the debate that ensued after the appeals court verdict the experts also failed to agree. Sceptics pointed to a generally gullible climate of opinion in which everything that Yolanda said was swallowed lock, stock and barrel by the media and the legal authorities, including her far-fetched stories about satanic sects. While the sceptics were up in arms against this widespread naivety, the victim's sympathizers were dismayed by the general disbelief. The doubts about Yolanda's credibility, they argued, added to the prevailing atmosphere of denial, thus violating the integrity of the victim twice over, this time by calling her a liar. Nobody would dare to bring any charges any more if things went on like this.

The most persuasive advocate of the sceptical line was the psychologist and expert witness Wagenaar. According to Wagenaar (1994) criminal proceedings do not revolve around whether one feels sorry for the victim, but are concerned to prove an indictment. In his view the evidence for Yolanda's story was extremely weak. It has never been proven that satanic sects exist. None of Yolanda's allegations against large numbers of people from Epe outside the small circle of kith and kin have been taken up by the Public Prosecutor. Her statements on a number of points were demonstrably untrue. She stated for instance that at the end of October 1989 a new-born baby was murdered, while a medical test showed that in August 1989 she wasn't pregnant. Wagenaar's conclusion is that only a limited part of Yolanda's story is credible.

As against this, a number of sympathizers advocated a view of the role of criminal proceedings in incest cases that deviates sharply from Wagenaar's emphasis on ascertaing the truth. According to staff of the Clara Wichman Institute for women and law Yolanda's integrity in the proceedings was insufficiently respected by the defendants' lawyers who tried to undermine her credibility as much as possible.[7] Since the law governing criminal proceedings only offers the suspect any protection against the superior power of the authority that brings the charges, the victim who is also the crucial witness is unfairly put in the position of the accused. Critics who point out inconsistencies and unverifiable elements in Yolanda's story, do not realize that what is legally unprovable may still be true. Since in many incest cases the truth is impossible to ascertain, criminal law should be more supportive of the victim, and not listen to so-called expert witnesses who undermine her allegations and accuse the victim of lying behaviour. Potentially criminal proceedings can help the victim to work through her past.

Other experts, among them the psychologist Van der Hart, do in fact regard it as possible to establish the truth in an incest trial in favour of the victim. In his afterword to Yolanda's book, *The terror of disbelief,* Van der Hart explains the prevailing scepticism as being based on a human need for security and justice. This is really an illusion, he argues; under certain circumstances most people are capable of extreme violence. Under pressure of a general climate of disbelief and the overwhelming intimidation practiced by the perpetrators, it is rare for victims to dare to open their mouths. Furthermore the process of *dissociation* often induces them to deny the event, even to themselves – dissociation is a psychological defence mechanism that Van der Hart has made his special study. In order to survive the horrific experience of incest the victim detaches herself from the event, isolating the memory in a split part of the personality, banishing it from the conscious mind. Nonetheless a psychologist can indirectly deduce from symptoms such as depression or eating disorders that the client must have experienced sexual abuse in her childhood.

Dissociation and Multiple Personality Disorders

In some cases of incest the narrative character is exacerbated still more by a far more thoroughgoing appeal to dissociation than was the case with Yolanda. According to psychologists and psychiatrists such as Terr (1994) and Van der Hart (1995), incest is also plausible when people enter therapy for completely different kinds of complaints such as nightmares, depression, forms of sexual deviancy or eating disorders. During treatment women who do not have any conscious memory of incest in their past can come to realize that their psychological difficulties were caused by traumatic experiences of incest in their early years. In the ensuing period the conscious ego had no knowledge of this, since the terrifying experience was driven from the conscious mind through dissociation. In cases of mild dissociation one's personality is split into the roles of victim and spectator; by mentally stepping out of oneself the victim also distances herself from her pain. In cases of 'total dissociation' one's personality is definitively split, so that the part that was subjected to the traumatic experience is isolated in a separate part of the consciousness which is then repressed. Incest and other forms of abuse are then completely forgotten. Total dissociation can lead to a *multiple personality disorder* which, according to the expert witness Nel

Draijer, may explain the contradictions in Yolanda's story. The victim divides herself into different partial *personae* with divergent lifestyles that in turn play the leading role in everyday life.[8]

According to these experts dissociation is painful for the victim, but does in the end make it possible to unearth the truth. Most memories undergo a pronounced distortion in the long term due to the fact that they are encapsulated in schematic memory structures. Owing to its isolation however, the traumatic memory of incest remains preserved in its pure form, so that years later it can rise to the surface during therapy without any distortions. The dissociation theory can thus integrate the conflicting accounts of the victim in a more general story that offers an outward coherence. Within this framework the victim often rewrites her life story so that it becomes an internally coherent whole. On the basis of memories of incest that victims reappropriate during adulthood, they can still bring charges against their parents. This is a development that has been taken to extremes in the USA.

On the basis of their empirical research into how memory operates, psychologists and psychiatrists such as Wagenaar et al. (1993), Loftus (1994), Reviere (1996) and Crombag and Merckelbach (1996) discount the diagnostic value of dissociation. In their survey of this kind of empirical research Crombag and Merckelbach (1996) systematically explore four assumptions behind the theory of recovered memories: (1) that children tend to forget traumatic experiences totally (2) as a consequence of repression or dissociation, (3) but that the forgotten trauma continues to disrupt their later lives resulting in pathological symptoms, (4) until psychotherapeutic techniques such as hypnosis enable them to trace these symptoms to their hidden traumatic origin and integrate them in normal consciousness. In the view of Crombag and Merckelbach, empirical research casts doubt on all these hypotheses.

According to this research into human memory, you don't remember anything before your second year; memory only begins to function at an average age of three-and-a-half years. The many recovered memories of incest concerning the first two years of one's life are thus not plausible. Once the memory has begun to operate it does not function like a video camera recording things passively; instead it offers a selective reconstruction of experiences from the past. In general people forget much more than they remember. Your strongest memories are of things you have experienced during the past two years. In the long run the memory works selectively constructing its own scenarios: it adds new events, turning them into scenarios, general patterns that are a deposit of experiences from the past. The details fall into oblivion, with the exception of events with a remarkable character; these continue to play a much more lively role in one's memory. Research into war traumas stresses this point. The same goes for intense negative childhood experiences, even when a loyalty conflict with one of one's parents plays a role in them. Information that is forgotten is not completely lost. Exceptional associative stimuli can bring it to the surface again so that it acquires a place in one's current memory bank. Distortion can occur here, partly under influence of information about the event that is obtained later from another source. Memories of remarkable events are also falsified in this manner. 55% of a group of subjects interviewed about an air crash said they recalled TV images of the plane hitting a block of flats. In fact there were no images of that moment. Association can also give rise to pseudo-memories. To sum up, precisely because of its extraordinary character, a traumatic experience of incest will surely remain a powerful presence in one's memory, instead of being completely forgotten. Present memories of incest can however be considerably distorted.

According to Crombag and Merckelbach then, there is no convincing empirical evidence for the existence of psychological defence mechanisms such as repression or dissociation. The diagnosis of a dissociated 'multiple personality', consisting of at least 2 (sometimes as many as 147) separate identities that are not aware of each other's existence or history and which in turn can influence a patient's behaviour, is not so different from that of a normal personality that also displays countless contradictions while largely forgetting its own past.[9] Human consciousness is not a single entity, but consists rather of numerous processes that either coexist or else conflict with each other. The multiple personality would seem to be a hypothetical self-image supplied by the psychiatrist. In the first instance patients come with completely different complaints such as depression or sexual disorders. It is only after a diagnosis of a 'multiple personality disorder' that *alter egos* are classified and named, after which the therapist immediately summons them up and speaks to them. Furthermore the diagnosis meets patients' need for a definite external cause for their complaints: all their suffering can be attributed to incest traumas.

The fact that therapists can also play a crucial role in the construction of memories of sexual abuse is convincingly stated by the memory special-

156 Reasoning in Ethics and Law

ist, Elizabeth Loftus (1994). A researcher for instance succeeded in inducing an incest suspect to come to the erroneous conclusion that he had forced his son and daughter to have sexual intercourse with each other. This is why, Loftus writes, researchers into memory conclude 'that memories are reconstructed using bits of fact and fiction, and that false memories can be induced by expectation and suggestion' (p. 79). In short, if the conclusions reached in this experimental research into our memory by Loftus and Crombag and Merckelbach are correct, 'recovered memories' of incest cannot make any privileged claim to be taken as the truth.[10]

This debate about dissociation is taking place between two groups of academics with conflicting theories. At this meta-level then no coherence has been reached either; as against the appeal to practical clinical experience of clinical psychologists and psychiatrists such as Van der Hart and Terr, experimental psychologists such as Wagenaar and Loftus put their trust in the empirically obtained facts of experimental research. The clinical psychologists defend themselves against the experimentalists with the argument that laboratory research does not take any account of their practical observations. Traumatic experiences such as infanticide, rape and kidnapping are moreover too damaging to be organized artificially in a laboratory situation. A psychiatrist such as Lenore Terr argues that it is these experiences, precisely because of their extraordinary character, that fall outside the normal operations of the memory, making the experiments of Loftus not applicable. 'Trauma drafts new rules for the memory' (p. 75). What is a judge supposed to make of all these conflicting narratives?

Both clinical and experimental psychologists agree that the memory works in the way suggested by narrative theory: memories are organised in a narrative structure. Both groups also concur that this narrative framework can result in a misrepresentation that gets in the way of a proper furnishing of proof. According to the clinicians the dissociated memory of incest fails to provide proof precisely because it corresponds so directly with reality. Like the experimentalists, they assume in the end that there is a correspondence theory of truth, even though you can only approach this truth by way of a coherentist reconstruction.

The clinical standpoint however is internally incoherent. Even if the essence of traumatic experiences continues to be preserved through dissociation, the interpretative integration achieved during therapy still misrepresents the past because it is affected by the schematic prejudices of the client and therapist. According to Van der Hart and Terr, the dissociated experience has preserved its purity precisely because it is not embedded in existing patterns of signification. The therapeutic activities of naming and integration nevertheless still bring with them the delayed normal distortion. Van der Hart (1995) moreover has in the meantime retracted earlier publications in which he attributed a greater accuracy and degree of truth to traumatic memories than to normal narrative memories. He now acknowledges that these can also be affected by hallucinations and thus be completely untrue. This undermines his standpoint that therapists can still uncover the historical truth, on condition that they do not impose their own viewpoint on their patients and provided they verify their stories for coherence.

On the basis of considerations like this Reviere (1996) argues for making a clear distinction between the hypothetical narrative that is valid within the therapeutic relationship and the objective historical truth that is required in a lawcourt or elsewhere. The practical experience that clinical psychologists use as argument against empirical research into the memory, is after all limited to the stories of their clients. In therapy it is a matter of integrating disordered elements of the personality into a coherent story so that the patient can see his or her existence as structured and meaningful. This is by no means sufficient however for establishing a more objective truth, says Reviere. In terms of the coherence theory, the coherence of the therapeutic narrative is too local to pass for truth in law.

All in all, the dissociation theory is unable to incorporate the incoherences in the narratives of the parties to an incest trial in a more inclusive Great Narrative that would give a judge adequate external narrative coherence.

Research in the Social Sciences: Shifting Disclosure

This conclusion is not applicable however to allegations of incest that are not based on *recovered* memories, as in the case of Yolanda. How far is *My Story* supported by sociological research into incest and how does this relate to narrativity?

The most important Dutch study of incest victims is that of Draijer (1988), which resembles D.E.H. Russell's investigation in the USA of 1986 in its structure and findings. Draijer's research was based on 1054 detailed interviews with women from 20 to 40 years old. Of this group 164 women (15.6%) reported sexual assault before the age of 16 by members of their family, namely by fathers (3.2%) uncles (4.4%), brothers (4.4%) grandfathers (1.6%), cousins (1.6%) and brothers-in-law or other members of the household (1.5%).[11] 8.3% suffered sexual abuse by more than one family member. The abuse began at an average age of 11.4 (in 3.8% cases it begun when they were under 10 and in 7.4% under 12). It stopped at an average age of 14.1. With 37% of the victims it occurred only once. In two-thirds of the cases abuse continued over a period of two years or longer. Incestuous abuse varied from lighter cases (physical harassment with the victim dressed, 18.3%; with her naked, 34.6%) to more serious cases (attempted rape, 20.6% and actual penetration, 26.5%). A little less than half of the victims, 6.4% of the total, suffered serious abuse. Draijer concludes that at least one out of fifteen women has been confronted during her childhood with serious traumatic forms of sexual abuse by family members.

Most of the victims (84%) attempted unsuccessfully to resist the abuse. When this proved vain, they tried to survive the experience by adjusting their emotional lives with repression, flights into fantasy or dissociation:

> Denial of experiences of abuse, pretending they never happened, forgetting them as quickly as possible – behaviour like this appears to have occurred in virtually all the cases in this enquiry (five out of six), suggesting therefore that it is inherent in cases of sexual abuse in general. (p. 176)

Draijer discusses the possibility of her research offering misleading results. It poses questions about the past of only one of the parties possibly involved in incest. The later experiences or present state of mind of the victims can colour their memories. Draijer moreover stresses that repression and a partial or total forgetting of the occurrence are important defence mechanisms for them that would have considerable influence on their memory. Traumatic experiences can even lead to total amnesia. 'We have to take a paradox into account – can those people who cut off their feelings at the time have any possibility of access to these feelings now?' (p. 176). Draijer concludes: 'It is by definition doubtful if it is possible to research unconscious processes by questioning them directly' (p. 178).

According to Draijer the expected distortion will result in too low rather than too high a figure for incest victims. Initially incest victims tend to deny or make light of the event either from fear or from shame. There are more drawbacks than advantages for the victim in pressing a charge; the perpetrator will reject her, other family members will get angry. Preliminary research into a group of women who were able to speak about their experience more openly because they had previously talked about it has shown that in reality abuse occurs much more often and is much more serious than one would conclude from Draijer's random sample.

Against these arguments that cases of incest are under-reported counts the fact that Draijer's interview methods assume in advance that this will occur. Inconsistencies in the stories of the subjects about the seriousness, duration and frequency of the abuse, the identity of the perpetrator and the age of the victim are not treated by Draijer as a sign of unreliability, but as part of a process of what she calls 'shifting disclosure':

> Firstly there is denial that there was any case of sexual experiences, then come statements that it happened only once, then that the perpetrator came 'far from home', then that it occurred frequently and at a young age and finally that there was more than one perpetrator and that they lived 'closer to home' – this development is inherent in conversations about incest experiences. (p. 59)

On the basis of these assumptions the interviewers were trained to pick up non-verbal signals from the interviewees, even when they initially denied that they had been abused. With this selection of women the interviewers then had to continue asking the same questions very directly. To reduce the victim's anxiety it was the (female) interviewer who named the painful or taboo sexual experiences, while the respondent only had to give a yes or no answer. Outside Holland similar methods in research, such as that of Russell, also led to very high incest scores:

> Studies where use is made of interviews by trained female interviewers and a large number of 'entrance questions' that could cause the subjects to recall possible questions of abuse (...) give the highest scores for the prevalence of sexual abuse by family members (these vary from 15% to 18%). (p. 103)

Sceptics might argue against this form of enquiry that the active role played by the interviewers could have an influence on suggestible interviewees, thus producing the expected result and exaggerated figures. In people with severe traumatic complaints such as depressions and anxiety neuroses, possibly as a result of far-reaching affective neglect, guidance of this sort can play on a need to find a definite external cause for their suffering. The story of the interviewee is then made externally coherent by matching the general psychological story of the researcher.

Although Crombag and Merckelbach implicitly accept Draijer's findings about the factual scope and seriousness of incest, their argument undermines the part of her conclusions that is based on recovered memories. According to Draijer, 57% of her victims of repeated incest completely forgot the abuse they had suffered: 'I still don't know exactly what happened. It is an empty spot in my memory' (p. 174). 80% of the repeated cases had in one form or another mentally blocked out what had happened, making it unclear whether what was involved was dissociation or deliberate denial. With these respondents Draijer's interviewers used the sort of directive questions that Reviere and later, more cautiously, Van der Hart deemed unacceptable. Therapy is not supposed to be structured like 'an archaeological dig of sorts to find a hidden trauma' (Reviere, 1996, p. 118), but sociological studies of incest do look like this. Narrative coherence is forced here by the fact that the stories of the interviewees are fitted in with the postulated theoretical narrative of the researcher.

Draijer's conclusions can be seen as a narrative reconstruction of the stories of the women interviewed which in turn contain reconstructions of their past. The risk of distortion is thus considerable, especially where loss of memory is involved. Nonetheless, even if one subtracts from Draijer's findings about the extent of serious cases of incest the 57% where there is doubt, there are still enough cases to speak of a disturbing phenomenon that deserves serious attention in criminal proceedings. In cases of conflicting stories about a concrete allegation of incest however it is insufficient in itself to suggest that the indictment is true. There is, for that matter, no lack of well-documented instances of false accusations. Here too Yolanda's story is not made sufficiently plausible by any external coherence with a Great Narrative about incest.

Narrative Incoherence

Cases of incest therefore correspond precisely with the narrativist theory of theoreticians such as 't Hart (1983):

> ... if the law turns out to be a form of 'a story' it is in any case no longer an adequate evaluation (by the subject) of the reality (as object). (p. 416)

Cases like Yolanda's are dominated exclusively by contradictory stories; outside of them, it is impossible to find any evidence of the controversial incest. The narrative character of incest cases is reinforced by the fact that more and more voices are taking part in the debate. Due to feminism, it is currently not only the male perpetrator's story that gets heard; the female victim has been given a voice too. Furthermore, in the previous century the unconscious was discovered. The narrative of the victim is now split into the contradictory stories of the conscious and the unconscious. A number of the victims have later given written descriptions of their own stories of incest: it is only when they reach adulthood that they remember that they were sexually abused in their childhood. In the years in between the conscious ego had no knowledge of it because the terrifying experience had been driven from the conscious mind through dissociation. This at least is what a number of psychiatrists would have us believe. There is however no agreement among the experts about the likelihood of lost memories of this sort. Some psychologists cast doubt on them appealing to empirical research into the functioning of memory and arguing that when someone has really gone through such traumatic experiences, she is likely to remember them all too well. According to these experts memories that surface much later during therapy are based on therapeutic suggestion. The same criticism also pertains to detailed questionnaires of women such as that carried out by Draijer who showed that 6.4% of all women had suffered from incestuous abuse in childhood and that 3.2% of them had been abused by their father figure. Here too the interviewers may well have bent the stories of the women interviewed to fit the theoretical narrative of the researcher. In short, incest would seem to be the prototype of the narrativist court case: there are stories everywhere but the referent is nowhere.

According to 't Hart the narrative nature of criminal law means that lawyers and judges should abandon their claim

> ... that the criminal procedure is about the ascertaining of the material truth, usually in the sense of what 'really happened'. The perpetrator is then deemed really to have committed what has been declared proven concerning him, with the guilty verdict forming the core of what 'really happened'. (p. 438)

Focqué and 't Hart see this as a way of liberating the law from a too rigid juridical formalism; they want criminal proceedings to become more open to the diversity of stories that are presently excluded by the prevailing legal dogma. The ultimate consequences of such a view would almost amount to accepting free association as acceptable evidence; it would make the practice of criminal law as speculative as Freud's interpretation of dreams.

In a story like Yolanda's, how can one ever achieve the narrative coherence that the narrativists regard as a criterion for ascertaining the punishable facts in the minor premise? The stories of the victims are internally incoherent and the suspects deny everything. At a theoretical level the experts contradict each other about the reliability of memory. This conflict between specialists is in part due to a clash at the meta-level of epistemology and scientific methodology: should you prove a theory of human consciousness with empirical data or can you arrive at it by way of the hermeneutic perceptions of psychotherapists?

The same sort of conflict recurs in legal epistemology when it is a matter of proving a punishable offence. As against the notion that truth means a correspondence with the facts, narrativists propose a hermeneutic criterion for the plausibility of narrative coherence; the credibility of a witness is determined by comparing his testimony with model stories, or social constructions that reflect everyday experience. The whole has to conform to the narrative pattern of the world-view of the parties to the case. This all-embracing coherence criterion is based on the optimistic assumption that something more than a purely local coherence is possible – otherwise narrative plausibility would cease the moment that stories conflict. But in the light of the Yolanda case there is no guarantee whatsoever that the different stories can be arranged to form a coherent all-inclusive whole. In a pluralistic world, where is the 'model narrative' about incest that can decide the issue once and for all? The more narrative a situation, the less coherent it is.

Coherentism versus Foundationalism

Reference

Suppose that even given all the difficulties it were possible within the western world-view to construct a Great Narrative about a problem such as incest, that could serve as a framework for testing the external narrative coherence of concrete stories of incest. Even then no case in criminal law can dispense with any reference to basic experiential data.

Nonetheless, in a confrontation between foundationalists and coherentists, coherentism is in the first instance stronger than the foundationalist theory that sensory experience forms the basis for our knowledge of reality. Coherentists contest the two central propositions of the theory known as *foundationalism*: (1) That a privileged subclass of beliefs based on direct sensory and introspective experience is justifiable as such, independently of whether it is confirmed by other beliefs; (2) that these empirical beliefs serve as a basis for justifying all other beliefs. Coherentism also opposes the ontological claim of *realism* with which this foundationalist epistemology is often combined, namely that (3) this empirical belief is the product of an independent external reality (including introspective observation caused by one's own processes of consciousness). *Coherentism* rejects the foundationalist division into foundation and superstructure, making the justification of every belief dependent on whether it is consistent with other beliefs. Against (1) the coherentists offer the holistic theory that every observation is contained in a network of interpretations, so that an empirical belief derives its meaning from its place within a system of concepts.[12] In contrast with the realist position therefore (3) Jackson also refuses to speak of any reference to any reality outside language:

> The question of the referent is then reduced to the question of the correlation between two semiotic systems (for example, natural languages and natural semiotics ...). This is a problem of inter-semioticity (cf. intertextuality). (Jackson, 1985, p. 15)

Coherentists often add here that sensory impressions permit a great variety of interpretations, so that theories about reality remain empirically underdetermined.

The first round is won by coherentism, because this conflict between foundationalists-cum-realists on the one hand and coherentists on the other can only be resolved through the coherence criterion. Anyone who assumes the foundation in advance in order to provide his foundationalism with a foundation is guilty of circular dogmatism. Moreover the basic empirical beliefs of the foundationalist position (1) offer insufficient support to the realist assumption (3) of the existence of an external reality: human experience is internal to consciousness and does not therefore immediately give us access to any independent external world. In accordance with Descartes' sceptical argument, sensory perceptions are just as likely to be illusions produced by an evil demon. In that case there is also no reason for allowing experience a privileged position. Consequently only a coherentist reconstruction of the totality of beliefs can indicate which notion about reality and knowledge is plausible.

There follows a second round between coherentism and foundationalism; this time however a more moderate form of foundationalism takes the lead as the most convincing theory of knowledge. Admittedly Cartesian scepticism is theoretically difficult to disprove, but it is incoherent with the pragmatic beliefs of the majority of people: in their everyday transactions the latter base themselves on a common sense idea of an outside world. If scepticism is put in parentheses as being unpractical, then the hypotheses of foundationalism and realism do offer a reasonable alternative. The assumption that our perceptions are directed causally by an external reality gives our system of everyday and scientific convictions the greatest degree of coherence. It makes it plausible that sensory perceptions surface involuntarily, that the empirical world shows continuity and coherence and that other people experience it in the same way. It also takes account of the practical success of science and of the role that experiments play in this. The scientific doctrine of evolution may add to this the argument that human capacity for knowledge adapts adequately to its environment: for this reason one can assume *prima facie* that under normal circumstances everyday experience offers us a reliable reflection of reality, thus forming a foundation stone for human knowledge.

The coherentism that in the second instance as well refuses to grant special status to empirical beliefs is implausible however from the point of view of its own coherence criterion. It takes no account of the special place granted to experience in substantiating the truth on the basis of which we make a distinction between a coherent empirical theory and a coherent fairy story. The coherentist perception that empirical beliefs are affected by theories does however undermine a number of overly radical assumptions of classical foundationalist tenets: legitimation is not a one-way street from foundation to superstructure, because empirical beliefs are not indubitable facts but fallible interpretations; their justification depends in part on conceptual consistencies and background theories.

By way of a similar sort of coherentist argument at a meta-level Susan Haack (1995) arrives in the second instance at her *foundherentism*, that unites the plausible elements of foundationalism and coherentism in a more coherent synthesis. Haack offers her alternative as an explication of the common sense notion of justification: it is aimed at truth, thus the criteria must be truth-indicative, and reference to an external reality is posited. In this respect second-instance coherence falls short of the mark, because coherence is no guarantee of a connection with any reality. Furthermore the involuntary character of perception supports the realistic supposition that human beings are organisms with sense organs that provide information about the outside world. The theory of evolution makes it plausible that human beings have survived because our cognitive faculty is tuned into our surroundings: we can arrive by trial and error at classifications that correspond to natural kinds, clusters of real comparisons. In the process of justification, Haack attributes a privileged position to empirical beliefs on the grounds of this coherentist reconstruction. She regards an empirical belief such as 'I am now seeing a piece of white paper' as only trustworthy *prima facie*. A direct report of a sensory experience too is based on fallible interpretation; on closer inspection it can turn out to be a hallucination. If reasons arise for doubting the reliability of a concrete empirical belief, it can draw support from non-empirical beliefs. The circumstances under which the empirical belief came about can for instance be tested against a theory about the process of perception: if the subject is influenced by serious anxieties or by alcohol then the reliability of his experience is diminished. Something similar is also true of the reliability of memories. Coherentist criteria then do play a role here, so that unlike in classical foundationalism an interchange does occur between foundation and superstructure. The degree to which a belief about one's direct experience is justified, depends, in Haack's view, on the nature of independent certainty, the degree of corroboration, and the extent to which it is consistent with all the remaining evidence (above all negative evidence: it is not justified when it takes no account of relevant evidence to the contrary).

> A is more justified in believing that p the better this belief is anchored in experience and supported by other beliefs by being integrated into an explanatory story the components of which are also anchored in experience and supported by other beliefs ... etc. (p. 212)

The 'superstructural' beliefs do not depend entirely for their justification on empirical beliefs either; they also require mutual support.

Coherentism in short is only plausible when it draws a distinction between two different levels. On the meta-level of the philosophical theory of knowledge neither foundationalism nor Haack's foundherentism are a match for it. At the level of the actual ascertaining of truth however it must still ascribe a basic role to an independent and knowable reality.

Coherence and Reference in Criminal Law

The same train of thought is applicable to the search for the truth in criminal proceedings. From his meta-level coherentism Jackson arrives incorrectly at a second instance coherentism: in furnishing proof in the law-courts what is involved is persuasion by means of a plausible story without any referent. For example the words of a witness

> ... do not 'refer' to the past events; these words construct a reality of their own, and the witness claims that we should believe that this constructed reality corresponds to what actually happened. However, since any account of what actually happened is constructed within a particular discourse, we cannot ultimately establish any link between the claim made in language and the outside reality, other than noting that the truth-claim is actually made. (Jackson, 1990, p. 381)

Against Jackson's narrativism, a first order coherentist reconstruction also results in a leading role for an empirical foundation in the second instance.

Internal coherence in a story means more than just its consistency: not only should the different elements not be in contradiction, they should also support each other in a hierarchical structure that is determined by the point or points of the story. In this way it is possible to distinguish subordinate parts that have a supportive function with regard to more central elements. In a nineteenth century novel for instance the descriptions of nature often provide a background that suggests the mood for the dramatic confrontations among the leading characters.[13] A coherentist reconstruction of a practice such as criminal law offers the same structure. A central point of criminal law is to sentence offenders on the basis of legally obtained adequate evidence. The gathering of evidence is subordinate to this end and presupposes reference to real events: if all the parties to the case believed that the witnesses had nothing to offer but rhetoric without a scrap of truth, criminal law would be meaningless. In the practice of law the common sense assumption prevails of an external reality that can be reproduced by the furnishing of proof. It is a matter of condemning the real perpetrator of a real crime. There is also a general agreement here about what transactions count as such and what sufficient proof consists of. In arriving at the truth empirical evidence is granted a privileged place, and scientific knowledge is regarded as having authority.[14] The weighing of witches no longer belongs to the acceptable means of proof; instead of trial by ordeal, we have the opinions of expert witnesses. If I kill someone with a knife, this qualifies as murder, and if, on arrested, a bloody knife is found in my pocket, this can qualify as proof of my guilt. This empirical evidence is reinforced when scientific analysis shows that the blood is that of the victim. Even if an empirical basis such as this is purely conventional as narrative coherentists argue, the conventions are granted a privileged place in establishing the truth. The assumption of a separate reality is also inherent in Jackson's own concept of external coherence in legal discourse: the minor story has to fit in with the prevailing 'standard narratives' and world-view.[15] Their everyday view of reality is indeed based on a naive realism pertaining to the distinction between subject and object, illusion and reality, fact and fiction. A reconstruction of the criminal law on the basis of an internal coherence should then take into account this function of empirical evidence in view of the tenor of the practice of criminal law, so that the coherence theory still leads to a correspondence criterion even if by a roundabout route.

The coherentist may then conclude that this reconstruction is unsustainable due to external incoherence – for instance because an independent reality existing outside language is unknowable – as a result however the whole point of the practice in question is undermined. As long as it is only

168 Reasoning in Ethics and Law

at a meta-level that he announces that the posited empirical basis is eventually determined by narrative conventions, there is no great problem; however, as soon as he posits his own meta-insight *instead* of the prevailing notions, the practice of criminal law acquires a meaningless make-believe character.[16] A judge cannot take sides in a conflict such as that between Yolanda and her parents without being open to the charge of cynicism, if he is not permitted to assume that one story demonstrably corresponds with the reality more than the other.

And this departure point is justified: a cynical redefinition of criminal law in a narrativist sense is not necessary now that it has been shown that at a general epistemic level a moderate foundationalism and realism are plausible, amongst other things because of the dominant role played by experience in the process of acquiring knowledge. Even if you acknowledge that there isn't any such thing as a pure, uninterpreted fact, you can still differentiate within people's thought processes between interpretations that tally closely with a presumably independent reality on the one hand and pure fiction on the other. In criminal proceedings too a place still emerges for a moderate form of foundationalism within coherentism.

It is in this spirit that the psychologists Wagenaar, Van der Koppen and Crombag (1993) have proposed further empirical requirements for proof in criminal proceedings. In the first place the narrative element must be *plausible* with a coherent, true-to-life story being told with a clear central transaction that occurs under circumstances that account for this transaction. Secondly the story must be *anchored* by way of evidence in knowledge of the empirical world as this is generally understood by reasonable people. In legal practice however one is often satisfied with a plausible story without ensuring that it is sufficiently anchored. Those elements that don't tally with the story are erroneously ignored. According to the authors there should at least be sufficient empirical evidence for the identity of the perpetrator, for the way that the crime occurred in accordance with the description of the offence and for the guilt of the perpetrator. The judge may not base himself on notions about reality that are demonstrably incorrect, for instance that the evidence of a police officer is automatically reliable. He must also explicitly indicate why he does not regard as convincing any alternative stories or empirical evidence to the contrary. Such empirical proof can only be given in an indirect fashion – so far the narrative theory of law is correct. In Dutch criminal proceedings the following elements are considered as lawful means of establishing proof: the observations of the judge during the proceedings, the explanations of suspects, witnesses and experts and of written documents. These verbal and written narratives however do have to be anchored in external reality. Due to the indirect character of this empirical proof, there is a risk of a process of infinite regress of justification, that the judge must respond to by making the anchoring explicit in his verdict. In short, Wagenaar, Van der Koppen and Crombag assume that it is possible to achieve a reasonable agreement about the empirical reality against which the legal narrative must be tested.[17]

Due to anchored empirical beliefs being given a privileged position in the furnishing of proof in criminal proceedings a distinction can be made between justified and non-justified narratives. No longer then does the judge drown in a plurality of incoherent attributions of meaning that narrativists such as Focqué and 't Hart serve him up with. Even in polysemic incest cases it is still possible then to reach verdicts that can be justified.

Truth in Incest Cases

What does this theory of justification mean for incest cases? In the present debate a reasonable consensus prevails about the core definition of incest, or rather about which actual transactions can in any case be considered as grievous incest.[18] As usual it is the borderline cases that need discussion, but the description of the offence itself of incest is not theoretically in question. The rational dissensus concentrates on the ascertaining of the minor premise of the juridical syllogism and on what qualifies as proof there: can you point to a correspondence between the allegation that incest has taken place and what actually occurred?

But this difference of opinion about the relation between narrative and reality also remains limited. The matter is clear when the victim's statement is supported by evidence from other sources, such as the existence of offspring, traces of sperm, photos, videos, accounts of third parties and a confession by the perpetrator, as long as it is not contradicted by evidence to the contrary.

What if, as in Yolanda's case, all one has is the opposing accounts of the litigants about what actually took place? The disputed event took place in the past and is not therefore directly accessible. Experts moreover disagree about the question as to whether it is possible to assess the veracity of such stories after the fact by means of psychological interpretation. With good reason and to ensure that innocent people are not found guilty the Dutch penal code imposes the burden of proof on the public prosecutor. According to the unwritten rules of the law of proof, the suspect is considered innocent till there is proof to the contrary; where there is doubt, this is explained to his advantage. The judge must be convinced that the suspect has in fact committed the crime, and his belief must be based on lawful proof.[19] Proof would be insufficient mean for instance if there was no more than one statement from one witness (art. 342 section 3 Sv) or from the suspect himself (art. 341 section 4 Sv). An allegation of incest does not in itself offer sufficient proof.[20] In Dutch law then a reasonable degree of agreement prevails over what the extreme cases are and of what in any case should qualify as sufficient or insufficient proof. The dispute concentrates around the twilight areas.

What if the victim's narrative is supported by the claim of a psychotherapist that his psychological investigation of the plaintiff shows that the charge is true? In 1995 The Dutch Supreme Court (Hoge Raad) in a civil lawsuit – where less stringent rules of proof apply than in criminal law – established that a report by experts can provide sufficient complementary evidence to arrive at a verdict (HR 17.11.1995, NJ 1996, 666). In doing so the Supreme Court quashed the Court of Appeal's statement that a report like this has no independent value because its only source is the information of the plaintiff. The grounds for appeal against the verdict of the Appeals Court was that an expert also bases his knowledge on his research at the university and his practical experience, so that he has objective criteria by which he can check the plaintiff's story. The expert states that he can deduce from the present subjective experiential world of the woman what must have occurred objectively in her childhood; her current psychological traumas made it plausible that she was sexually abused in her youth; her information about being abused by her father and brother was extremely convincing, so that one can assume that it was based on authentic memories; the fact that the perpetrator denied all this was in the expert's view typical of the behaviour of sexual offenders. According to the victim, in view of this evidence the accused now had to prove that he had not abused his sister. The Supreme Court endorsed that the statement of an expert could be sufficient evidence, especially in cases such as incest where only the plaintiff and defendant had direct knowledge. The judge should however treat the experts' reports with great circumspection.

Indeed expert reports should be treated very critically due to their fundamental theoretical and methodological differences of opinion. As a solution for 'the battle of experts' Wagenaar et al. (1993) propose at any rate to make a thorough investigation of the competence of the expert in question and the reliability of his method. An expert should thus himself make a statement about the diagnostic value of his research method. According to the research carried out by Jampole and Weber for instance, the test with 'anatomical dolls' has led to 18% of mistaken convictions of sexual abuse of children. The test therefore does not offer much basis in itself.[21] As for the directive method that a remedial educationalist added to the dolls' test, it is without question unsound: like Draijer's interviewers it indicated the assumed sexual transactions and got the children to give yes or no answers (Wagenaar et al., 1993, p. 190 ff.)

A similar unreliability also taints clinical psychologists' interpretations of such narratives. A psychologist cannot state the causes of a psychological trauma with the same degree of confidence as a doctor can with a physical injury. A stab would suggest a blow with a knife, but for eating disorders various conflicting explanations are given; not only sexual abuse but also more symbolic problems may play a role; anorexia nervosa in women for instance has been attributed to an exaggerated need to meet an ideal of slenderness, but also to an attempt to deny one's own femininity by becoming shapeless. As we saw earlier, clinical interpretations have turned out to be so controversial that they cannot reasonably be regarded as providing sufficient grounds for persuading a judge that the suspect is guilty of the offence. In this regard the 'battle of the experts' goes against clinical psychologists and psychiatrists such as Terr and Van der Hart. This conclusion also affects the value of the non-verbal grounds of proof that Draijer regards as important.

Suppose however that the accusation is supplemented with a suspect's confession that is later withdrawn as in the case of Yolanda. According to Dutch law, if it was a matter of a single isolated confession, proof would be insufficient, even if the suspect hadn't later withdrawn his confession. The English and American legal systems take a different view, but their stance is not all that convincing here. Although a confession in any normal case does serve as a good indication of the guilt of the perpetrator – in by far the greater majority of criminal proceedings this remains uncontested – it cannot escape a suspicion of reasonable doubt, due to the danger of false confessions. Wagenaar et al. (1993) point to the murder of the well-known millionaire Gerrit Jan Hein for which a number of pseudo-perpetrators claimed responsibility. According to them voluntary false confessions can be prompted by pathological fantasies or a neurotic need for punishment, or out of a need to protect the party who is actually guilty. A confession may moreover come about under pressure from police officers who take the suspect's statement. More simple-minded suspects are very vulnerable to suggestion by authority figures.

The confessions of Yolanda's parents did not exist in isolation however; they also tallied with the victim's allegations. Against this counts the fact that they were later replaced by decisive disavowals. What value then does a confession have as incidental proof? The same criteria apply to confessions as to all types of evidence. According to Van der Koppen (1994) the initial hearing is particularly important, because it is then that the slightest distortion caused by influencing and fixing of the memory will appear. The interrogation must be carried out in a neutral fashion by specialised detectives – not by therapists because they do not see the difference between establishing the truth and social work. These initial interrogations must be recorded on sound cassettes so that they can be reproduced and verified. After this you can check the contents of the confession for coherence (is the story the same as that of earlier and later statements?) and correspondence (does it contain intimate information and does it contain plenty of details that can be verified?). The same applies however to the disavowals. If both stories are coherent, only correspondence can decide the issue.

In the case of Yolanda the police of Epe were clearly implicated in Yolanda's story. A detective admitted that he had told the father that Yolanda would commit suicide if he didn't make a confession. The parents moreover seem to have been very suggestible. Just as, according to Loftus (1994) an incest suspect can be persuaded to believe that he had forced his son and daughter to have sexual intercourse with each other, so a lawyer as a test succeeded in getting Yolanda's mother to make the untrue statement that she had murdered her neighbour. According to Wagenaar (1994), under unacceptable pressure from the police the confessions of Yolanda's parents showed such untrue or impossible statements that the consistent parts were also tainted.

In short, as long as all one has are conflicting statements by the parties involved and the interpretations by experts of these statements, we have narratives but no justification.

Conclusion

In recent years the classical syllogistic model for legal debate has often been linked with a coherentist viewpoint of the major and minor premises in concrete lawsuits. This means that a requirement of *narrative coherence* applies to the minor premise that in combination with the major premise indicates the relevant facts.

The general perception is that the 'legal facts' represented in the minor premise do not form any objective reflection of observable reality such as a correspondence criterion of truth would require: that which is regarded as a fact as such is a product of interpretation and construction. The most extreme form of this mode of thinking is the *narrative theory of law*, that treats both the normative and the empirical part of the juridical verdict as a story that doesn't refer to any external non-narrative reality. What alternative truth does a notion of law offer when it makes no theoretical distinction between fact and fiction? According to the narrativists you should judge the plausibility of stories like this on the basis of a coherence criterion. It should comprise an internally coherent whole, it must conform with other stories and it must be tally with the prevailing narrative world- view.

In this extreme form the narrative theory of law falls short of its mark, because the accusation remains fatally underdetermined. This is particularly clear in incest cases such as that of Yolanda. What we get there is a spectacle of conflicting versions of the litigants and their representatives, legal authorities and psychologists clashing with each other as they weave a tangle of stories without any referent, because the original crime cannot be ascertained. If every case contained so much narrative judges would have to give up the struggle and seek employment writing thrillers.

The narrative theory is an understandable response to the decline of classical metaphysics, in which reality as a whole is presented as rational and coherent, with human knowledge being viewed as ideally speaking a rational reflection of this. When science as successor to classical meta-physics failed to fulfil the modernist expectation that its theories would be an exact reflection of the pure facts, it became evident that human knowl-edge should be conceived of as a narrative arrangement of different patterns of interpretation. From this standpoint coherence is no longer a token of re-ality itself but rather of human cognitive organisation.

The question arises however of whether truth as coherence can have any meaning any longer. The classical metaphysical unity of the True, the Good and the Beautiful has disintegrated into a plurality of heterogeneous practices. The danger is that all that will remain will be fragmented partial theories; at most they will show an internal coherence, but they will not tally with each other, nor can they be tested against each other for their plausibility. The Surrealists saw life itself as being so incoherent that they rejected every attempt to come up with a consistent story. The narrative theoretician 't Hart was no less radical in rejecting the rigidity of legal dogmatism. As Louis Aragon wrote:

> It would seem, it is said, or to put it more precisely it is insinuated that all of this will end up as a story. Maybe for bastards, that's what I say. They see novels or novelettes in everything. There are people who only need to see a man with a red hat to make a whole story of it. For people like that everything is material for a story: a piece of wood, adultery or a gardenia. A tedious mountain of stories. (...) It is a bourgeois habit to want to turn everything everywhere into a narrative. (p. 78)

Narrativism degenerates thus into a cacophony of narrators making pro-nouncements one on top of the other, without any criterion that might still preserve something of the classical *harmony of the spheres*. In such a plu-ralist world it is impossible for a judge to reach a rational verdict that would comply with the criterion for external coherence.

The radical identification of reality and law with literary fiction or nar-rative is however a romantic exaggeration. One has every reason for making a distinction between truth and fancy. According to my own theory of Critical Schizoism, you cannot refute scepticism if you take the role of an outside spectator to an extreme, but in everyday life you can suspend your sceptical judgement.[22] From the point of view of a coherentist recon-struction at the meta-level or epistemology it is plausible for the level of the concrete search for the truth to draw a distinction between fact and fiction.

The coherence requirement needs further definition to comply with the human practice of knowledge. Maybe coherence is perfect in the imaginary world of literature, but in the sciences it must be supplemented by a moderate form of empirical foundationalism, due to the central role that experience plays there. In the latter case this leads to a moderate correspondence theory of truth that rejects the extreme requirement that a story should offer an exact copy of this reality. In the justification of claims to truth then it is a matter of an interaction between coherence and basic empirical beliefs.

Because of its hybrid normative character, the law calls for a fairly complicated set of criteria. In judicial procedures you can discern a variety of narrative structures that reach a syllogism in the verdict: judicial dogmatism, social reality and the reality of the law – each of these factors tells its own story. But normative reality can be constructed more freely than empirical reality, due to the limitations imposed by experience on itself in the case of the latter. Even if every statement about empirical reality is based on hypotheses, the building blocks of these hypotheses are not purely fictitious in character; the person constructing them cannot create them out of nothing. The coherence criterion for truth can thus be applied in law at most in a differentiated form. In the judicial search for the truth plausible coherent stories do play an important role. In the domain of the narrative coherence of the minor premise however a reasonable, experience-based agreement must prevail over what qualifies as empirical referents, and how a narrative reconstruction of a crime can be anchored in it.

Even in cases of incest it is theoretically not impossible to make it convincing beyond reasonable doubt that the allegation corresponds to reality: fundamentally speaking it is not controversial what transactions qualify as incest, nor what qualifies as compelling evidence – for instance, traces of sperm on a woman who is under age that are identified as belonging to her father. In Yolanda's case there was no such evidence. If Yolanda's story were taken in itself, her single statement would in terms of Dutch law be insufficient to qualify as proof. In fact her statement was supported by that of psychologists who testified that her story was plausible. This additional evidence was also insufficient however, since it was contradicted by other psychologists; clinical interpretation in general moreover is regarded as not very reliable. A second validation of Yolanda's allegations comes from the initial confessions of her parents. These however were produced by unacceptable pressure from criminal investigators and contain too many material inaccuracies. Yolanda's own statements also lack credibility, since they are both implausible and have insufficient empirical anchoring. Her accusation is demonstrably in conflict with the facts at certain points: the numerous alleged abortions and maltreatments would have had to leave some physical scars, the constant series of pregnancies and abortions is biologically impossible. The sadistic universe in Yolanda's story can moreover more readily be explained in terms of her own obsessions than of the actual sadistic inclinations of half the population of a small Dutch town: even though it is believable that they may have benefitted from Yolanda's prostitution, it is improbable that they all participated eagerly in far-reaching practices of mutilation and torture. This leaves unanswered the question of how to account for the prevailing atmosphere of sadism in Yolanda's tale. She may well have suffered some traumatic experience, but speculation like this does not qualify as evidence in criminal proceedings. In Yolanda's case then the Appeals Court was erroneous in coming to the verdicts it did.

The narrative theory of law is based on a romantic exaggeration of the story-telling element in law. While scientific positivism was naive in expecting to obtain direct access to the pure facts of a case, it remains fundamentally important to follow the father of positivism Auguste Comte in drawing a firm distinction between the 'observing mind' and the 'imaginative mind'. In this spirit Dutch judges should take more care to ensure that their verdicts have an empirical foundation than is now the case. While it is true that you can sum up the whole dogmatism of law, everyday social reality and the entire world-view of a society as consisting of stories, you will still have to find a loophole to admit all the traditional notions of truth in order to make rational discussion possible within the different realms of life, including that of the law. This transcendental argument is supported by the overwhelming role that empirical experience plays in our acquisition of knowledge. Within a coherence theory about the juridical discourse you are still obliged to draw a line between fact and fiction and to assume the existence of an external reality that imposes restraints on too free an interpretation of the law. In this way the truth of law becomes an ordered interplay of coherence, rational consensus, pragmatism and correspondence: the story must be plausible in the terms of the reasonable expectations of all the parties to the law; at essential points moreover it must display a demonstrable conformity with the empirical reality as this is critically defined on the basis of human experience and scientific knowledge, and which is validated in part at least by successful practical application.

Notes

1   This article is translated from the Dutch by Donald Gardner. I would like to thank M. den Boer, B.S. Jackson, F.C.L.M. Jacobs, A.W. Musschenga, G.J. Postema and S.A.M. Stolwijk for their helpful suggestions.

2   Dutch criminal law (article 246, penal code) punishes anyone who coerces another person to commit indecent acts with penalties of up to eight years prison on the charge of 'offences against morality'; article 242 punishes rape (forcible sexual penetration, with a maximum penalty of twelve years. Furthermore, if the victim suffers grievous bodily harm, then the penalty is a maximum of twelve years. Voluntary sexual intercourse and indecent behaviour with minors under sixteen years old is also punishable. Sexual intercourse and indecent behaviour with minors of between twelve and sixteen is dealt with in articles 245 and 247 (maximums of eight and six years respectively), but prosecution is only initiated after an official indictment. If the victim is under twelve, article 244 raises the sentence for sexual intercourse to a maximum of twelve years. Article 249 imposes sentences of a maximum of six years on defendants who have committed indecent acts with one of their children.

3   In this regard Den Boer (1990) points out that the language of the law creates its own institutionalised reality with lawyers and judges playing the role of second narrator: the stories of the subjects of the law such as plaintiff and defendants in a case of incest are 'translated' by legal narrators such as the investigating detectives, judges or magistrates into the structure of the legal text. The story of the suspect gets distorted moreover due to the fact that the power relation between him and his cross-examiners is asymmetric.

4   Criminal lawyers and judges should moreover read more novels to enlarge their imagination and capacity for empathy. The literary narrative provides us with a far deeper insight into human life than does science or scholarship. It can 'tell of paradoxes, contradictions and aporias that prevail in concrete human existence (...) in a different way than that suggested in the unambiguous patterns and seamless descriptions of reality one gets in the law or the social sciences' (p. 364). More authors have pointed out the similarities between law and literature – for instance, Cardozo (1921), White (1973), Dworkin (1986),

Weisberg (1992), Nussbaum (1995). Others have emphasized the narrative rather than the literary character of the law, for instance Van Roermund (1993) and Den Boer (1990).

5 I will discuss the 'normative coherence' of the major premise in cases of incest in another article. Also see note 18.

6 In as much as *My Story* is internally coherent this is due to the way that the editor, Bob Snoijink, a professional writer, has arranged this material of incoherent fragments of interviews. 'After countless days of interviews I have fitted the hundred pieces of her mammoth jigsaw puzzle, giving them some shape (...)' (Foreword).

7 Marianne Cense and Gerdie Ketelaars (1994).

8 The term was recently rechristened *Dissociative Identity Disorder* because 'personality' was felt to be too vague a term.

9 In a letter to a Dutch daily, *De Volkskrant* of 27 April 1996 Liz Bijnsdorp wrote, 'I will not tolerate being attacked by these two specialists because I suffer from multiple personality syndrome with 147 alter egos. I have fought for years to put this all too ingenious survival strategy behind me and have done so successfully.'

10 The objection of Crombag and Merckelbach to Linda Meyer's prospective research is that it is premature, not that it is wrong. In this research women who were treated in a hospital in connection with sexual abuse were interviewed seventeen years later. A good third of them said that they did not remember anything of the abuse they suffered. Crombag and Merckelbach argue that this still does not prove that traumatic occurrences are inevitably forgotten for many years. It is possible that the victims don't remember anything because they were younger than two years old at the time; perhaps they were not informed of the real reason for their being hospitalised, or else the abuse did not actually take place or the interviewees may have felt ashamed and thus denied that anything took place.

11 24.4% reported abuse by non-family members, with 77.5% of the instances being perpetrated by people they knew. In general 34% had experienced some form of sexual abuse. Two thirds of the interviewees had voluntarily taken part before they were thirteen in non-traumatizing sexual experiments with people of their own age.

12 I only discuss the holistic version of coherentism here; for a more detailed theory, see Lehrer (1974). A coherentist justification in a linear sense diminishes in infinite regress.

13 In the semiotic structure of narrative the central component is the purpose of the behaviour of a protagonist.

14 Inasmuch as research into decision-making by juries shows that in fact they are more likely to treat as true a plausible untrue story than a truthful but im-

plausible one (see Bennett and Feldman, 1981, but criticised by Jackson, 1996), this doesn't prove anything except that people can make mistakes: when members of a jury are confronted with the factual untruth of their reconstruction, they will correct their mistake.

15   The same goes for the psychologists and psychiatrists. Both empiricists and clinicians assume that memories may refer to real events.

16   Jackson (1996) does not himself come to the 'strongly sceptical' conclusion that the law must therefore disappear as an ideological sham. Rather he opts for the 'moderately sceptical' theory that plausibility does not contain any truth, but can provide confirmation. For a narrativist however this is hardly coherent.

17   Jackson's criticism of Wagenaar's theory of anchored narratives (1996) is that it tries to have its cake and eat it, by drawing on two conflicting epistemological theories – both narrativism and traditional correspondence theory. Wagenaar erroneously makes a distinction between the plausibility of a narrative and the evidence, so that the latter acquires an autonomous referential character. According to Jackson that which presents itself as evidence is itself a part of the narrative coherence of the story as a whole. On the other hand, see Morley (1996). I present Wagenaar's 'anchored narratives' here as making an adequate synthesis of foundationalism and coherentism.

18   The prohibition on incest in the major premise meets with the criterion of 'normative coherence'; it fits in perfectly with the principles of individual integrity and autonomy that are fundamental in western legal tradition. As persons in the process of growing up, children are exceptionally dependent on their parents. The abuse of power by their father or mother, especially in the intimate domain of their sexuality, implies a serious hazard for their future development.

19   Dutch criminal law has a negative system of proof that only imposes certain formal limits on what is acceptable evidence. Otherwise it is up to the judge to assess it. In this regard Holland belongs to the other legal systems of continental Europe that, unlike the United States, do not impose any detailed stipulations on what counts as evidence.

20   Wagenaar et al. (1993) also point out that Dutch judges impose extremely loose requirements on additional evidence. It does not need to be any direct confirmation of the indictment. Additional evidence in an incest trial may include the medical statement that the daughter (in the meantime cohabiting with her friend) was no longer a virgin, plus the statement by the father that he had on occasion been alone at home with his daughter (HR 8.11.1988, no. 83, p. 887).

21   According to the Supreme Court the judge is obliged to state explicitly why he wants the results of this test to be used even though the defence is critical of it (HR 28 February 1989, NJ 1989, p. 748).
22   Maris, 1990.

References

Audi, R. (1993), *The Structure of Justification*, Cambridge University Press, Cambridge, Mass.

Bender, J.W. (ed.) (1989), *The Current State of Coherence Theory*, Kluwer Academic Publishers, Dordrecht.

Bennett, W.L. and Feldman, M.S. (1981), *Constructing Reality in the Courtroom*, Tavistock, London.

Boer, M. den (1980), 'A Linguistic Analysis of Narrative Coherence in the Court-Room', in P. Nerhot (ed.), *Law, Interpretation and Reality*, Kluwer Academic Publishers, Dordrecht/Boston/London.

Boer, M. den (1990), *Legal Whispers. Narrative Transformations in Dutch Criminal Evidence*, EUI, Florence.

BonJour, L. (1985), *The Structure of Empirical Knowledge*, Harvard University Press, Cambridge, Mass.

Caruth, C. (ed.) (1995), *Trauma. Explorations in Memory*, The John Hopkins University Press, Baltimore and London.

Cense, M. and Ketelaars, G. (1994), 'Slachtoffers van seksueel misbruik verdienen respectvolle behandeling', *de Volkskrant* (15 February 1994).

Coffeng, T. (1994), 'Juist Wagenaar zou de feiten moeten kennen', *de Volkskrant* (19 February 1994).

Crombag, H.F.M. and Merckelbach, H.L.G.J. (1996), *Hervonden herinneringen en andere misverstanden*, Uitgeverij Contact, Amsterdam/Antwerp.

Draijer, N. (1988), *Seksueel misbruik van meisjes door verwanten*, Ministry of Employment and Social Security, The Hague.

Ellenberger, H.F. (1970), *The Discovery of the Unconscious. The History and Evolution of Dynamic Psychiatry*, Basic Books Inc. Publishers, New York.

Focqué, R. and 't Hart, A.C. (1990), *Instrumentaliteit en rechtsbescherming*, Gouda Quint bv, Arnhem.

Ford, C.S. and Beach, F.A. (1951), *Patterns of Sexual Behavior*, Harper & Row, Publishers and Hoeber Medical Division, New York.

Haack, S. (1995), *Evidence and Inquiry*, Blackwell Publishers Ltd., Oxford.

Hart, A.C. 't (1983), *Strafrecht en beleid*, Acco, Louvain.

Hart, O. van der (1995), *Trauma, dissociatie en hypnose. Handboek*, Swets & Zeitlinger B.V. Publishers, Lisse.

Haveman, R. and Staffeleu, J. (1990), *Daders van seksueel geweld: straffen of behandelen?*, Bohn Stafleu Van Loghum, Houten.

HR 17 November 1995, *Nederlandse Jurisprudentie* 1996, p. 666.

Jackson, B.S. (1987), *Semiotics and Legal Theory*, Routledge & Kegan Paul, London and New York.

Jackson, B.S. (1988), *Law, Fact and Narrative Coherence*, Deborah Charles Publications, Liverpool.

Jackson, B.S. (1990), *The Normative Syllogism and the Problem of Reference*, in Nerhot.

Jackson, B.S. (1996), "Anchored narratives' and the interface of law, psychology and semiotics', in *Legal and Criminal Psychology*, vol. 1, pp. 17-45.

Jampole, L. and Weber, M.K. (1987), 'An Assessment of the Behavior of Sexually Abused Children with Anatomically Correct Dolls', in *Child Abuse and Neglect*, vol. 11, pp. 187-192.

Janssens, C.A.P. (1959), 'Op zoek naar Yolanda. Het verhaal van een rechtszaak', in *Nemesis*, no. 2, pp. 52-60.

Jordan, A. de (1897), *Lettres d'Amour*, Éditions Laclos, Paris.

Kolk, B.A. van der and Hart, O. van der (1995), *The Intrusive Past: The Flexiblity of Memory and the Engraving of Trauma,* in Caruth.

Koppen, P.J. van der (1994), 'Het allereerste verhoor door de politie, dàt telt', interview by Jan Tromp, *de Volkskrant*, 19 January 1994.

Korterink, H.J. (1994), *Epe, het proces*, Uitgeverij Elmar B.V., Rijswijk.

Lehrer, K. (1974), *Knowledge*, Oxford University Press, Oxford.

Loftus, Dr. E. and Ketcham, K. (1994), *The Myth of Repressed Memory; False Memories and Allegations of Sexual Abuse*, St. Martin's Press, New York.

MacCormick, N. (1984), *Coherence in Legal Justification*, in Peczenik, pp. 235-251.

MacCormick, N. (1978), *Legal Reasoning and Legal Theory*, Clarendon Press, Oxford.

Maris, C.W. (1990), *Horror Vacui*, 1001, Amsterdam.

Maris, C.W. (1991), 'Romantisch recht', *NJB*, jaargang 66, no. 22, 30 May 1991, pp. 887-898.

Morley, I.E. (1996), 'Narratives, anchored narratives and the interface between law and psychology: A commentary on Jackson (1996)', *Legal and Criminal Psychology*, vol. 1, pp. 271-286.

Nerhot, P. (ed.) (1990), *Law, Interpretation and Reality*, Kluwer Academic Publishers, Dordrecht/Boston/London.

Nussbaum, M.C. (1995), *Poetic Justice. The Literary Imagination and Public Life*, Beacon Press, Boston.

Peczenik, A., Lindahl, L. and Roermund, B. van (eds.) (1984), *Theory of Legal Science*, D. Reidel Publishing Company, Dordrecht/Boston/Lancaster.

Pollock, J.L. (1986), *Contemporary Theories of Knowledge*, Roman & Littlefield, Savage, MD.

Pyck, K. (1994), 'Yolanda en het virus van de massahysterie', *de Volkskrant*, 21 May 1994.

Reviere, S.L. (1996), *Memory of Childhood Tauma; A Clinician's Guide to the Literature*, The Guilford Press, New York, London.

Roermund, B. van (1993), *Recht, verhaal en werkelijkheid*, Coutinho, Bussum.

Rümke, R. (1994), 'Ontkennen van seksueel geweld werkt averechts', *de Volkskrant*, 27 July 1994.

Russell, D.E.H. (1986), *The Secret Trauma, Incest in the Lives of Girls and Women*, Basic Books Inc. Publishers, New York.

Terr, L. (1993), *Unchained Memories: True Stories of Traumatic Memories Lost and Found*, Basic Books, New York.

Wagenaar, W.A. (1994), 'Yolanda, de Eper zaak en een 'broodje aap'', *de Volkskrant*, 12 February 1994.

Wagenaar, W.A., Koppen, P.J. van, and Crombag, H.F.M. (1993), *Ancored Narratives. The Psychology of Criminal Evidence*, Harvester Wheatsheaf/St. Martin's Press, Hertfordshire/New York.

Westermarck, E. (1934), *Three Essays on Sex and Marriage*, Macmillan & Co, New York.

White, J.B. (1973), *The Legal Imagination. Studies in the Nature of Legal Thought and Expression*. Little, Brown & Co, Boston/Toronto.

Yolanda/Snoijink, B. (1994), *Yolanda, Mijn verhaal; De Eper incestaffaire*, Uitgeverij BZZTÔH, The Hague.

8 Empirical Science and Ethical Theory: The Case of Informed Consent

ALBERT W. MUSSCHENGA

In the Netherlands, as in many other countries, the law nowadays requires that researchers and doctors need to obtain the informed consent of subjects or patients before involving them in an experiment or initiating a medical plan. In case of medical experiments the informed consent has often to be given by signing a form. The requirement to obtain informed consent is based on the principle of respect for the autonomy of persons. In the analysis by Faden & Beauchamp (1986), informed consent is an autonomous action by a subject or a patient that authorises a professional to involve the subject in research or to execute a medical plan. The most important condition for giving informed consent is substantial understanding. A patient who is asked to participate in a phase II-study, e.g. to test a new drug, needs to understand the information about the risks, burdens and benefits of the use not only of the experimental drug, but also about the risks etc. of the standard treatment – if such a treatment is available. However, medical experiments are often very complicated. That is why patients sometimes are overloaded with information which precludes substantial understanding. Moreover, they often have to decide under stress. In many cases patients tend to overestimate the possible benefits for themselves of participating in an experiment. Empirical researches show that the conditions for informed consent are often not met and are also very difficult to fulfil in practice. This raises the question whether the doctrine of informed consent has to be rejected because of the shallowness of its empirical presuppositions about patients' actual capacity to understand information.

The general problem that lies behind this question concerns the role of empirical presuppositions in ethical theory. Should ethical theories be rejected if their empirical presuppositions are implausible? In this chapter I first discuss this general problem, and then apply my findings to the case of informed consent.

Introduction

In his contribution to this volume and in his book *Facts, Values, and Methodology*, Wim van der Steen pleads that, for various reasons, moral philosophers should get more acquainted with the results of empirical science. Ethics aims to provide guidelines for human conduct. It can hardly do that if it does not account for human nature. Empirical premises are often needed to move from general to specific normative theses. Normative statements are linked up with facts through concepts with empirical reference (Van der Steen 1995, 46).

Nowadays, a growing awareness exists among philosophers who are doing 'applied ethics' that they must know about the results of empirical research, if they do not want to end up with general and abstract principles which are only valid under ideal conditions. More and more ethicists appear on the scene who are not only trained in philosophy, but also in one of the empirical sciences.

Empirical assumptions and facts always play a role at the level of situational application of rules and principles. Attempts to accommodate material from empirical science in ethical *theories* are still rare, and reflection on the methodology needed for this is largely absent.

The mere fact that most ethicists have no training in disciplines outside philosophy does not suffice to explain this lacuna. The gap between ethics and science is also reinforced by ethical theories which regard facts as irrelevant (cf. some Kantian theories) or problematic (cf. relativist theories). Van der Steen refers to Thomas Nagel, who argues in his account of altruism in *The Possibility of Altruism* (1970, 82), that we should ignore insights from empirical sciences into human motivation (Van der Steen 1995, 42 ff.).[1]

I agree with Van der Steen that moral philosophy should become more empirically informed. However, if one wants to avoid naive forms of scientism, it is imperative to reflect seriously on the methodology of relating ethical theory to empirical sciences. What are the limits of a scientific approach to ethics? In what ways can scientific material be used to strengthen, correct and evaluate ethical theories? In this contribution I explore the possibilities and the limits of connecting ethical theory to empirical sciences. I present a framework for an empirical evaluation of normative ethical theories. Before doing that, I deal with a particular philosophical obstacle, viz. the argument of relativistic philosophers that there is no such thing as human nature. After sketching the framework, I will apply it to an important doctrine of medical ethics, that of respect for autonomy and informed consent.

Abraham Edel, who belongs to the older generation of contemporary moral philosophers, has done important groundwork on the relevance of empirical science to ethical theory. He used insights from the human, social and historical sciences to tackle the problem of ethical relativity and to reduce what he called 'ethical indeterminacy' in *Ethical Judgement: The Use of Science in Ethics* (1955). His program of relating science to ethics is summarised in a little book entitled *Science and the Structure of Ethics* (1961). I recapitulate the program in the next section.

Abraham Edel on Evaluating Ethical Theories

Edel distinguishes the role of scientific results in ethical theory from the application of scientific method to ethical theory. They are, however, interrelated. 'If the human field is sufficiently determinate and scientific results have a constitutive place in ethics, then the wider use of scientific method within ethical theory may be possible' (Edel 1961, 6). I confine myself here to the relevance of empirical findings to ethical theory.

A central concept in Edel's account is 'Existential Perspective' (EP). The EP comprises assumptions about the world, human nature, human community, unavoidables in human life (such as birth and death) etc. which are operative in ethical theory. The concept of EP is narrower than concepts such as 'world view' and 'ideology' in that it only concerns the stage-setting for morality, which need not coincide with total world-outlook (1961, 13). The assumptions guide and help shape an ethical theory, although the precise pattern of influence varies with the type of the theory. Edel distinguishes three types of ethical theory: theories with an 'overtly scientific existential perspective' which are more or less based on scientific insights prevalent in the time they were formulated (such as utilitarianism, moral sense theories, evolutionary ethics), theories with 'theological and metaphysical existential perspectives' (such as religious theories and the theories of Aristotle and Hegel), and theories with a 'science in transcendence existential perspective' 'which disparage the role of existential assumptions in the internal workings of ethical theory and, in varying degrees, propound the autonomy of ethics' (a category to which he reckons Kant, G.E. Moore, N. Hartmann and existentialist theories) (1961, 30). He argues that theories of the second type like those of the first type, include EP-assumptions in domains covered by empirical science. By fitting various theories into the third category, Edel suggests that they have a common view of existence that furnishes a special type of stage-setting for ethics. 'But we have the task of showing that in such views the stage-setting is inarticulate or incomplete or even displaced and that, when uncovered, it is found to pose scientific questions' (31).

Edel's categorisation of ethical theories is a useful tool for discussing the relevance of empirical science for ethical theory. It should be comparatively easy to confront theories of the first type, such as utilitarianism or Hume's theory, with empirical science, because their founders themselves aspired to be scientific in theorising about morality. Theories of the second and the third type are not that tractable.

Edel's purpose was not only to make a comparative study of the EP's of diverse ethical theories, but also to stimulate the construction of a more adequate EP for contemporary ethical theory. For that purpose, an evaluation of the EP's of ethical theories is also necessary. One of the standards that have to be applied in evaluating EP's are truth standards. 'Since an EP purports to give a picture of ethically relevant aspects of the world, man's nature and condition, the accuracy of any picture may be called to account, and, insofar as science has penetrated any field, to scientific account. Truth is embedded in the aims of an EP; it is not merely giving a pleasant account (36).'

Few contemporary philosophers, if any, have dealt with the evaluation of ethical theories as extensively as Edel did. His distinction of evaluating ethical theories and evaluating the EP's of ethical theories is still useful.

The Role of Empirical Background Assumptions in Moral Justification

One can but agree with Edel that empirical facts and assumptions which are part of an ethical theory's EP should be true, or at least plausible. The question I want to discuss is whether the plausibility of these empirical facts and assumptions affect the justification of the theory's basic moral principles. Theories of moral justification usually lack the insight that questions of empirical truth could be relevant in judging the plausibility of an ethical theory. If the plausibility of the empirical core of an ethical theory affects the justification of its basic moral principles, that has consequences for the agenda and thereby for the nature of a theory of moral justification. Theories of moral justification should at least recognise the connections between basic moral principles and related empirical assumptions. This happens in some coherence theories of moral justification in ethics. Some proponents of such theories do account for the role of non-moral beliefs in the justification of basic principles and are therefore more willing to rely on empirical science. A coherence theory of justification in ethics holds that one's moral belief p is justified insofar as p is part of a coherent system of beliefs, both moral and non-moral, and $p's$ coherence at least partially explains why one holds p. According to coherentism, justification is inferential, but it need not be linear and deductive. One's belief p is justified by one's belief q, which is justified by one's belief r which is ultimately justified by one's belief p.

Central in any coherence theory of justification in ethics is the method of reflective equilibrium. John Rawls first made the distinction between narrow and wide reflective equilibrium, which was subsequently further elaborated by Norman Daniels (Rawls 1974/5; Daniels 1979, 1980). A narrow reflective equilibrium is reached when a good fit exists between a person's well-considered judgements and a set of principles. This equilibrium is reached in a process of mutually adjusting judgements and principles. However, alternative sets of principles might also fit the well-considered judgements. In that case one has to determine, in the view of Rawls and Daniels, the relative strengths and weaknesses of the alternative sets of principles, by considering their relevant background theories. That is how one arrives at a 'wide reflective equilibrium'. 'The method of wide reflective equilibrium is an attempt to produce coherence in an ordered triple of sets of beliefs held by a particular person, namely (a) a set of considered moral judgements, (b) a set of moral principles, and (c) a set of relevant background theories' (Daniels 1979, 258). The role of background theories in Daniels' approach is comparable to that of the EP in Edel's theory.

Rawls used the method of wide reflective equilibrium in explicating and defending his theory of justice. He departs from a hypothetical contract behind a veil of ignorance as a device for selecting between rival conceptions of justice. The contract should provide arguments by which one can judge the relative strengths and weaknesses of these conceptions. According Norman Daniels, these arguments can be viewed as inferences from a number of relevant background theories: a theory of the person, a theory of procedural justice, general social theory and a theory of the role of morality in society (1979, 260). The theories in (c) must show that the principles in (b) are more acceptable than alternatives on grounds that are to some degree *independent* of (b)'s match with relevant considered judgements in (a). This is what Daniels calls 'the independence constraint' (1980, 85 ff.).

What is the nature of background theories? Daniels shows that in Rawls' theory of justice, the background theories are not empirical theories; they rather formulate ideals. The 'theory of the person' in Rawls' theory is not an empirical theory, but a Kantian, philosophical view of the nature of persons. But as Edel already argued, even metaphysical conceptions such as the Kantian theory of persons are related to empirical assumptions. I therefore assume that background theories in the method of wide reflective equilibrium may also be empirical theories or theories with an empirical core. Alan Gibbard, who himself rejects the method of wide reflective equilibrium, believes that views of human nature are indispensable in any search for a wide reflective equilibrium (Gibbard 1990, 25). Rawls himself refers to psychological literature when formulating his Aristotelian Principle (1971, 426, note 20).

When a conflict exists between background beliefs and principles, coherence is attained by mutual adjustment. Conflicts may call for a revision of principles, background beliefs, or both. The nature of revisions depends on the degree of a person's commitment to the propositions involved, and logical and evidentiary relations among the propositions, and other propositions he accepts or rejects (DePaul 1993, 20). This means that it is impossible to make general statements about what happens when an empirical assumption which is part of a basic principle's network of supporting beliefs turns out to be false. It depends on the logical and evidentiary relations between the assumption and the principle.

Daniels believes that resolving disagreements about background theories might contribute to reaching moral agreement because they are more tractable than disagreements about moral judgements and principles (Daniels 1979, 262). I would rather doubt that. Only if well-considered judgements converge sufficiently, while principles do not converge, an appeal to background theories may help to solve problems of moral disagreement. Besides that, whether agreement on particular background beliefs does foster moral agreement depends on the place of those beliefs in the entire network of assumptions underlying moral beliefs.

I will give two examples in which particular empirical beliefs play a central role in the acceptance or rejection of ethical theories. The first one I derive from Derek Parfit's *Reasons and Persons* (1984). In that book Parfit argues that we are not separately existing entities, apart from our brains and bodies, and various interrelated physical and mental events. What is usually at stake in discussions about personal identity are two unities: the unity of consciousness at any time and the unity of a whole life. Parfit states that these unities cannot be explained by claiming that different experiences are had by the same person. They must be explained by describing the relations between these many experiences and their relations to a person's brains. According to Parfit, what matters to persons asking themselves whether they still are the person they were twenty years ago, is not personal identity, but the psychological connectedness and/or continuity with the right kind of cause (Parfit 1984, 214 ff.). This view on identity is central to Parfit's rejection of the belief in 'the separateness of persons' which is held by authors such as Sidgwick and Rawls, and his defense of an utilitarian view on distributive justice (329 ff.). He argues that since persons are nor separately existing entities, the impersonality of utilitarianism is less implausible than most of us believe (346). The evidentiary relations between idea of the separateness of persons and Rawls' deontological conception of justice are pretty close. If it could be convincingly shown that the idea is implausible, that would force Rawls to at least revise his theory.

The other example is classical utilitarianism. Classical utilitarianism consists of three theories: a psychological theory of motivation, a subjectivist theory of non-moral value and a theory of moral obligation. In his *Principles of Morals and Legislation* Bentham founds the principle of utility – the cornerstone of utilitarianism's theory of obligation – on the empirical observation that human actions are governed by pain and pleasure: 'Nature has placed mankind under the governance of two sovereign masters, *pain* and *pleasure*. It is for them alone to point out what we ought to do, as well as to determine what we shall do' (1948, 1). This crude theory of motivation does not find much support nowadays.

Empirical Justification of Background Assumptions

Domains of background beliefs supporting ethical theories which are in principle open to empirical justification, contain assumptions about the nature and the structure of human motivation, and about the capacities of human beings to reason and to take decisions. Both are often lumped together under the concept of 'human nature'.

The nature of empirical justification, like moral justification, is subject to many controversies. Relativists in regard to science contend that the natural world and evidence about it hardly constrain our beliefs (Laudan 1990, viii). Empirical statements are always theory-laden and underdetermined by observation data. Besides that, rules and methods for testing theories are socially sanctioned conventions. That implies that they will deny that conclusive statements about (aspects of) human nature are possible. Since there are diverse, incommensurable theories about human nature, it is impossible to speak of 'the' human nature.

Empirical background beliefs of ethical theories are usually not subjected to any kind of empirical justification. Therefore one could argue that ethical theories are not sufficiently justified if their empirical background beliefs are not justified according to *some* criteria of justification. This is the direction in which Michael DePaul seeks to complement conventional coherence theories of moral justification. DePaul's suggestion is that it is compatible with the internalist character of wide reflective equilibrium to demand that someone's background beliefs meet the epistemic standard they themselves explicitly or implicitly endorse. In his view a person is not justified in holding certain non-moral background beliefs, if these do not meet his own epistemic standards. If they do not, they have to be regarded as irrational from his own perspective. DePaul defines rationality as a matter of believing upon due reflection, in accord with our own epistemic standards. Beliefs are irrational if they do not meet the obligations defined by these standards (DePaul 1993, 67 ff.). If someone is not able to prove that the beliefs of which their moral principles are a part, are rational, this does in my view not necessarily lead to the conclusion that their principles are irrational. It might still be possible that someone else who is holding the same epistemic principles, does succeed in showing that the beliefs are rational.

This account of justification stays, as I already noted, within an internalist framework. It is possible that a person's epistemic standards are not widely shared. He may endorse a controversial theory, for example the motivation theory of psychological egoism. He will then at least have to show that this theory is empirically adequate and well-confirmed according to his own epistemic standards. For many who believe that at least empirical assertions have to be checked against the world, this epistemic internalism is unsatisfactorily. This might be a reason to return to a version of foundationalism. However, the objections against foundationalism are well-known. Foundationalist theories distinguish between justified beliefs which are basic, and those which are derived from one or more basic beliefs. Basic beliefs have a higher epistemic status because they are supported by the subject's empirical or non-empirical experience. But, as Popper already argued, all observations are theory-impregnated. This also applies to the 'basic statements' against which scientific theories should be tested. Although the decision to accept a basic statement is causally connected with our experiences, it cannot be justified or supported by experience.

A promising alternative for both coherentism and foundationalism is Susan Haack's 'foundherentism'. She argues that justification comes in degrees. Beliefs are more or less justified. The degree of justification depends on the extent to which a belief is supported by other beliefs, and how secure these supporting beliefs are. Her favourite analogy is the cross-word puzzle. How reasonable one's confidence is that a certain entry in a cross-word puzzle is right, depends on (i) how much support is given to this entry by the clue and any intersecting entries that have already been filled in, (ii) how reasonable, independently of the entry in question, one's confidence is that those already filled-in entries are correct, and (iii) how many of the intersecting entries have been filled in (Haack 1993, 82). How important mutual support may be, with respect to empirical beliefs the *only* ultimate evidence we have is experiential evidence – sensory and introspective (Haack ch. 10). A certain empirical belief may be well supported by very secure other beliefs. However, as long as there is no direct experiential evidence for that belief, it cannot be regarded as justified.

Let me summarise my findings. Ethical theories' claims on being true and/or justified are supported by background beliefs including empirical beliefs. The quality of these beliefs' support depends for their part on whether they are well-supported by other beliefs and by experiential evidence. The impact of the discovery that certain of its empirical background beliefs are false or implausible, on a theory's justification, depends on the nature of the evidentiary relation between these beliefs and the theory. The history of ethics shows that hardly any ethical theory has disappeared because its empirical background assumptions proved to be implausible. What has happened again and again is that problematic empirical background assumptions are dropped or replaced by other, more plausible ones. This may be accompanied by a revision of the theory. This is what happens continuously. Although for Bentham his motivation theory is an important background theory in his defence of utilitarianism, hardly any modern utilitarian holds such a theory on human motivation. This proves that the evidentiary relation between hedonism and the utilitarian theory of moral obligation is weak. Lawrence Becker argues in his book *A New Stoicism* that once we abandon the bad science and theology of the Stoics, and put in its place the latest theories about normal human development, we can see how Stoicism offers us the best perspective from which to lead flourishing lives (Becker 1997).

I noticed above that the empirical background assumptions which serve to support the justification of ethical theories, are themselves rarely subjected to scientific scrutiny. I would therefore propose that we do not regard an ethical theory as justified if its adherents do not succeed to show that its empirical background beliefs are sufficiently supported by other empirical beliefs and experiential evidence.

Ought Implies Can

The discussion in the previous sections has shown that empirical scrutiny of the background assumption of ethical theories often leads to a revision of theories, but rarely to the complete rejection of a theory. But there is still another way to make the findings of empirical science relevant for ethical theorising and practical ethics. Empirical science can tell us whether what 'ought' to be done also 'can' be done.

'Ought implies can' means that ethical theories and principles have to be feasible. I discuss the validity of the criterion of feasibility, and consider how empirical sciences bear on it. A central point in my argument will be that judgements about feasibility should depend on the theory's own meta-ethical view of the task of ethics

What does it mean that principles should be feasible? Principles are standards for the evaluation of the moral quality of actions and the character of actors. They are also meant to guide actions. There are several kinds of situations in which it is impossible to satisfy a moral requirement. For example, in the case of a moral dilemma an agent cannot do what he ought to do unless he also does what he ought not to do. I will concentrate on those cases in which empirical sciences can show that the nature of human beings makes it unreasonable to expect that they satisfy a certain requirement. The observation that the actions of most people do not comply with some principles, could be considered as an indication of a non-feasibility.

Owen Flanagan is one of the few authors who elaborated a standard of feasibility. I discuss his views, to determine whether his standard of feasibility is plausible and helps us evaluate ethical theories. Flanagan argues that almost all traditions of ethical thought are committed to 'psychological realism'. This core commitment, he says, can be formulated in terms of a meta-ethical principle, which he calls 'the Principle of Minimal Psychological Realism' (PMPR) (1991, 32):

> Make sure when constructing a moral theory or projecting a moral ideal that the character, decision processing, and behaviour prescribed are possible, or are perceived to be possible, for creatures like us.

PMPR is meant to be both descriptive and prescriptive. It picks out an aspiration of almost all ethical theories, and sets out a criterion for evaluating theories in terms of this aspiration (33). His PMPR applies to human motivation as well as capacities of reasoning and deciding, but Flanagan only considers motivation.

Flanagan's demand of psychological realism can easily be translated into the terminology used in the previous sections. It corresponds with the demand that the background theories or the EP of an ethical theory or moral ideal should be plausible. In some places Flanagan formulates the demands of his PMPR in a positive way: ethical theories must specify their motivational requirements and make plausible that these can be met by what they regard as mature moral beings. In other places he speaks of natural features which lay down basic constraints on the possible shades of human personality, our ability to realise a particular psychology. Ethical theories, in drawing a picture of what they regard as mature moral beings, must respect these basic constraints. Here the PMPR seems to function as a negative standard for evaluating ethical theories. I discuss the positive version of the PMPR first.

Some authors deny the validity of standards of feasibility. In their view it is the task of ethics to formulate ideals which people should strive for, even if it is rarely possible to meet them. One could indeed question whether the belief that feasibility is a valid standard for evaluating ethical theories is theory-neutral. It presupposes a division within morality between 'ordinary morality' and 'supererogatory morality', between what is morally required and what is morally laudable. Such a division is widely accepted and explicitly defended by theorists who contend that impartiality is not *the* moral point of view; there are moral limits to what can be required from the point of view of impartiality. Two classes of such limits are distinguished. First, morality permits persons to perform actions which from an impartial point of view are less than optimal, and favour things they care about. Second, morality forbids certain actions which are required from a impartial point of view, if they conflict with obligations which arise from special relations.

Persons who always favour the interests of others and the common good over their self-regarding projects perform supererogatory actions and can rightly be called moral heroes. A division between ordinary and supererogatory morality is rejected by Shelley Kagan (Kagan 1989). He says that we are always required to do what is morally best. It is not pleasant to admit that we often fail. 'Faced with this realization what we must do is change: change our beliefs, our actions, and our interests. What we must not do – is deny our failure' (1989, 403).

Flanagan knows the objections of authors such as Kagan, and therefore tries to distinguish psychological realisability from demandingness and degree of difficulty. He notes that, although demandingness and degree of difficulty are related in a complex way, they are easily confused (Flanagan 1991, 39). Ethical theories may rightly formulate highly demanding principles and ideals which are not easily met, if it is plausible that people are able to develop into the kind of beings the theories want them to be. Normative conceptions which fail to meet certain standards of psychological realisation, will fail to grip us, and in failing to grip us will fail to gain our attention, respect and effort (1991, 26).

I agree with Flanagan that even highly demanding ethical theories presuppose that at least some persons are able to comply with their demands. These persons need not be 'real existing' persons. Ethical theories are only then psychologically unrealisable if '... no future members of our species, in any possible social contexts, could instantiate, or even closely approximate, the motivational structure required by the theory' (26). In this interpretation of PMPR, ethical theories which do not answer to the principle must be very rare. Thus interpreted, the potential of the PMPR to discriminate between ethical theories is not very high.

In my view, the test may have more actual usefulness if one takes account of the distinction between *supererogatory ethical theories* and *theories of social morality*. The aspiration level in Jesus' ethics of love, for example, is not what normal, decent, and reasonable people may be expected to attain. Jesus prescribes that one should do what one wants others to do to oneself (Luke 6, 31). An unbridgeable gulf exists between such a supererogatory ethics of love and contractualist theories of narrow, social morality in which reciprocity is the basic principle. Contrary to supererogatory theories, theories of social morality explicitly aim to lay down principles and rules for the social interaction between average human beings which are neither morally bad, nor morally perfect, for human beings with limited rationality, limited sympathy and limited strength. Narrow morality is restricted to rules and principles which regulate the social interactions between members of a society. The criterion of feasibility is not neutral between these different types of ethical theories. In supererogatory theories low compliance is not an indication of the nonfeasibility of a principle or an ideal, but of man's weakness of will or moral imperfection.

In the negative version of the PMPR, ethical theories, in drawing a picture of mature moral beings, respect the natural constraints on the possible shades of human personality. What are these constraints? Candidates for such constraints are features which turn up in some recognisable form regardless of cultural context and historical time, and therefore are taken to lie closer to our basic biological and cognitive architecture than certain other traits. According to Flanagan legitimate contenders for such traits are the six basic emotions of anger, fear, disgust, happiness, sadness, and surprise; the perceptual system; the propositional attitudes (but not their contents); biological sex, sexual desire, hunger, thirst, linguistic capacity, and the capacities to be classically and operantly conditioned, to reason, and to remember (1991, 42f.). Natural traits are the raw material underlying social behaviour. The traits constrain human personality. That is why ethical theory has to reckon with them in assumptions about human motivation.

Flanagan distinguishes *natural* traits from *narrow* psychological traits which are socially constructed and internalised during education. Narrow psychological traits also heavily constrain realisable psychological make-ups. The examples he gives are racial hate and sexism. So, in Flanagan's view, an ethical theory can be unrealisable in two different ways. First, 'It may be unrealisable in principle because it requires that we not possess certain characteristics that typically come with our kind of biology and cannot be modified, suppressed or otherwise be inactivated'. Second, it may be unrealisable because it requires us not to have some narrow traits which are deeply entrenched in our identity and culture (1991, 46). The PMPR is meant to refer only to the first kind of unrealisability.

The distinction between natural traits and narrow psychological traits is actually untenable. Flanagan himself implicitly concedes that the traits we meet in humans are always cultural expressions and elaborations of the raw material of natural traits. To some extent, all traits that reveal themselves in actual attitudes and behaviour are cultural. Also, the narrow psychological traits are connected with basic emotions such as fear and disgust, the expression of which depends on culture. Racism is an attitude of scorn towards people with racial characteristics other than one's own. It is intimately linked with culturally variable beliefs about racial characteristics deemed relevant for judging and treating human beings. Sexual desire, according to Flanagan a natural trait, is also connected with cultural beliefs about appropriate objects of desire. Apart from that, many examples exist of ascetic people who manage to suppress or inactivate sexual desire.

All in all, feasibility as interpreted by Flanagan, cannot be used as a general standard for evaluating ethical theories and principles for several reasons. First, it is not neutral between theories with different aspiration levels. Second, the concept of natural traits of human motivation and cognitive processes which constitute basic constraints on what ethical theories can reasonably expect human beings to do or not to do, is highly problematic. This is not to say that the criterion of feasibility is entirely useless. I am inclined to take the stand that the standard is relevant for a general evaluation of only those theories and principles which aim to guide other-regarding, interpersonal actions. Much more relevant than the *general* feasibility of theories and principles is whether these are feasible in *particular contexts*. Theories and principles might be feasible under some, and not under other conditions. Empirical research is needed to determine whether empirical background assumptions and presuppositions can be met in a specific context. I will illustrate this approach by examining whether the empirical assumptions which are presupposed by the doctrine of informed consent, are justified if one takes into account the specific characteristics of the actual context in which very ill patients have to make their decision. The assumptions regard the capacity of humans to grasp and understand information and take autonomous decisions.

Informed Consent

In many countries, the law nowadays requires that researchers and doctors need to obtain the informed consent of subjects or patients before involving them in an experiment or initiating a medical plan. In case of medical experiments the informed consent has to be given by signing a form. The requirement to obtain informed consent is based on the principle of respect for the autonomy of persons. In the analysis by Faden & Beauchamp, informed consent is an autonomous action by a subject or a patient that authorises a professional to involve the subject in research or to execute a medical plan. An informed consent is given by a subject or a patient who with (1) substantial understanding and (2) in substantial absence of control by others (3) intentionally (4) authorises a professional (to do an action R) (1986, 278). According to Faden & Beauchamp acts of consent to medical or research procedures – signing forms, saying 'okay' or the like – rarely fail to be informed consents because they fail to satisfy *only* the condition of intentionality or that of authorisation. If these conditions are not satisfied, almost invariably there are also problems with satisfying the condition of substantial understanding. Conversely, if there are no problems with the condition of substantial non-control, the securing of substantial understanding *generally* (not always) turns out to be sufficient to secure informed consent. Faden & Beauchamp argue that if the condition of substantial understanding is adequately satisfied, the conditions of intentionality and authorisation usually present no problem -

(299). That is why Faden & Beauchamp focus almost exclusively on the condition of substantial understanding.

What does it mean for a person to have substantial understanding of an act of consenting (or refusing)? Faden & Beauchamp distinguish *substantial* from *full* understanding. X has a full understanding of X's action if X apprehends with full adequacy all the relevant propositions that correctly describe (1) the nature of the action R, and (2) the foreseeable consequences and possible outcomes that might follow as a result of performing or not performing the action (300). Substantial understanding means that a person understands *that* he is authorising and *what* he is authorising. Sometimes doctors and patients regard informed consenting solely as informing about one's condition and about treatment options, and not as giving permission or authorisation. Inadequacy in the understanding of informed consent as an act of authorisation is easy to detect. More difficult is it to be precise about what a patient has to understand to have a substantial understanding of the nature of his act as one of authorisation. In Faden & Beauchamp's elaboration of the condition of substantial understanding, the condition demands apprehension of all those descriptions of R that the person regards as important or material for the decision to authorise R. That is a subjective criterion (304).[2]

In summarising Faden & Beauchamp, I have tried to make clear what conditions have to be met in obtaining informed consent from a subject or a patient. The principle of respect for autonomy on which the demand of informed consent is based, is not a supererogatory one. It is meant to regulate the interaction between physicians and patients. According to the principle 'ought implies can', the principle of respect for autonomy is valid in the context of obtaining consent for participation in medical research, if and only if it can be shown that it is feasible in that context. Failure of compliance is at least an indication of non-feasibility.

I will primarily focus on empirical assumptions regarding the capacity of persons to come to a substantial understanding of what is material for a decision to authorise R. In my view it makes no sense to evaluate in the abstract the capacity of understanding. Therefore I focus on the context of obtaining informed consent from patients involved in therapeutic experiments. Especially in such experiments, informed consent is of important, because they are usually burdensome while the nature and probability of the outcome are uncertain. Faden & Beauchamp themselves discuss several factors that may impede effective communication between patients and doctors and substantial understanding by patients of what is material for their giving informed consent.

Many problems of understanding and communication have to do with the information about risks and probabilities, an area which, as Faden & Beauchamp note, has special relevance in informed consent (319). Research, especially that by David Kahneman and Amos Tversky, has shown that people have problems with processing information about risks and that these problems introduce inferential errors and disproportionate exaggeration of risks in making choices (Kahneman & Tversky 1974, 1981, 1984). These errors are not unique to patients, not even to lay persons. Also experts can suffer from distortions in their assessment of risks. One of the troublesome biases in informed consent is the so-called 'framing' or 'formulation' effect (Kahneman & Tversky 1984, 344.) Choices between risky alternatives can be influenced predictably by the way risk information is presented. A well-known example from everyday life of differences in framing is the description of a glass as half *full* or half *empty*. Framing effects have been demonstrated in several studies of medical risk information (e.g. McNeill et al. 1982). Faden & Beauchamp argue that framing effects do not invariably diminish understanding in ways that render acts less than substantially autonomous. Nevertheless they argue that professionals seeking informed consent from subjects and patients should provide patients, if relevant, with both sides of the story (the 'half full' and the 'half empty' side) (321).

Effects of the framing of information point to biases in making choices. Information is however not distorted, but only selectively understood. Some studies have demonstrated that half of the participants in comparative research on a standard treatment and an experimental treatment falsely believe that the experimental treatment is the more effective one, although the consent form suggested that the new treatment was promising but that evidence failed to indicate how it compared with the standard treatment (Gallo et al. 1995, 1062). Their perception of possible benefits of the experimental treatment is undoubtedly distorted by their need to keep hope alive. Participating in a medical experiment is for many patients with a life-threatening disease the last straw to catch. If a patient, in giving consent, falsely believes that the experimental treatment is more effective than the standard one, his consent is not based on a substantial understanding of the experiment. It is possible that such distortions of information can be minimised when the doctor and others such as research nurses again and again repeat the correct information about risks and benefits and their probabilities. However, a substantial percentage of patients will probably continue to hold false beliefs about risks and benefits because it is in their interest to have them. Many doctors hold that one should not take away a patient's last hope. That may be true, but consent based on false hope, does not meet Faden & Beauchamp's conditions of informed consent.

Another factor working against the condition of substantial understanding is that human beings can process only limited amounts of information (Faden & Beauchamp 323 f.). The information load problem is exacerbated by the fact that the information is mostly novel and alien. Time pressure in many informed consent discussions also affects the comprehension of information negatively. A nice illustration of the information load problem stems from my own experience as a member of the ethics committee of a hospital specialised in oncology. Researchers of that hospital presented a proposal for a randomised phase III-trial of surgery versus radiotherapy to patients with stage-III non-small cell lung cancer who showed a positive response to an initial treatment with chemotherapy. Radiotherapy is the standard treatment and surgery the experimental one. The aim of the trial was to determine whether surgery is superior to radiotherapy. Lung surgery is a very invasive treatment. The researchers also wanted to conduct a phase-II trial in which the response rate and the nature of the toxicity of the initial treatment with a combination of two different drugs – Gemcitabine and Cisplatin – was to be determined. These two trials were linked. The Gemcitabine-Cisplatin combination was to be used as the induction regime for the next treatment which would be either surgery or radiotherapy. Therefore, some of the patients who were eligible for the phase-III trial, should also have to participate in the phase-II trial. They had to be asked to give consent for participation in two succeeding trials. Both consents had to be given before the first trial. In my view, this is a typical example of an information overload problem. The average patient is hardly able to process all the information concerning two trials in a relatively short time.

Faden & Beauchamp mention fear, anxiety and uncertainty as causes of distraction from optimum information processing and also as stressors with physiological consequences that further reduce cognitive abilities. However, it is not evident that stress always has a negative effect on cognitive abilities. Research by Dorner & Pfeiffer shows that subjects under stress who had to solve a series of tasks of strategic thinking, compared to subjects not under stress, exhibited a more analytical behaviour and increased their workload, instead of decreasing it, while there were no differences with respect to performance (Dorner & Pfeifer 1993). As Faden & Beauchamp state, the cognitive functions most susceptible to disruption by illness and others stressors are those actively involved in linguistic communication: the ability to store, recall, and dismiss information in active memory, the maintenance of vigilance in attentive focus, and the ability to suppress distractions. Many disease states also directly affect cognitive functions and communication.

Faden & Beauchamp offer valuable suggestions as to how professionals can check whether a subject has an understanding adequate to make a substantially autonomous choice. They can build 'feedback loops' into their communication with subjects, for example by letting persons restate in their own words the information given to them. However, the overall picture that emerges from diverse empirical studies about the capacity of patients to understand information, is bleak. We should seriously doubt if the consent given by some categories of patients in medical experiments, such as end-stage cancer patients, does meet the condition of substantial understanding. The picture becomes even worse when one takes into account the opportunity doctors have to influence decisions by manipulating information (withholding information; selective presentation of information), psychological manipulation (appeals to emotions, and feelings such as guilt or feelings of obligation), and the effect of role-constraints such as the tendency of patients to be passive in the interaction with a doctor and the desire to be 'a good patient' and to please the doctor.

In many cases one can seriously question whether the benefits of participating in a research project are proportional to the burdens. In some countries, e.g. in The Netherlands, such proportionality is required by law. The side-effects of experimental treatments are often burdensome, the risks serious, while the benefits for the patient are uncertain. In my experience as a member of an ethics committee medical researchers tend to emphasise especially in such hard cases that the patients, and not the doctors and researchers, have to weigh and compare the benefits and burdens of the available options. Whether the researchers themselves would decide to participate, is irrelevant in their own view. If they have provided the patients with all the relevant information and answered all questions, it is up to them to decide. However, it can be expected that the information overload problem will arise especially in hard cases in which substantial understanding is even more important than in other cases. If it is an empirical fact that the condition of substantial understanding is often not met in such cases, we should reconsider the doctrine and the procedures of informed consent, and above all the role and the responsibilities of the researchers. If the researcher is the same person as the patient's primarily responsible physician in attendance, she should not limit herself to providing information. She should act as the advisor of the patient. The responsibility for deciding (not) to participate should be a shared one. Doctors should give more weight to the traditional principle of medical ethics *'primum non nocere'*, instead of complying with the legal principle *'volenti non fiat injuria'* which sometimes seems to be the rationale behind the requirement of informed consent.

Conclusion

The question I set my self to discuss in this paper is whether the plausibility or implausibility of empirical background assumptions facts and assumptions affects the justification of an ethical theory and its basic moral principles. I concluded that the impact on a theory's justification of the discovery that certain of its empirical background beliefs are false or very implausible, depends on the nature of the evidentiary relation between these beliefs and the theory. Hardly any ethical theory has disappeared because its empirical background assumptions proved to be implausible. What has happened again and again is that problematic empirical background assumptions are dropped or replaced by other, more plausible ones.

Subsequently I discussed another way to make the findings of empirical science relevant for ethical theorising and practical ethics: empirical science can tell us whether what 'ought' to be done also 'can' be done. My conclusion was that the standard of feasibility is only relevant for a general evaluation of theories and principles which aim to guide other-regarding, interpersonal actions, and not for supererogatory ones. I argued that perhaps much more relevant than the *general* feasibility of theories and principles is whether these are feasible in *particular contexts*. Theories and principles might be feasible under some, and not under other conditions. In the last section on informed consent, I showed that this approach is indeed relevant. Empirical research is needed to determine whether empirical background assumptions and presuppositions can be met in a specific context.

Notes

1   Contemporary exceptions are Owen Flanagan's *Varieties of Moral Personalities* (1991) and Alan Gibbard's *Wise Choices, Apt Feelings* (1990).
2   Although for Faden & Beauchamp the subjective criterion is the central one in determining the adequacy of a person's understanding of R, it is not the sole standard for them. Sometimes the set of propositions a person views as material for his or her decision to authorise R is not sufficiently comprehensive to ensure that the 'R' the person intends to authorise is, by an 'objective' account, the same R the person being authorised believes he or she has been given permission to implement (Faden & Beauchamp 1986, 309). Sometimes an extrasubjective component is needed in the knowledge base necessary for substantial understanding. Faden & Beauchamp operationalise this demand as follows: Person X must not only understand those propositions about R that he views as material for a decision whether to authorise, but also what Y (the professional) believes to be of value for such a decision. As a result X and Y come to share an understanding about the terms of authorisation and about the nature of what is authorised (309). Such an understanding requires effective communication between doctor and patient, in a climate of trust.

References

Becker, L.C. (1997), *A New Stoicism,* Princeton University Press, Princeton.
Bentham, J. (1948), *The Principles of Morals and Legislation* [1780], with an Introduction by L.J. Lafleur, Hafner Press, New York.
Brink, D.O. (1989), *Moral Realism and the Foundations of Ethics,* Cambridge University Press, Cambridge.
Daniels, N. (1979), 'Wide Reflective Equilibrium and Theory Acceptance in Ethics', *The Journal of Philosophy* 76, pp. 256-282.
Daniels, N. (1980), 'Reflective Equilibrium and Archimedean Points', *Canadian Journal of Philosophy* 10, pp. 83-103.
DePaul, M.R. (1993), *Balance and Refinement,* Routledge, London.
Dorner D., & Pfeifer, E. (1993), 'Strategic Thinking and Stress', *Ergonomics* 36, pp. 1345-1360.
Edel, A. (1955), *Ethical Judgment,* The Free Press, Glencoe, Illinois.
Edel, A. (1961), *Science and the Structure of Ethics*, University of Chicago Press, Chicago/London.
Faden, R.R., & Beauchamp, T.L. (1986), *A History and Theory of Informed Consent,* Oxford University Press, New York/Oxford.

Flanagan, O. (1991), *Varieties of Moral Personality*, Harvard University Press, Cambridge, Mass.

Gallo, C., Perrone, F., De Placido S., & Giusti, C. (1995), 'Informed Versus Randomised Consent to Clinical Trials', *The Lancet* 346, pp. 1060-1064.

Gibbard, A. (1990), *Wise Choices, Apt Feelings,* Clarendon Press, Oxford.

Haack, S. (1995), *Evidence and Inquiry*, Blackwell, Oxford.

Kagan, S. (1989), *The Limits of Morality*, Clarendon Press, Oxford.

Kahneman, D., & Tversky, A. (1974), 'Judgment Under Uncertainty: Heuristics and Biases', *Science* 185, pp. 1124-1131.

Kahneman, D. & Tversky, A. (1981), 'The Framing of Decisions and the Psychology of Choice', *Science* 211, pp. 453-458.

Kahneman, D., & Tversky, A. (1984), 'Choices, Values and Frames', *American Psychologist* 29, pp. 341-350.

Laudan, L. (1990), *Science and Relativism*, University of Chicago Press, Chicago.

Parfit, D. (1984), *Reasons and Actions,* Clarendon Press, Oxford.

Rawls, J. (1974), 'The Independence of Moral Theory', *Proceedings and Addresses of the Aristotelian Society* 47, 1974/5, pp. 5-22.

Rawls, J. (1972), *A Theory of Justice*, Oxford University Press, London.

Van der Steen, W.J. (1995), *Facts, Values, and Methodology: A New Approach to Ethics,* Rodopi, Amsterdam/Atlanta.

Index